THE DIFFICULTY OF DIFFERENCE

PSYCHOANALYSIS
SEXUAL DIFFERENCE
& FILM THEORY

D. N. RODOWICK

ROUTLEDGE ▪ New York & London

For R. B. and L. M.

Was du ererbt von deinen Vätern [und Muttern] hast,
Erwirb es, um es zu besitzen.

—Goethe, *Faust*, I, 1

Published in 1991 by

Routledge
An imprint of Routledge, Chapman and Hall, Inc.
29 West 35 Street
New York, NY 10001

Published in Great Britain by

Routledge
11 New Fetter Lane
London EC4P 4EE

Copyright © 1991 by Routledge, Chapman and Hall, Inc.

Printed in the United States of America

Library of Congress Cataloging in Publication Data

Rodowick, David Norman.
    The difficulty of difference   :   psychoanalysis, sexual difference,
  and film theory / D. N. (David Norman) Rodowick.
        p.   cm.
    Includes bibliographical references and index.
    ISBN 0-415-90331-9 (HB). —ISBN 0-415-90332-7 (PB)
    1. Film criticism.   2. Sex differences (Psychology)
  3. Psychoanalysis.   I. Title.
    [DNLM: 1. Motion Pictures.   2. Psychoanalytic Theory. 3. Sex
  Factors.   WM 460 R695d]
  PN1995.R619   1990
  791.43′013—dc20   90-20695

British Library Cataloguing in Publication Data
Rodowick, D. N. (David Norman)
    The difficulty of difference   :   psychoanalysis, sexual
  difference and film theory.
    1. Cinema films. Feminist theories
    I. Title
    791.4301

ISBN 0-415-90331-9
ISBN 0-415-90332-7 pbk

Contents

Note on Abbreviations

This book cites liberally from the works of Sigmund Freud and Jacques Lacan in both original and translated versions. All citations from Freud in English are from *The Standard Edition of the Complete Psychological Works of Sigmund Freud,* ed. James Strachey (London: Hogarth Press and the Institute for Psychoanalysis, 1953–1974), abbreviated in my text as SE followed by the relevant volume and page numbers. Simple references to Freud's works are referenced by the date assigned to them in the international Freud Bibliography. Citations referring to the original German are from the Freud *Studienausgabe* (Frankfurt am Main: S. Fischer Verlag GmbH, 1975), abbreviated as Stud., followed by volume and page number.

All translations from Lacan are cited from the Norton editions. The abbreviation E refers to *Écrits: A Selection,* trans. Alan Sheridan (New York: W. W. Norton and Co., Inc., 1977). References to the translated *Séminaires* are abbreviated as S followed by the relevant volume and page numbers.

Preface

Readers familiar with my work may have a sense of *déjà* vu when seeing the title of this book. Eight years ago I published an essay entitled "The Difficulty of Difference." Although it was widely read and cited, I have always been struck by several paradoxes in how this article was received. That my essay, a study of the problem of sexual *difference,* was accepted as a contribution to *feminist* film theory was a welcome if unforeseen event. More significantly, I was struck by how "The Difficulty of Difference" was read, mistakenly in my view, simply as a critique of Laura Mulvey's important and influential article on "Visual Pleasure and Narrative Cinema." At that time, my concern was how the theme of Mulvey's provocative and polemical argument was taken to be axiomatic. Every film student knows well this catechism: "In a world ordered by sexual imbalance, pleasure in looking has been split between active/male and passive/female."[1]

In retrospect, I never meant to imply that Mulvey's argument was necessarily wrong. In fact, the more I read this inescapably important essay, the more complex and thought-provoking it becomes. Instead, my concern was the way in which Mulvey's work was being appropriated and canonized by professional film theory which seemed to me to close off many of the perplexing questions and problems that the essay was determined to ask and to confront. Included among them are complex methodological issues involving the appropriation of psychoanalysis by film theory, the question of sexual identification and sexual difference in spectators—above all through the problem of enunciation or "subject-positioning"—and the methods and objectives of ideological criticism. To me, these remain crucial and unresolved problems in film theory's encounter with psychoanalysis.

Over the years, my students have urged me to readdress the issues raised in my earlier work. It is to my students, then, that I owe the inspiration for this book, also called *The Difficulty of Difference.* Attentive readers may find the "original" essay appearing ghost-like beneath the palimpsest of ideas that have now been layered upon it. This is especially true in my discussion of the influence of Laura Mulvey in Chapter One and my reconsideration of Freud's study of infantile beating phantasies in Chapter Four. In this respect, I am grateful to the journal *Wide Angle* for their indulgence. However, in repeating the title of an earlier work I do not want to imply that I am appearing eight years after the fact to say "what I really meant." Rather, I want to stress that for me problems of sexual difference and psychoanalytic theory, above all with respect to their possible contributions to cultural theory and ideological criticism, should not be considered as closed off, finished, or resolved. My purpose in writing this book is to make some very familiar territory once again unfamiliar and thought-provoking. I will be most concerned here with problems of film theory, especially the discursive contexts through which the meanings of mass cultural artifacts are formulated, appropriated, sometimes compromised, hopefully changed.

A year ago I was asked by the journal *Camera Obscura*, along with dozens of other scholars, to comment on the place of my research within the debate on the "female spectator."[2] This controversy has provided an interesting touchstone for my current work. This debate was initiated by many responses to Mulvey's work, including my own. While commenting at length on the forms of male spectatorship and identification built on phantasies of the female body, Mulvey was criticized for not speculating on the possibilities of desire and identification for the female spectator. Quite a few interesting essays and several books have since appeared, all of which are determined to identify specifically feminine forms of identification and spectatorship as distinct from the masculine. This is a logic based on sexual *opposition*. However, I would characterize my own work as concerned less with the female spectator than with the problem of *sexual difference* in the forms of narration historically presented in film and other media, in the possibilities of identification organized by film texts, and in the languages of film theory and psychoanalysis.

The first issue I might clarify in my own work is that my position on the problem of identification in film is paradoxical in every sense of the word. In the wake of my book, *The Crisis of Political Modernism*, I have tried to displace the centrality of the problem of *identification* in contemporary film theory in favor of a theory of *reading*.[3] Despite the achievements of psychoanalytic film theory and textual analysis in the past twenty years, I would insist that all claims made about processes of identification in actual spectators, powerful and important as they may be, are speculative. In my view the analysis of forms of enunciation, or point of view, in fiction films may tell us a great deal about ideological representations of gender difference. However, they can tell us nothing definitive about the forms of sexual identification, or the potential meanings, produced with respect to actual spectators. This also holds true for equally important studies of reception and reading formations as attempts to delimit the range of meanings historically attributable to the texts of mass culture. Textual analysis has accomplished much in suggesting how positions of identification and meaning are coded by film texts. But in my view, one must accept fundamentally that these positions exist only as potentialities that are ultimately undecidable with respect to any given spectator. This, for me, is an indispensable political *a priori*. The more I work on this problem, the more I believe that ultimately each encounter between text and subject is historically contingent and unpredictable. Film theory has too often envisioned this encounter as one of ideological overdetermination (where filmic text and cinematic apparatus set the formal conditions for reception) rather than as a potential site of resistance, reappropriation, and rereading. Therefore, we should be prepared to interrogate our theories themselves to understand to what degree they impede rather than enable the transformative work of critical reading.

In this respect, the very question of the female spectator—which so strongly organizes current feminist film theory—presents certain political and theoretical risks. This is especially true of its appeal to psychoanalytic theory. Initially, psychoanalysis was appropriated by feminist film and cultural theory to formulate a critique of "essentialism"; that is, the idea that the female body grounds an experience of subjectivity, sexuality, desire, and language that is essentially other to masculinity. Presented in this manner, the question of sexual identity suggests opposed ontological categories based on a biological experience of genital sex, which is, of course, antithetical to Freud's thought. This critique of essentialism was largely the project of the British journal *m/f*, to which I still feel strongly allied. However, even when carefully deployed as critiques of biological essentialism, the current attempts to define the self-identity of female spectators through psychoanalytic theory are nonetheless based on ontological arguments. The singularity and self-identity of this concept—emphatically *the* female spectator—can only be preserved by a binary logic that opposes it to what it is not, or what it must negate: the definition of phallocentric subjectivity as "male." I will ask in a moment whether Freud's version of psychoanalysis can support this binary logic. There are, however, advantages to envisioning "femaleness" as an ontological category, best represented by Gayatri Spivak's suggestion that feminist theory might have to accept the risk of essentialism.[4] I take this to mean that it is incumbent upon feminist theory—and in fact all critiques of domination—to attempt to create new positions of interpretation, meaning, desire, and subjectivity even while acknowledging they sometimes stand on shaky philosophical legs. Moreover, left intellectuals and artists have the responsibility not only of criticism, but also of the imagination of utopias.

In this book, I return to Freud's case studies to explore how his complex and contradictory analyses of phantasy militate against understanding sexual identification as opposition. Among these analyses, the essay "'A Child is being Beaten'" (1919e) remains one of the most important and most commented on of Freud's works. Here Freud demonstrates clearly that sexual subjectivity can never be simply nor singularly aligned with femininity or masculinity. Indeed Freud's version of the acquisition of gender understands all subjectivity as divided within itself according to identifications that are continually traversed by sexual difference. These divisions are described by Freud in several, sometimes confusing ways. As it has often been pointed out, Freud uses the terms *Männlichkeit* and *Weiblichkeit* simultaneously to refer to biological sex, to "social" gender defined by object choice, and to sexual identification according to an active or passive organization of the drives. To be sure, this often confusing and contradictory range of references is partly explained by ideological biases on Freud's part.

Nevertheless, if Freud's multiple uses of the terms femininity and masculinity are clear only in the context of specific analyses, this underscores a vital point. While Freud's analysis of the "child is being beaten" phantasy divides its enunciators and structural versions into male and female, the essay is nonetheless about the difficulty of aligning masculine and feminine identifications with a "final" sexed subjectivity. Freud divides the phantasy spatially across three strata, only two of which are available to conscious articulation. What defines a version as "male" or "female" are the *particular* transactions between masculine and feminine identifications within *each* of the three stages of the phantasy. The structural complexity of this schema is intensified by the fact that the unconscious is governed by neither time nor negation. All three stages, with their particular ratios of masculinity and femininity, coexist in the male and female patients analyzed. In this respect, I believe that Laura Mulvey's and Teresa de Lauretis's account of identification as "oscillation" is correct, but cannot be seen as specific only to female spectators.[5] Furthermore, the characterization of this form of identification as "transvestite" or "transsexual" is unfortunate with its suggestion of opposed, self-identical forms that can be reversed or transgressed. In Chapter Four I argue that the relation between masculine and feminine identification is best represented as *transactional*. In Freud's essay, what distinguishes male from female subjectivity are the transactional modalities between masculine and feminine identifications in each individual.

That Freud can decide between male and female versions of the phantasy and determine three stages of development for each is admittedly a retroactive construction. Because there is no negation in the unconscious, there is also no totalization of identity where each subsequent phase of the phantasy would dialectically incorporate and superintend the preceding ones. Repression is the ego's only means of defense for maintaining its alleged unity against the contradictory desires articulated in the three phases of the phantasy. But as Kaja Silverman so eloquently points out in a recent essay on deviant male subjectivity, the structural element of greatest interest in this phantasy is masochism, defined not as a "perversion," but as the inherently entropic, or what Freud called the "destructive," character of the drives.[6] To the extent that the Oedipus complex is the agent of patriarchal ideologies, its goal is to divide sexual identity onto the two routes of reproductive heterosexuality. But the most radical lesson of psychoanalysis is that this goal is never fully nor finally achieved; sexual identity always remains fragile and in flux. If the binding of subjectivity to sexual representations was not inherently unstable, how else could one explain the repetitiveness and pervasiveness of the ideological forms attempting to shore up these representations in aesthetic, as well as medical, legal, economic, and political discourses? Appealing to Freud's theories of phantasy and the late essays on masochism, I propose that the entropic character of desire provides the elements for a theory of utopian readings of aesthetic texts and modes of reception as sites of resistance. In Chapter Five, I develop this idea in a reading of Jacques Rivette's *Céline and Julie Go Boating,* originally published in *Art & Text,* included in this book with their permission in a revised form.[7] My reading of *Céline and Julie* is not a textual analysis in the usual sense of the term. I am neither particularly interested in the formal work of the film as an alternative text, nor in making claims about its strategies of identification. But because the film addresses so directly questions of phantasy, narrative, and female spectatorship, I find that it presents exemplary opportunities for demonstrating how my more abstract theoretical arguments might be put to work in the activity of close reading. A simple way of stating my position might be to say that, as opposed to a critic like Raymond Bellour who understands film narrative as perfectly realized Oedipal phantasy, my position is that phantasy is always a form imperfectly realized.[8] Narrative is not a machine for producing desire in texts and in spectators. Rather, the systemic and normative dispositions of aesthetic work should be understood as historically specific attempts to shore up ideological representations against the entropic character of desire. Rather than being manufactured or contained by narrative, I consider desire as a historical force that continually erodes proper forms, producing contradiction in the texts themselves, and in spectators' relations with texts.

My own pleasure in writing this book was considerably enhanced by the support of many friends. In his usual spirit of comradeship and collegiality, Dana Polan carefully commented on each chapter of this book as it was written, keeping me on course when my arguments strayed. Toril Moi was kind enough to read the manuscript, providing much encouragement and advice. I am also grateful to Bill Germano and Diane Gibbons at Routledge for their invaluable editorial help. Janet Bergstrom, Tom Levin, Brigitte Peucker, Michael Levine, and Allen S. Weiss also read and commented on various drafts. Shiobhan Somerville exhaustively explored the nooks and crannies of the manuscript, correcting mistaken and misplaced references as well as other follies of an absent-minded author. To John Montagu at New Yorker Films goes my sincere thanks for loaning me a 35mm print of *Céline and Julie* and permitting me to make frame enlargements from the film. A number of friends, colleagues, and students also provided helpful insights, encouragement and advice, including Laura Mulvey, Miriam Hansen, Hillis Miller, Al La Valley, Bernhard Riff, August Ruhs, M.D., Paul Sandro, Lynn

Wardley, Dudley Andrew, David Bordwell, Kristin Thompson, Jan Matlock, Anne Higonnet, Shoshana Felman, Dori Laub, M.D., Hanna Weg, Kirsten Evans, Lynn Whisnant Reiser, M.D., Georges May, Jennifer Wicke, and John Guillory. Audiences who heard presentations from this work—at Dartmouth University, the Gesellschaft für Filmtheorie and the Tiefenpsychologisches Institut at the University of Vienna, Miami University, the Whitney Humanities Center at Yale University, and the University of California, Riverside—challenged me to hone and refine my arguments. A Morse Fellowship granted by Yale University enabled me to develop this book in its early stages. I am also grateful for research support from the Whitney Humanities Center at Yale and for help from the Yale Department of Audio-Visual Services.

Chapter 1
The Difficulty of Difference

Binary Machines

In *Dialogues,* a book cowritten with Gilles Deleuze, Claire Parnet comments on the function of "the binary machine."[1] In these interesting pages she resumes an argument begun by Deleuze concerning the relation of philosophy to the State. Every college educator knows well the official version of this story, defined according to the theory of progress that was the nineteenth century's contribution to Enlightenment philosophy. As philosophy becomes more specialized and departmentalized, its role is to contribute in a "detached" way to the refinement of procedures of thought. Increasingly, the "image" of thought invoked, along with criteria for its perfectibility, is associated with procedures of "language" but of a special sort: that defined by linguistics and related logico-mathematical protocols.

Deleuze's position and his ongoing practice of reading philosophy is motivated by a different emphasis. Philosophy is confronted as an "image of thought" that in its historical manifestations all too perfectly prevents people from thinking. And not only because "thought" is left to specialists, but also because the definitions of thought produced by specialists accord perfectly with the State's image of power and its juridical definitions of identity. As critics and educators, the language we use to describe "identity"—as a difference from or conforming to an image of gender, class, or race—is intricately tied to the mechanics of power.

What Parnet calls the binary machine perfectly describes this technology of thought and the notions of identity it fabricates. Its components are easily elucidated: divide into two mutually exclusive terms or categories and thus produce two perfectly self-identical "ideas" that brook no contradiction or invasion from the outside. Hegel's dialectic is the utopia of this technology, dividing and reconciling into ever higher unities and hierarchies until spirit and subject became one in an image of universal rationality. Nowadays binary thought—which has reproduced itself in the discourses of law, economy, medicine, science, and politics no less than epistemology and aesthetics—is content with cellular division and horizontal replication. According to Parnet,

> Dualisms no longer relate to unities, but to successive choices: are you white or black, man or woman, rich or poor, etc.? Do you take the left half or the right

half? There is always a binary machine which governs the distribution of roles and which means that all the answers must go through preformed questions, since the questions are already worked out on the basis of the answer assumed to be probable according to the dominant meanings. Thus a grille is constituted such that everything which does not pass through the grille cannot be materially understood . . . .

[The] binary machine is an important component of apparatuses of power. So many dichotomies will be established that there will be enough for everyone to be pinned to the wall, sunk in a hole. Even the divergences of deviancy will be measured according to the degree of binary choice; you are neither white nor black, Arab then? Or half-breed? You are neither man nor woman, transvestite then? (D 19–21)

The binary machine always pretends to totality and universality. And to a certain extent, Parnet sees the working of language by the binary machine to have been imminently successful. In this context, one could ask if the picture of language developed in structural linguistics differs so much from the image of thought in the Hegelian dialectic.[2] The smallest possible unities—phonemic—are integrated into ever higher levels of unity—morphemic, syntactic, syntagmatic, narratological—that are simultaneously equivalent to "higher" levels of thought. And when grafted on to structural anthropology, these branching divisions and hierarchies become equivalent to the "meaningful" organization of human collectivities. This is one way of understanding the feminist critique of Lévi-Strauss, for example, where the binary division and hierarchy of the sexes informs the intelligibility of language, labor, and social life. But Parnet's point is that granting linguistics' recognition and exacting description of the dualities that work language and society is to leave untouched its own language—its patterns of logic, rhetoric, and argumentation—which, tautologically, only produce the legibility and intelligibility of that which is already structured by binary division. A similar tautological situation is no less evident in the ways that contemporary film theory has appropriated the logic of structural semiology and psychoanalysis for the formal analysis of films and the spectatorial relations they imply.

If language and linguistics so perfectly replicate one another, the latter reproducing the "thought" of language as the limit of what language can render "thinkable," what alternatives can be imagined? Parnet and Deleuze warn that it is futile to propose a thought "outside" of language. (How many theories of avant-garde literature and art have been wrecked on this utopian island?) Nor can it be said that language deforms identities, concepts, or realities that can be returned to their proper states. "We must pass through [*passer par*] dualisms," writes Parnet, "because they are in language, it's not a question of getting rid of them, but we must fight against language, invent stammering . . . to trace a vocal or written line which will make language flow between these dualisms, and which will define a minority use of language" (D

34). Rather, it is a matter of reconsidering what "language" is or could be, of understanding what it leaves aside, and of remembering that totality is a pretension that displaces recognition of the multiplicities it covers over. It is a question above all of reading differently.

The question of reading can now be rephrased: how to understand otherwise these schemata of language and thought? How can one recover the "individuations without 'subject' " that fall between the terms of binary division and are de-territorialized by the law of the excluded middle? How can one apprehend the minority languages and the multiple collectivities that are displaced and overcome by the universalizing unity of binary thought? For Parnet, the Achilles' heel of this logic is the term that not only constitutes the middle, but also guarantees the contiguity and multiplication of binary modules:

> And even if there are only two terms, there is an AND between the two, which is neither the one nor the other, nor the one which becomes the other, but which constitutes the multiplicity. This is why it is always possible to undo dualisms from the inside, by tracing the line of flight which passes between the two terms or the two sets, the narrow stream which belongs neither to the one nor to the other, but draws both into a non-parallel evolution, into a heterochronous becoming. At least this does not belong to the dialectic. (D 34–35)

I have left to one side the principal targets of Parnet and Deleuze's criticisms: structural linguistics, psychoanalysis, and more profoundly, the alliance between them represented by the work of Jacques Lacan. There is much to be said for this critique of psychoanalysis which is more complex and compelling in the *Anti-Oedipus* than it is in the pages of *Dialogues*. The questions that interest me, however, are on one hand how contemporary film theory has read and incorporated psychoanalysis, and on the other, to what degree the logic of psychoanalysis, above all the work of Freud, is inflected by the binary machine? In *The Crisis of Political Modernism*, I argued that the most substantial accomplishment of contemporary film theory was its formulation of new practices of reading that profoundly transformed our notions of filmic and literary texts.[3] But blocked by a formal conception of text, spectator, and the relation between them, Anglo-American film theory has been unable to comprehend historically or theoretically the implications of these reading practices. Despite the gains they have enabled, neither semiology, psychoanalysis, nor feminist theory have entirely eluded the logic of the binary machine in their theoretical language and in their formal conceptualization of film text and film spectators.

The consequences of this situation must be addressed. What I question now is the way that Freud has been mobilized in film theory to address questions of textual analysis, on one hand, and sexual difference in spectatorship on the other. Do Freud's writings implicitly propose a model of reading that might erode the version of language and power formulated by the binary machine? Does the work of Freud enable a different way of understanding sexual difference? Rather than following the "law" of unity and identity, is Freud among the first to understand the possibilities of "individuations without 'subject' " and a minority language of sexuality? Is there in Freud a theory of reading that renders legible otherwise deterritorialzed languages, identities, and meanings?

Pleasure and its Discontents

"In a world ordered by sexual imbalance, pleasure in looking has been split between active/male and passive/female." This phrase from Laura Mulvey's "Visual Pleasure and Narrative Cinema" is undoubtedly and deservedly one of the most well known in contemporary film theory.[4] I begin with Mulvey's essay not because I disagree with what it "says," but to open up tensions in Mulvey's own reading of Freud, and, more importantly, in how Mulvey's work has been read and appropriated. Without doubt, it is and will remain one of the most important essays in contemporary film theory. "Visual Pleasure and Narrative Cinema" has indeed been successful in its original, polemical objective: to place questions of sexual difference at the center of the debate concerning film theory's appeal to psychoanalysis. But what was offered as a polemic and a stepping stone to further analysis has instead too often been treated as axiomatic. What is at stake is how film theory has read Freud in order to understand the construction of "femininity" by audiovisual media and to reconceptualize the value of psychoanalysis for a theory of narration and spectatorship.

Mulvey's early argument, which is still the subject of an ongoing debate in her own work, remains the best and most brilliant exposition of the reading of Freud produced by Anglo-American film theory in the seventies.[5] Mulvey's project and the many essays inspired by it are organized around the question of identification. The first task of this project is to target and examine the codes and mechanisms through which the classical cinema has traditionally exploited sexual difference as a function of its narrative and representational forms. The second task is to ascertain the affects these mechanisms might inspire in the spectatorial experience of sexed individuals as well as their role within the more general ideological machinery of patriarchal culture. The analysis of narrative forms, and the forms of spectatorship implied by them, are thus intimately related. Similarly, the analysis and criticism of patriarchal ideology by film theory has had a historic impact on these questions.

One of the most striking aspects of Mulvey's argument is the association of a fundamental negativity with the figuration of femininity characteristic of the classic, Hollywood cinema. The great strength of Mulvey's analysis is that it is not a simple condemnation of how women are represented on the screen. Instead she identifies a powerful contradiction in the heart of the structure of image and narrative in Hollywood films. In order to begin to define these issues more precisely I have isolated a rather long citation from Mulvey's essay. My motive is neither to completely sustain nor subvert Mulvey's argument, but rather to illuminate a series of assumptions and a system of oppositions that organize her discussion of sexual difference and mechanisms of visual pleasure in film. In a section entitled "Woman as Image, Man as Bearer of the Look," Mulvey makes the following argument:

> But in psychoanalytic terms, the female figure poses a deeper problem. She also connotes something that the look continually circles around but disavows: her lack of a penis, implying a threat of castration and hence unpleasure. Ultimately, the meaning of woman is sexual difference, the absence of the penis as visually ascertainable, the material evidence on which is based the castration complex essential for the organisation of entrance to the symbolic order and the law of the father. Thus the woman as icon, displayed for the gaze and enjoyment of men, the active controllers of the look, always threatens to evoke the anxiety it originally signified. The male unconscious has two avenues of escape from this castration anxiety: preoccupation with the re-enactment of the original trauma (investigating the woman, demystifying her mystery), counterbalanced by the devaluation, punishment or saving of the guilty object (an avenue typified by the concerns of the *film noir*); or else complete disavowal of castration by the substitution of a fetish object or turning the represented figure itself into a fetish so that it becomes reassuring rather than dangerous (hence over-valuation, the cult of the female star). This second avenue, fetishistic scopophilia, builds up the physical beauty of the object transforming it into something satisfying in itself. The first avenue, voyeurism, on the contrary, has associations with sadism: pleasure lies in ascertaining guilt (immediately associated with castration), asserting control and subjecting the guilty person through punishment or forgiveness. This sadistic side fits in well with narrative. Sadism demands a story, depends on making something happen, forcing a change in another person, a battle of will and strength, victory and defeat, all occurring in linear time with a beginning and an end. Fetishistic scopophilia, on the other hand, can exist outside linear time as the erotic instinct is focused on the look alone. (VP 13–14)

Unlike Raymond Bellour, whose work has many affinities with Mulvey's, Mulvey is less concerned with problems of textual analysis than with the definition of structures of identification and the mechanisms of pleasure or unpleasure that accompany them. I am now using the term identification in its strictly psychoanalytic sense: "Psychological process whereby the subject assimilates an aspect, property or attribute of the other and is transformed, wholly or partially, after the model the other provides. It is by means of a series of identifications that the personality is constituted and specified."[6]

Mulvey herself does not develop the argument in precisely these terms. Her argument does presume, however, a potentially transformative relation between the object (the narrative film and the mechanisms of visual pleasure characterizing it) and the spectatorial subject such that the libidinal economy of the latter is organized and sustained by the signifying economy of the former. In fact all theories of the subject invoked by psychoanalytic film criticism cast signifying processes in film as the "other" with the power to transform or sustain categories of subjectivity.

For Mulvey these subject/object relations are a product of the point of view mechanisms of Hollywood cinema. This idea is emphasized by the division of gender and labor in the title of this section: "Woman as Image, Man as Bearer of the Look." In the interlacing of diegetic looks between the characters, the look of the camera, and that of the spectator, an economy is preserved where set subject-positions are continually reconfirmed and reproduced by avoiding avenues of identification leading to unpleasure and by seeking out avenues leading to pleasure. That the analysis of sexual difference reveals an imbalance in the social system represented in films is of course important. But of greater significance is the suggestion that visual and narrative forms produce pleasure, that this pleasure is produced for someone, and that this production sustains an imaginary situation where real relations of social imbalance are maintained for a given culture. According to Mulvey, the forms of point of view institutionalized by the cinema as mechanisms of pleasure have defined themselves historically in the same manner as the ego forms itself in relation to the objective world: that which promotes pleasure is introjected and that which promotes unpleasure is systematically rejected.[7] The various forms defining cinematic imaging and point of view at a given historical moment are objectively produced and sustained only to the extent that they maintain a pleasurable relation with the subject at whom they are aimed—the cinema consumer. If these mechanisms perform their social and ideological function efficiently, the production of pleasure will sustain and reinforce the place of the subject in a given structure of representation. An imaginary place is created for this subject in and by the film text that he or she may choose to inhabit. As in Marx's suggestive epigram from the *Grundrisse*, "production not only creates an object for the subject, but also a subject for the object."

In sum, processes of identification in the cinema and the various forms of looking that organize their functioning in film narratives regulate an economy of exchange where the production of pleasure guarantees the place of the subject both in and for the text. What constitutes this place and the imaginary from which it is derived, as well as how it is placed and for whom, are the central questions and the greatest difficulties of Mulvey's essay.

The terms and the logic evoked by Mulvey in the long citation above should now be sorted out. Mulvey is primarily concerned with the organization of looking by, for, and in the text of the narrative film. Again, the concept of identification is understood as the linch-pin on which the relations between subject and object turn. Identification also organizes, or attempts to organize, the vision and the libidinal aims of the spectatorial subject. Drawing on terms from Freud's "Instincts and their Vicissitudes" (1915c), Mulvey undertakes a classification of the forms of visual pleasure characteristic of the narrative cinema.[8] Her primary distinction is:

active: male

passive: female

At first glance this polarization of terms seems faithful to Freud's own schema. Later I will examine whether or not Freud's arguments concerning sexual difference are not somewhat more complex.

Nevertheless, Mulvey's discussion of forms of "pleasure in looking" crystallizes around this schema. To maintain this polarization of terms, she establishes two crucial sets of distinctions. The first involves the following pairing of terms in section II C, where Mulvey describes fundamental structures of identification in the strictly psychoanalytic sense:

sexual instincts	ego-libido
scopophilia	narcissism
[separation of subject and object]	[identity of subject with object]

Mulvey is careful to differentiate the first pair, sexual instincts/ego-libido, while maintaining the intimate link between them. The nature of this linking of opposites is clarified by examining Freud's distinction between ego-libido and object-libido. Although he was not strictly consistent, Freud often used the terms "libido" and "sexual instincts" interchangeably. However, in the distinction between object- and ego-libido he refers primarily to the direction in which the libido is channeled; that is, whether it is being directed toward an exterior object or being reinvested in the ego itself. Obviously the concept of ego-libido is indissolubly linked to narcissism which Mulvey correctly points out in her description of the mirror stage and its apparent similarities with cinematic perception. Mulvey understands the economy of the ego-libido as attached fundamentally to the phenomenon of primary narcissism characterizing Lacan's scenario for the mirror stage. In this scenario the formation of the ego, the potential "I" of the speaking subject, is understood as a splitting—first in a division between the sexual instincts and the ego-instincts through the organization of narcissistic libido, and second in the formation of an image to which this libido is attached. The formation of this image constitutes an economic relationship with the ego that is *imaginary* in the full sense that Lacan gives to the term. The joy of recognition that the child receives through identifying itself in this exterior image is located in a fundamental misperception where the distance between subject and object is simultaneously formed and canceled. The terms for perceiving, knowing, and desiring are thus constituted and verified by the setting in place of this imaginary other who both is and is not the child. The ego is formed through a simultaneous externalization and internalization of an object constituted by a visual and imaginary structure that governs the child's perception of self.

A first caution is in order here. This scenario of the formative moments of the ego is not yet a scenario of sexual difference. And Mulvey, with great care, has not yet introduced the distinction between active:male/passive:female. To be sure, in both Freudian and Lacanian accounts this scenario establishes the "first" sexual relations: those attached to the imago of the mother and to the autoeroticism associated with narcissism. In addition, this period of development sets the stage for the complicated and fragile set of sexual identifications that are carried through in the formation of the castration and Oedipus complexes. But in this preoedipal phase of psychological development there is no evidence that masculinity or femininity will follow predetermined routes. In fact, Freud himself is adamant that gender difference is a product of a retroactive "understanding" of Oedipal relations during puberty. For Freud, up until this point any child's relation to sexual difference is fundamentally undetermined, unformed, and unsure; after puberty sexual identifications remain fragile. Moreover, the anxiety produced by the residue of preoedipal relations characterizes all questions of identity that plague the subject for the rest of its psychological life.[9] The complex of Oedipal identifications is only the first attempt to address questions of sexual identity whose indecisiveness is never fully resolved.

Unquestionably, the problem of the persistence of this anxiety is central to Mulvey's argument. For the structures of desire and pleasurable looking perpetuated by the Hollywood cinema demonstrate for Mulvey both the insistent patriarchal bias of cinematic representations and the potential for eroding that bias:

> During its history, the cinema seems to have evolved a particular illusion of reality in which this contradiction between libido and ego has found a beautifully complementary phantasy world. In *reality* the phantasy world of the screen is subject to the law which produces it. Sexual instincts and identification processes have a meaning within the symbolic order which articulates desire. Desire, born with language, allows the possibility of transcending the instinctual and the imaginary, but its point of reference continually returns to the traumatic moment of its birth: the castration complex. Hence the look, pleasurable in form, can be threatening in content, and it is woman as representation/image that crystallizes this paradox. (VP 11)

For Mulvey, the imaging of the woman's body evokes a fundamental negativity that always places the pleasure and security of cinematic looking at risk. The fundamental mechanisms of pleasurable looking are meant to displace the castration anxiety suggested to the male spectator by the representation of the woman's body, and the male spectator obsessively requires this representation to alleviate his anxiety. Yet each repetition simultaneously renews a possibility of threat: the potential negation of Hollywood codes of looking and the security of the male ego they support.

This leads to a second point that Mulvey is careful to emphasize: the drives may only be apprehended through their investment in representations. Or, as Mulvey puts it, they "are formative structures, mechanisms not meaning. In themselves they have no signification, they have to be attached to an idealisation" (VP 10). Indeed in the citation above Mulvey characterizes the formation of the ego as a kind of "phantasmization" of the subject. Certainly, almost all of Freud's discussions of instinctual vicissitudes rely on the analysis of representations or phantasy scenarios. This is the fundamental link between the "instinctual" theory and Freud's analytic method concerning manifestations of phantasy life, including dreams, parapraxes, jokes, and the scattered comments on painting and literature. And any concrete discussion of the construction and dissemination of subject-positions must presuppose that there are historically and socially determined mechanisms, both formal and technological, that organize the desire of the subject and account for the structuring of that desire. But it is not Freud, but rather Lacan's account of the relation between the imaginary and the symbolic that Mulvey follows.

The implications of this choice must be addressed at the risk of oversimplifying Lacan's thought. Lacan's account of the processes of identification and subject formation are often more deterministic than Freud's. Each stage of the formation of the ego, from the mirror stage to the dissolution of the castration and Oedipus complexes, is driven by a process of dialectical incorporation. As Miriam Hansen points out, ". . . in Lacanian models of spectatorship scopic desire is conceptually inseparable from voyeurism, fetishism and, thus, the regime of castration. Not that these are unrelated or free of determinism in Freud. The Freudian speculation, however, does not posit earlier stages of psychic development as always already negated by later ones, in a Hegelian sense of 'Aufhebung' which Lacan assimilated to psychoanalysis."[10] Alternatively, as I hope to demonstrate in greater depth in Chapters Three and Four, Freud understands the relation between the drives and their representatives as causally and temporally more complex, fragile, and historically mobile. In sum, terms that Freud develops on the basis of shifting "polarities" [Polarität] are simultaneously divided and linked through the mechanism of Lacan's dialectic. Moreover, Mulvey has specific reasons for preferring Lacan's scenario of negation even if she thereby fixes Freud's polarities in a system of binary division: to preserve an image of the female body as a site of negativity that can erode rather than sustain the security of the male look.

Returning to Mulvey's argument, some of the assumptions characterizing the long citation above can now be reconsidered. The best place to begin is with the following pairs of oppositions:

male	female
active	passive
scopophilia	narcissism

I have already suggested two cautions in my discussion of primary narcissism. First, the strict distinction between what is "male" and what is "female" in processes of identification is undoubtedly the trickiest problem in reading Freud and should be approached with great caution. And where film theory wishes to sustain the analogy between Lacan's mirror stage and the "primary identification" organized by the cinematographic apparatus, additional care is called for. There is no doubt that sexual difference plays an important role in Lacan's account, both explicitly and symptomatically. But the *a priori* alignment of scopophilia and narcissism with active and passive aims on one hand, and maleness and femaleness on the other, is not clear. None of Freud's texts on sexual difference suggests an unequivocal distinctiveness between maleness and femaleness in this relation as I will make more clear in a moment. Second, if primary narcissism formulates an identification whose visual structure supports pleasure in looking, this structure implicitly contains both active and passive components. It is maintained not only in the *act* of the look, but also in the *return* of the look from the imaginary other who verifies the apparent corporeal and psychical integrity of the "I" of the subject. Pleasure in looking contains both passive *and* active forms. Mulvey implies as much in the passage cited above, especially in the reference to "fetishistic scopophilia" which in her schema would have both "active" scopophilic and "passive" fetishistic components.

Similarly, for Mulvey the avoidance of castration anxiety (unpleasure), is made possible by two distinctive types of looking:

active	passive
voyeurism	fetishistic scopophilia
sadism	?

There is an implicit blind spot here. For example, Mulvey defines fetishism as an overvaluation of the object, a point Freud would support. But he would also add that this phenomenon is one of the fundamental sources of authority defined as passive submission to the object: in sum, *masochism*.[11] Why is the relation of masochism to "fetishistic scopophilia" elided in Mulvey's essay?

Her emphasis considers the structure of the look not only in terms of the pleasure it allows, but also in how it organizes relations of power and control in and through narrative form. This claim, as powerful as it is provocative, deserves greater theoretical elaboration. Within Mulvey's thesis, though, the structure of the look is based on two givens: it is fundamentally a source of control or mastery and as a product of patriarchal society it is fundamentally masculine. The concept of masochism is deferred by the political nature of her argument. She wishes, justly I believe, neither to underestimate the extensiveness of a "masculinization" of point of view in the cinema, nor does she want to equate femaleness with masochism.

No one will have missed the reference to Freud in naming this section "pleasure and its discontents." But the nature of that "discontent" has yet to be explicitly addressed. In *Civilization and Its Discontents* [*Das Unbehagen in der Kultur* (1930a)] Freud himself uses the word *Unbehagen*, more aptly translated as discomfort, uneasiness, or restlessness. The idea of pleasure [*Lust*], then, is inseparable from this uneasiness [*Unlust*] as Mulvey herself implies in her discussion of castration anxiety. Nonetheless, Mulvey's account, and in fact most contemporary film theory follows her in this, is relatively unwelcoming to Freud's own complex remarks in the case histories on the restlessness of identification and the contradictoriness of desire that traverses and problematizes any strict binary distinction between "maleness"/"femaleness" and activity/passivity.[12] My own view is that the most productive area for a turn to Freud in film theory is to derive a theory of signification from the Freudian theory of phantasy. This theory would first have to account for permutations in the signification of the look in relation to the variations and shiftings of the subject and object of enunciation as transactions in sexual difference. Secondly, I would caution that although this theory could describe *possibilities* of cinematic identification, its claims for the positions adopted by any spectator would be purely speculative. Mulvey has undoubtedly helped to lay the groundwork for such a theory but her own considerations are deficient on several points. For example, Mulvey discusses the male star as an object of the look but denies him the function of an erotic object for either the female or male spectator.[13] Because Mulvey considers the look to be essentially active in its aims, identification with the male protagonist is only considered from a point of view that associates it with a sense of omnipotence and of assuming control in the narrative. She makes no distinction between identification and object-choice where active sexual aims may be directed towards the male figure nor does she consider the signification of authority in the male figure from the point of view of an economy of masochism. On the other hand, her discussion of the female figure is restricted only to its function as a male object-choice. In this manner, the place of maleness is discussed as both the subject and the object of the gaze (though only in a restricted fashion) and femaleness is discussed only as an object structuring the male look according to its active (voyeuristic) and passive (fetishistic) forms. In "Visual Pleasure and Narrative Cinema" the vicissitudes of identification—whether in its pleasurable or anxious forms, or whether it involves taking the other as an object (scopophilia) or identifying with attributes of a more perfect other (narcissism)—is reserved for the male alone, despite the suggestion of distinctive male and female forms. Where is the place of the female subject in this scenario?

In order to unravel this problem, or at least clarify its contours, here again is Mulvey's schema as I have reconsidered it:

male	female
active	passive
object-libido	ego-libido
scopophilia [object-choice	narcissism identification]
voyeurism	fetishistic scopophilia
sadism	[masochism]
masculine unconscious	?

In this context Mulvey must be questioned, as she herself questions Freud, as to whether or not "anatomy is destiny." In her schema psychological subjects and the libidinal economies that characterize them are typed according to a bodily definition of sexual difference. In other words, when describing the organization and the economy of the scopic drive, the sets of oppositions defining psychological characteristics are implicitly derived from biological difference. However, it would be too easy and undoubtedly unfair to Mulvey's sensitive and powerful reading of Freud to write off her argument as promoting a biological essentialism. Rather her argument is searching to define the specificity of the female body as the locus of a repressed yet articulate being. Recognition of this body and the representations proper to it, would thus enable both the recognition of a subjectivity so far elided under patriarchy and the overthrow of the discursive and social practices that censor this subjectivity.[14] In short, Mulvey discovers in the patriarchal construction of an image of the female body the materials for negation and critique that allow new possibilities of subjectivity and desire.

Freud's own texts, from the *Studies on Hysteria* (1895d) to *The New Introductory Lectures on Psychoanalysis* (1933a), are marked by a certain ambivalence in this respect to which the comment about anatomy and destiny will always bear witness. Similarly, Freud's anthropological and phylogenetic arguments, with their suggestion of a primitive memory of sexual difference and the universality of a patriarchal social life, must be regarded with a high degree of suspicion.[15] Alternatively, Freud's lifelong reflection on femininity and female sexuality led him to profoundly question the idea of a biological or instinctual determination of sexual difference. This is indeed where the theory of "instincts" and the theory of the drives diverge. Especially in the case histories, questions of sexual difference, femininity and masculinity, and homosexualities, are understood as highly complex yet not the least determined by inherent biological factors. This is after all the same Freud who was hooted by the Vienna society of physicians in 1886 for suggesting the possibility of "male" hysteria.

Freud was always uncomfortable with the concept of biological determinism in speaking about sexual difference and cautioned against it in several essays. For example, in a footnote to *Civilization and its Discontents*, Freud writes:

> We are accustomed to say that every human being displays both male and female instinctual impulses, needs and attributes; but though anatomy, it is true, can point out the characteristic of maleness and femaleness, psychology cannot. For psychology the contrast between the sexes fades away into one between activity and passivity [that is, in describing the organization of the drives], in which we far too readily identify activity with maleness and passivity with femaleness, a view which is by no means universally confirmed. . . . However this may be, if we assume that it is a fact that each individual seeks to satisfy both male and female wishes in his sexual life, we are prepared for the possibility that those [two sets of] demands are not fulfilled by the same object, and that they interfere with each other unless they can be kept apart and each impulse guided into a particular channel that is suited to it.[16]

Above and beyond the inherent complexities of his arguments, the contradictory responses to Freud's views on sexual difference are explained by the variety of the situations referred to in his use of the terms *Männlichkeit* and *Weiblichkeit*. Freud understood at least three different senses of the distinction between "maleness" and "femaleness"—biological, psychological and cultural—and accepted that their interrelation was by no means univocal or unproblematic. Moreover, these three senses are only profitably understood by identifying how they are inscribed in the material representations that serve patriarchal ideology as its raw materials.

There is a passage in "Instincts and their Vicissitudes" that illuminates Mulvey's reading of Freud in this respect. Towards the end of the essay, Freud asserts that the fundamental polarities of mental life are subject (ego)-object (external world), pleasure-unpleasure, and active-passive. When describing the interaction between these polarities—which precisely define the economy of identification—Freud warns that relations of activity and passivity must not be confounded with the relation of the subject (ego) and the object (external world). For the psychical life of the ego is always characterized by a complex of active and passive relations motivated by its reception of and reaction to perceptual information. Moreover, the drives are inherently always active in their aims. To the extent that psychological significations are attached to the meaning of masculinity and femininity in relation to activity and passivity, they do not define mutually exclusive sets of oppositions and are always the product of a historical and social variability. Similarly, there could never be a unilateral response between object and subject when identification takes place.

The rigor of Mulvey's binary schema for describing the relation of the drives to the representation of sexual difference therefore belies the complexity of Freud's thought. The density of contradiction in which the *significations* of feminine and masculine are circulated in our culture is thereby confused in Mulvey's analysis with the related but nevertheless separate problem of *identification* in Freud. Similarly, Mulvey's schema collapses when any one of the three senses of sexual distinction in Freud are systematically applied. Why would this be so? The contradictions of Mulvey's argument derive from an implied ontological definition of feminine identity and the feminine body as the requirement for her theory of political modernism. If the possibility of a "female unconscious" is a question mark in her essay, it is because the potential for a feminine subjectivity and desire will only be defined by a feminist counter-cinema that will arise through the negation of Hollywood codes of looking and visual pleasure. In her essay, that possibility rests in the very representations of the female body formulated in Hollywood cinema as an uncanny, "alien presence" that must be contained or mastered.

The clearest way of understanding this aspect of Mulvey's essay is to examine her division of film form into narrative and spectacle. The former is aligned with the vicissitude of sadism and the latter with fetishism as exemplified in the films of Alfred Hitchcock and Joseph von Sternberg. Following the counter-cinema argument, if Hollywood narrative relies on conventions of linearity, continuity, and depth illusion no less than pleasurable looking, then for Mulvey the imaging of the female body "tends to work against the development of a story line, to freeze the flow of action in moments of erotic contemplation. This alien presence then has to be integrated into cohesion with the narrative" (VP 11). The conventions of Hollywood cinema are understood as an agonistic relation between coherence and contradiction, movement and stasis, containment and erosion. The imaging of the female body always threatens to disrupt the linearity, continuity, and cohesion of the narrative. Mulvey refers to it as a momentary "no-man's land" outside of the temporal and spatial coherence of the narrative. Similarly, the effort to eroticize and fetishize the female star by fragmenting her body in close-up "destroys the Renaissance space, the illusion of depth demanded by the narrative, it gives flatness, the quality of a cut-out or icon rather than verisimilitude to the screen" (VP 12).

The organization of looking around the female body thus preserves an anti-realist space and the potential for a narrative, political modernism. Moreover, Sternberg and Hitchcock are not "symptoms" in this respect; instead they are models, straining the envelope of narrative coherence and pointing the way to a possible counter-cinema. Through an overvaluation of the image, Sternberg's films stress pictorial rather than narrative values. He deemphasizes depth illusion, stresses the flatness of the screen, stages non-linear plots, and, most importantly, refuses to mediate the look through the agency of the male protagonist: "for him the pictorial space enclosed by the frame is paramount rather than narrative or identification processes" (VP 14). Alternatively, the interest of Hitchcock for Mulvey is that he foregrounds erotic looking, making it central to the plot. He portrays the processes of identification associated with the look in a way that reveals their perverse origins. In Hitchcock's films, "erotic involvement with the look is disorientating: the spectator's fascination is turned against him as the narrative carries him through and entwines him with the processes that he is himself exercising" (VP 16). In sum, for Mulvey the look of the camera and of the spectator are subordinated in Hollywood cinema to the narrative organization of point of view and its requirements of unity, coherence, linearity, depth illusion, and diegetic verisimilitude. On one hand, "the look of the audience is denied as an intrinsic force," but on the other, "the female image as a castration threat constantly endangers the unity of the diegesis and bursts through the world of illusion as an intrusive, static, one-dimensional fetish" (VP 18). Thus the binary schema of Mulvey's analysis really begins with the structured oppositions of the counter-cinema argument, mapping them back onto Freud to build a theory of identification and distanciation that will "free the look of the camera into its materiality in time and space and the look of the audience into dialectics, passionate detachment" (VP 18).[17] The entire essay is organized according to the question of the specificity of the female body-image, rather than the specificity of the female look or feminine identification. In turn, questions of signification and identification in film are structured by a system of binary division and exclusion devolving from that body.

In Freudian theory, however, the relation of the body to the drives is not governed by such a straightforward binary logic. Instead, Freud draws a complex picture of the relations that attach the aims of the drives to systems of representation. In "Instincts and their Vicissitudes," for example, Freud suggests a classification of drive-components that defines their aims and objects according to both active and passive forms. Here masculinity and femininity are defined solely as psychological and cultural distinctions. In addition, the distribution of terms in Freud's instinctual theory is neither static nor immutable. It relies, in fact, on a mobility where given terms exchange places and functions within the structure of their division. Thus the fundamental vicissitudes for Freud are the reversal of a component into its opposite and the turning around of a drive upon the subject's own self. The examples he gives are especially apposite to Mulvey's analysis. The paired opposites Freud uses to explain the reversal of a form into its opposite are *voyeurism* (desire in looking)/*exhibitionism* (desire in being looked at); for the turning around of a form upon the subject's own self Freud uses the pair *sadism* (desire in controlling or hurting an other)/*masochism* (desire to be controlled or hurt). Thus Mulvey draws upon Freud's schema only to substitute fetishism for exhibitionism, and to exclude masochism. And where her schema is marked by a logic of binary opposition, Freud characterizes the mutability of his pairs as "ambivalence."

Once again the forms that channel the drives are understood to be active and passive by turns rather than being fixed immutably in their oppositions. Paradoxically, despite the power and the suggestiveness of her argument, Mulvey's thesis ultimately falters by imagining the female subject through the binary logic of the counter-cinema argument. And if the female subject becomes somewhat unimaginable in this context, it is not only because of difficulties in Freudian thought. In Mulvey's analysis the spectating subject is forcibly the male subject. When Mulvey defines the look according to its objective and subjective, as well as active and passive, relations, it is a look made for the male subject. Consequently, the only place for the female subject in her scenario is as an object defined in the receiving end of the glance or as the unrealized possibility of a counter-cinema. Her pairing of voyeurism and fetishism is also interesting in this respect because it is inconsistent with Freud's own schema.[18] Unlike exhibitionism, fetishism is not precisely a passive form of looking. Rather, it is better characterized by another vicissitude—repression. In this manner, a contradictory belief is set up within the ego in which the evidence of castration is elided. The ego is split into two epistemological scenes—one where the woman is phallic and undifferentiated and the other where she is understood to be without a penis.[19] The playing down of masochism is also interesting in Mulvey's essay. However, rather than being a misreading, this is better understood as a point necessitated by her political position. She hesitates—and not without justification—to characterize the position of the female subject as masochistic. This would define woman's place in representation solely as an object of aggression. Moreover, if she were to delimit a place for the female subject in this schema her logic would require that woman's relationship to representation, and to desire organized in representation, would of necessity be defined as masochistic economy.

But the question still remains: where is woman's place? Mulvey speaks of a male unconscious but a female unconscious takes place in her analysis only as an absence, a negativity defining castration and the not-masculine, or as a yet unrealized possibility. If the code of the look may be understood as a figure conjoining identification, desire, and the "phantasmization" of narrative as many theorists have suggested, what is the place and the function of the female subject with respect to this structure? How does this structure condition the possibility and even the knowledge of her desire through the politics of inclusion and exclusion so characteristic of the power relations of the classic, narrative text?

Chapter 2
The Return of the Exile

The universalization of subjectivity as maleness is without doubt, and justifiably, the primary target of feminist theory and criticism. While psychoanalysis has been imported to feminist theory and film theory as a tool for comprehending this problem, even the most sympathetic readers of Freud and Lacan have expressed ambivalence about this project.[1]

The work of Laura Mulvey, Stephen Heath, Raymond Bellour, and others has been indispensable for understanding the function of sexual difference in articulating narrative form and pleasure in the cinema. But the reasons for this ambivalence, even among the strongest adherents of psychoanalytic film theory, are twofold. First, a hegemonic and totalizing model of the ideological function of classic cinema has been constructed that leaves little room for historical variability. This seems true both with respect to accounting for historical changes in narrative form and to understanding the variability of the demands that ideology places on narrative forms. The most extreme version of this model is Raymond Bellour's *"blocage symbolique"* where the fantasy of the male, Oedipal trajectory is understood as informing effects of textual structuring from the most minute and specific to the most general and non-specific levels.[2] For Bellour identification is not anchored simply to a character or a look. It is organized by the imaginary "body" of the film itself as an effect of textual progression and expansion regulated by an Oedipal logic whose site of enunciation is the camera itself. In this respect, Bellour's work accords with that of Jean-Louis Baudry and Christian Metz on the cinematographic apparatus. Moreover, woman's place in this model has for the most part held a strictly determined position in even the most sympathetic analyses. Take for example these remarks by Raymond Bellour in an interview with Janet Bergstrom:

> It seems to me that the classical American cinema is founded on a systematicity which operates very precisely at the expense of woman, if one can put it that way, by determining her image, her images, in relation to the desire of the masculine subject who thus defines himself through this determination. Which means that the woman too finds herself involved, for herself, in relation to desire and the law, but in a perspective which always collapses the representations of the two sexes into the dominant logic of a single one. . . . To put it hastily, for of course things are somewhat more complicated than that, I think that a woman can love, accept and give a positive value to these films only from her

own masochism, and from a certain sadism that she can exercise in return on the masculine subject, within a system loaded with traps. All of which is far from being negligible![3]

The response by British and American feminists to this position has been to historicize the study of point of view structures, emphasizing the negativity associated with the staging of the look by the female body. Jacqueline Rose criticizes Bellour by focusing on the instability of the shot/reverse shot pattern as a function of paranoia and a return of the aggressivity of the look upon itself. Miriam Hansen's study of the films of Rudolph Valentino stresses the eroticizing of the male body by a desiring female gaze. Best known is the work of Mary Ann Doane on the vicissitudes of the female look in the woman's film of the 1940s.[4] In every case, however, the potential subversion or erosion of patriarchal ideology is shown to be contained ultimately by the overall narrative organization of the films.

There is a fundamental difference, however, between the position of Mulvey and the work she has inspired in Doane and others. Critics like Doane question the psychoanalytic paradigm itself, looking for alternative models in the work of Julia Kristeva, Luce Irigaray, and others that might allow the possibility of an "autonomous language" of subjectivity and desire. More importantly, where Mulvey anticipates the creation of new possibilities of subjectivity and desire for the woman by a feminist counter-cinema, Mary Ann Doane, Miriam Hansen, Kaja Silverman, Linda Williams, and Tania Modleski see important possibilities of female looking and identification to be already inscribed within the historical forms of Hollywood narrative as well as current independent, feminist cinema.[5]

This leads to the second reason why feminist film theory remains ambivalent towards Freud's thought. While psychoanalytic models of film analysis are criticized for totalizing film narrative within a phallocentric and patriarchal model, the work of Freud itself is questioned as to whether it can conceive a position for femaleness outside of a paradigm that universalizes subjectivity as male. In "Femininity and the Masquerade: Theorising the Female Spectator," Mary Ann Doane forcefully articulates this argument. Reading Freud's late essay on femininity from *The New Introductory Lectures,* Doane analyzes Freud's rhetoric demonstrating his exclusion of a "female spectator/auditor" in stating, "'. . . to those of you who are women this will not apply—you are yourselves the problem . . . .'"[6] According to Doane, Freud is unable to ask the riddle of femininity without invoking the ontological question of "what is man?" Freud introduces his riddle with four lines from Heinrich Heine's *The North Sea:* "Heads in hieroglyphic bonnets,/Heads in turbans and black birettas/Heads in wigs and thousand other/Wretched, sweating heads of humans . . ." In Doane's reading, Freud excises the line that immediately follows—"Tell me, what signifies Man?"—

as well as the fact that the stanza is presented as the address of a "young man." More importantly, Doane sees Freud's selection of these four lines as symptomatic: the riddle of femininity is associated in Freud's thought with clichéd images of masquerade, the enigmatic and undecipherable, and the language of hieroglyphics.

What is at stake, then, is how problems of sexual difference are addressed in psychoanalytic accounts of identification. In what terms do Freud and Lacan (the two are not necessarily equivalent) argue the problem of identification as a modeling process for the ego? To what extent are psychoanalytic accounts of identification coextensive with the "identification" of spectators in the viewing situation staged by the cinema? How has seventies film theory (Metz, Baudry, Bellour, Heath) incorporated the theoretical language of psychoanalysis, especially with respect to sexual difference? British and American film theory has produced two responses to these questions in the past 15 years. First, the gender "neutrality" of theoretical language has been questioned, demonstrating its universalization of the subject as male. The second response derives, from the critique of psychoanalysis and of the films purportedly addressed to women, an account of the specificity of the female spectator. For the most part, I believe the critique of "phallogocentricity" in psychoanalysis to be powerful and convincing. Following Luce Irigaray, special critical attention has been paid to Lacan's account of identification processes. For in his account of the castration and Oedipus complexes the acquisition of language and subjectivity seem welded dialectically by the signification of the phallus as the final arbitrator of difference. Paradoxically, this situation appears to leave women without language or a subjectivity.

The work of Mary Ann Doane provides one of the more interesting meditations on these problems. Without rejecting psychoanalysis outright she has consistently examined the possibilities for defining woman's "autonomous symbolic representation" in the language of psychoanalysis as well as the aesthetic forms of both Hollywood cinema and feminist independent cinema. For Doane, the question of the female spectator is epistemological: how do women establish a critical knowledge of their disenfranchisement with respect to language and vision? Her work, like many writing in the wake of Mulvey, gravitates between two approaches. One is to examine what terms are attributed historically and ideologically to "femininity" in theory and in film narratives. Doane finds the language of psychoanalysis and the forms of film narrative to be entirely complicit. Both present scenarios—in fact, strikingly visual and narrative scenarios—where "femininity, when it is infrequently and marginally discussed . . ., is analyzed in relation to a norm of masculine subjectivity and is inevitably found lacking or deficient" (DD 21). The reigning models of cinematic identification here are voyeurism and fetishism where pleasure in male looking is defined as seeing what is prohibited in relation to the woman's body. By the same token, "feminine" identification in psychoanalysis is often linked to masochism: pain, suffering, and aggression turned back on itself. Secondly, Doane suggests that in examining "the margins of the major masculine scenarios informing theories of the cinematic apparatus, one discovers a series of scenarios which construct the image of a specifically feminine subjectivity and spectatorial position as well" (DD 20). Psychoanalysis is open to a redemptive reading no less than the woman's film itself.

Describing "subjectivity," male or female, is not a simple issue and Doane is more careful than most in defining her range of references to this concept. In the opening chapter of *The Desire to Desire*, Doane carefully distinguishes between the problems of address, spectatorship, and subject-position. Where the woman's film of the 1940s is concerned, "address" indicates that the films are targeted—in terms of their marketing, themes, plot structures, and forms of point of view—to what is perceived to be a female audience: "The films deal with a female protagonist and often appear to allow her significant access to point of view structures and the enunciative level of the filmic discourse. They treat problems defined as "female" (problems revolving around domestic life, the family, children, self-sacrifice, and the relationship between women and production vs. that between women and reproduction), and, most crucially, are directed toward a female audience" (DD 3). Similarly, Doane emphasizes that the "projected image of the female spectator" in the woman's film cannot simply refer to the individual woman in the audience who is socially and psychically unique. As she describes it, *"femininity* and *masculinity, female spectatorship* and *male spectatorship,* do not refer to actual members of cinema audiences or do so only in a highly mediated fashion" (DD 8). Nonetheless, there is for Doane a powerful mediation of these terms that can be explained by psychoanalysis. Historically, the films encourage and perpetuate positions of identification aligned with the dominant definitions of sexual difference. She argues that men and woman enter the movie theater as social subjects who have been "compelled to align themselves" with one of the dominant binary divisions of sexual difference. Hence the importance in Doane's analysis of the isomorphism between the psychoanalytic and the cinematic scenarios of identity. For the ideological project of the films is to confirm the already determined sexual identities of the audience members. Doane does not challenge the binary division of gender across the terms of address, spectatorship, and position of identification. Rather, she examines the absence of a position of feminine identification that would fully coincide with an autonomous female subject. In this manner, she asserts that

> Men will be more likely to occupy the positions delineated as masculine, women those specified as feminine. What is interesting, from this point of view, is that masculinity is consistently theorized as a pure, unified, and self-sufficient

position. The male spectator, assuming the psychical positions of the voyeur and fetishist, can easily and comfortably identify with his like on the screen. But theories of female spectatorship constantly have recourse, at some level, to notions of bisexuality. . . . It is as though masculinity where required to effectively conceptualize access to activity or agency (whether illusory or not). (DD 8)

Doane also insists that this projection of a coherent and unified subjectivity, understood as the possession of men, is an illusory, if essential, function of the ego. Nevertheless, she remarks that the illusion of a coherent and controlling identity is valorized and made the property of men under patriarchy, while "the woman does not even possess the same access to the *fiction* as the man" (DD 11). In Doane's view, women simply do not have access to the terms for constructing a coherent identity (psychoanalytic or cinematic) in the same way as men, and this idea will be central to her argument. While these remarks accurately describe psychoanalytic film theory, there will be reason to challenge whether a careful reading of Freud supports them.

Thus Doane is careful to insist that the female spectator represented "in-the-text" is a virtual position and is not necessarily incumbent on any individual. However, no such reservations are extended to "the female spectator of theory"—that is, the position described for femininity by Freud—in psychoanalysis. Since Doane insists that the theoretical scenario of psychoanalysis and the narrative scenarios of the woman's film are in many respects isomorphic, difficulties arise in her argument. In each instance, these difficulties come about through the effort to describe an autonomous position for the woman as opposed to the man. And in every instance the division of the woman from the man relies on woman's different relation to castration. As Doane explores the margins of psychoanalytic theory, what she rehearses are the possible varieties of this difference with respect to identification-positions deemed attributable to women.

For Doane, the specificity of the female spectator (as psychoanalytic subject) is defined as "one who does not assume a masculine position with respect to the reflected image of her own body. . ." (DD 129). Her working assumption is that psychoanalytic theory can demonstrate that the woman is constructed differently from the man in relation to processes of looking and identification. To describe this difference, the criterion used by Doane in a number of essays involves the relation of proximity to distance.[7] In particular, Doane relies on Christian Metz's description of primary cinematic identification as modeled by Lacan's mirror phase and the perversions of voyeurism and fetishism in "The Imaginary Signifier."[8] For example, Doane's gloss in "Femininity and the Masquerade" asserts that the desire in seeing attached to voyeurism requires setting at a distance. In the Lacanian formula, desire blossoms in the gap where the subject pursues an absent and irrecoverable object. Thus Metz claims that "voyeuristic desire, along with certain forms of sadism, is the only desire whose principle of distance symbolically and spatially evokes this fundamental rent" (IS 60). Doane adds that the iconic density of cinema combined with the fundamental absence of the represented objects further duplicates and emphasizes the relation between distance and desire. Distance is also an epistemological figure. Earlier Doane remarks on the association of femininity with the image in patriarchal culture. Because signifier and referent are relatively indistinct, the image or iconic sign is understood as failing the representation of "proper nouns and abstract notions." In linking femininity and hieroglyphics as a writing in images, Freud, according to Doane, implies that women share the deficiency of the iconic system of representation: "it cannot disengage itself from the 'real', from the concrete; it lacks the gap necessary for generalisability (for Saussure, this is the idea that, 'Signs which are arbitrary realise better than others the ideal of the semiotic process')" (FM 76).

By the same token, Doane criticizes the work of Luce Irigaray, Sarah Kofman, Michèle Montrelay, and Hélène Cixous for describing the specificity of female subjectivity in terms of proximity, closeness, or the "overpresence" of the image characteristic of narcissism: "the female look demands a becoming. It thus appears to negate the very distance or gap specified by Metz and Burch as the essential precondition for voyeurism" (FM 78). This becoming, where the subject merges with the image itself rather than mastering it at a distance, is governed by the relation of the female body to the castration complex. Following Kofman, Doane suggests that the passing of the Oedipus complex—where the subject turns from the imaginary plenitude of the mother's body to the symbolic law of the father—is also understood by Freud as a passage from the senses to reason. This separation from the mother and identification with the father relies on having the bodily means to symbolize what the father possesses and the mother lacks—the signification of the phallus. Here Doane follows Montrelay claiming, "that while the male has the possibility of displacing the first object of desire (the mother), the female must become that object of desire. . . . This body so close, so excessive, prevents the woman from assuming a position similar to the man's in relation to signifying systems. For she is haunted by the loss of a loss, the lack of that lack so essential for the realisation of the ideals of semiotic systems" (FM 79). Not only woman's identity and language are at question here. In Doane's reading, the woman's access to desire is also difficult:

It is with the Oedipal complex, the intervention of a third (the father) in the mother-child dyad and the resulting series of displacements which reformulate the relation to the mother as a desire for a perpetually lost object, that the subject accedes to the active use of the signifier. Distance from the "origin" (the maternal) is the prerequisite to desire; and insofar as desire is defined as the excess of demand over a need aligned with the maternal figure, the woman is left behind. (DD 11–12)

Finally, where factors of spatial proximity and closeness to the body inform woman's problematic relation to identity, language, and desire, a temporal relation divides the sexes in relation to seeing and knowing. Like many others in film theory, Doane notes how Freud's narratives of childhood investigations of sexual difference rely on staging sight in relation to the body and the discovery of an other sex. In "Some Psychical Consequences of the Anatomical Distinction Between the Sexes," knowledge of sexual difference is predicated on the visibility of the penis and the child's rational-ization of its presence or absence. In Doane's gloss, for the girl seeing and knowing are simultaneous; no temporal gap divides them. On seeing the penis for the first time the little girl "'makes her judgment and her decision in a flash. She has seen it and knows that she is without it and wants to have it.' In the lecture on 'Femininity' Freud repeats this gesture, merging perception and intellection: 'The [girls] at once notice the difference and, it must be admitted, its significance too'" (FM 79).[9] The situation of boys is different. The sighting of the girl's body, perceived as a loss that threatens his own narcissistic integrity, is disavowed and delayed. In Doane's account, the threat of castration drives the boy to invest this sight with meaning after the fact. There are no snap judgments for the boy. This delay between seeing and understanding marks the quality of his knowledge with the capability of re-visioning, rereading, and of holding an image at a distance. And it is this balancing of knowledge and belief, this managing of distance between the visible and knowable, that informs Metz's and Doane's accounts of cinematic identification as an "epistemology" of the look in relation to the models of the mirror phase, voyeurism, and fetishism.

Thus voyeurism and fetishism are understood as the result of a particular structuring of the male look and identification in relation to the assumed castration of the woman's body and men's anxieties concerning that loss. For Doane, however, the difficulties of the woman—with nothing to lose and lacking the means to symbolize lack—must be understood differently. The psychical mechanisms that ground male looking, identification, and knowing are either not accessible to the woman or can be assumed only with difficulty. "The female," she writes,

> . . . must find it extremely difficult, if not impossible, to assume the position of fetishist. That body which is so close continually reminds her of the castration which cannot be 'fetishised away'. . . . The woman is constructed differently in relation to processes of looking. For Irigaray, this dichotomy between distance and proximity is described as the fact that: 'The masculine can partly look at itself, speculate about itself, represent itself and describe itself for what it is,

whilst the feminine can try to speak to itself through a new language, but cannot describe itself from outside or in formal terms, except by identifying itself with the masculine, thus by losing itself.' Irigaray goes even further: the woman always has a problematic relation to the visible, to form, to structures of seeing. (FM 80)[10]

Thus the special relation balancing proximity and distance is part and parcel of the system of masculine identification and the universalization of the subject as male under patriarchy. In Doane's account, however, ". . . identification on the part of the female reader or spectator cannot be, as it is for the male, a mechanism by which mastery is assured. On the contrary, if identification is even 'provisionally' linked with the woman (as it is for Irigaray), it can only be seen as reinforcing her submission" (DD 16). Here Doane suggests that "identification" is necessarily an ideological mechanism. Moreover, failing castration, women intrinsically have the capacity to "fail" identification or stand outside of ideology.

Doane is nonetheless ambivalent about this account. For in the degree to which she accepts Irigaray's arguments, in failing identification women would also fail identity, language, and a potentially critical, "distanced" relation to patriarchal ideology. She recognizes that the tropes of proximity, closeness, overidentification, and so forth are coincident with an ideological construction of femininity perpetuated by the woman's film no less than by "standard" psychoanalysis. Yet she feels that if these tropes appeal to woman spectators, no less than renegade woman psychoanalysts, then there must be some recognizable residue of an authentic, alternative feminine position with respect to seeing and knowing. In this respect, she places special emphasis on how two particular psychical mechanisms—narcissism and paranoia—are evoked and represented in the woman's film.

For Doane, figures of narcissism are the most ideological complicit components of the woman's film. Seducing women into "femininity," the staging of narcissistic relations in these films is meant to produce an identification for the woman that, paradoxically, dispossesses her of subjectivity. Following Irigaray, Doane holds to the idea that women fail even the phase of primary narcissism linked to the *stade du miroir* in Lacan. In patriarchal culture, the definition of the woman's body as the castrated body and its association with negativity means that

she has no separate unity which could ground an identity. In other words, she has no autonomous symbolic representation. But most importantly, and related to this failure with respect to identification, she cannot share the relationship of the man to the mirror. The male alone has access to the privileged specular process of the mirror's identification. And it is the confirmation of the self offered by the plane-mirror which, according to Irigaray, is "most adequate for the mastery of the image, of representation, and of self-representation." The term "identification" can only provisionally describe the woman's object relations—for the case of the woman "cannot concern either identity or non-identity." (DD 15–16)[11]

In the woman's film, figures of narcissism are attached to images of femininity to lure women as spectating and consuming subjects, encouraging them to refashion themselves as objects and commodities. This problem is clearest in Doane's analysis of *Caught* (Max Ophuls, 1949). The film opens within the look of the woman, as the character played by Barbara Bel Geddes thumbs through a fashion magazine commenting off screen: "I'll take this one" and "This one's for me." The character, whose desire for a fur coat is stimulated by the images of women in mink, will only obtain that desire by learning "to model" herself, to build herself into an image for men: "For the female spectator exemplified by Maxine and Leonora in this scene, to possess the image through the gaze is to become it. The gap which strictly separates identification and desire for the male spectator (whose possession of the cinematic woman at least partially depends on an identification with the male protagonist) is abolished in the case of the woman. Binding identification to desire (the basic strategy of narcissism), the teleological aim of the female look demands a becoming and, hence, a dispossession. She must give up the image in order to become it—the image is *too* present for her" (DD 157).

Doane makes a similar argument about the problematic of the female "transvestite" spectator, or the oscillation of identification between masculine and feminine polarities. In her "Afterthoughts on 'Visual Pleasure'. . .," Laura Mulvey criticizes her own universalization of masculine subjectivity by examining the possibility of how the active, female protagonists—and by extension, women in the audience—might gravitate between "regressive" masculine and passive feminine identifications. Inherently unstable, the female spectator is therefore understood as revolving between a narcissistic identification with her eroticized like on the screen and a transsexual identification with the active mastery of the masculine hero. But to the extent that the woman's film directs itself to a female audience, Doane argues, this "transvestite" economy is rechanneled to a more "proper," narcissistic, feminine identification.

For Doane, to the extent that the woman's film solicits the activity of scopophilia as a component drive, its purpose is to abolish the distance conducive to voyeurism. The woman's film stages the female spectator and encourages a narcissistic identification in order to encourage women to give up their subjectivity to be an image for the man. And if the narrative system fails to represent the protagonist as willingly adopting this position, the price is a "despecularization" of the image of the female body. This despecularization is represented as either the product of a fundamental masochism or the return of the sadistic activity of looking on the woman's own body. Since in the classical Hollywood cinema the appeal of the erotic and the specular is condensed in the body-image of woman, the despecularization of that image, as well as displacing the active, erotic look of the female protagonists, is tantamount to "disembodying" the female spectator: "the cinema, a mirror of control to the man, reflects nothing for the woman—or rather, it denies the imaginary identification which, uniting body and identity, supports the discursive mastery" (DD 19). In this manner, the option of a feminine and narcissistic identification is also contradicted. "In patriarchal society," Doane writes, "to desexualize the woman's body is ultimately to deny its very existence. The woman's film thus functions in a rather complex way to deny the woman the space of reading" (DD 19).

If strategies of narcissistic identification invoke the agency of female looking only to displace it by "despecularizing" the female body, for Doane, the role of paranoia in gothic narratives is even more disturbing. Nevertheless, there are two ways of reading this disturbance. First, the paranoid identifications of the gothic invest the activity of the female look itself with terror, anxiety, and horror because, in Doane's argument, it is "objectless." In its most literal sense, this is a fundamental mechanism of suspense in the cinema. Looking is invaded by terror where the desire to see is matched by the inability to discern an absent object of sight—to image or bring into focus an imagined hostile presence. By the same token, this anxiety attached to an imagined but indiscernible other is a fundamental mechanism of identification. Citing Lacan, Doane notes that the primary narcissism set in place by the mirror stage is always haunted by an aggressivity that threatens the unity and integrity of the subject's ego because the delineation between subject and object is still too imaginary, too fragile.[12] What is particularly at stake here is separation from the maternal body. This separation is at once the price of gaining a distinct identity as well as the inspiration of all the anxiety that the withdrawal of that body—source of nurturance, care, and love— may signify. Thus one of the functions of the paternal signifier in Lacan is to master difference by gaining access to the symbolic, the mastery of language and representation being equivalent to the fixing of distinctions between subject and object, inside and outside, and of course, male and not-male.

But the paranoid aspect of the gothic films has another, special interest for Doane. Following the arguments of Jacqueline Rose, Doane asserts that if paranoia is latent in the structure of the look as an aggressivity that threatens to destabilize the narrative system of the classic, Hollywood cinema, then the "paranoid woman's film" may constitute a special case: "While the mainstream Hollywood cinema organizes vision in relation to both spectacle and truth, and hence pleasure and fascination, the woman's film evinces a certain impoverishment of this mechanism" (DD 128). The very fact that the female look is represented as impoverished with respect to truth characterizes these films by an obsessive concern with epistemology as a potential negation of the relations between spectacle and truth, pleasure and fascination. This obsessiveness leads Doane to portray the paranoid woman's films as "metacommentaries" on sexual difference and Hollywood cinema: "There is, therefore, something about the filmic representation of paranoia, female paranoia in particular, which foregrounds and even, at points, interrogates a fundamental semiotic mechanism of the cinema" (DD 126).

For Doane, part of the interest of the relation between film and paranoia is their similar mobilization of auditory and visual representation. But the following three parallels are of even greater significance: the foregrounding of epistemology, destabilization of oppositions between subject and object, and "the foreclosure of the paternal signifier and corresponding fusion with the maternal" (DD 134). Each of these parallels has special consequences for the "metatextual" character of the films. The instability of the look has the gravest ideological consequences, for the very activity of the female look tends to return as an aggressive assault on the imaged female body, disenfranchising the protagonists of their activity and agency in the narration. Alternatively, the foreclosure of the paternal signifier, the defining characteristic of paranoia, suggests the possibility of interpreting the "disturbances" in the system of the gothic films as a non-phallic organization of representation: "The subject/object distinction, and hence access to the symbolic order, is predicated on absence. This is why Lacan defines paranoia as the foreclosure of the paternal signifier, that is, the phallus, the signifier of difference itself. Paranoia, in its repudiation of the Father, allies itself with the dyadic structure of narcissism, the imaginary, the pre-Oedipal" (DD 131).

The foregrounding of epistemology in these films is doubly motivated by the aggressive reversibility of the look and erosion of the coherence of representation of subjectivity promised by the paternal signifier. The desire to see and to know is characterized by the paranoid projection of anxiety onto the mise-en-scène of the films. For the female protagonist of the gothic films, the most familiar environment (the home) and the closest companion (the husband) are invested with an uncanny terror. In many respects, these mechanisms differ little from the usual strategies of suspense in the cinema. Referring to Freud's essay on "The Uncanny," Doane shows how the dialectic of concealing and revealing—attached to figures of point of view, no less than motifs of the door, windows, and staircases in the suspense and gothic films—devolves from the repressed sight of female genitals "because they represent, for the male, the possibility of castration and the concomitant rupture of the unified body image which supports a narcissistic identity" (DD 139). The castration anxiety invoked by uncanny figures causes a literal disturbance in the films as a crisis of visual perception. For Doane, what is interesting about the uncanny as a process of defense is its repetitiveness. Unable to master castration anxiety once and for all, it adopts a strategy of denial by an obsessive concern with the very process of seeing: "The uncanny defense against castration consists, paradoxically, not simply of blinding itself to the image of the castrated female body but of looking and looking again, as if replaying the original trauma would somehow ameliorate it. The foregrounding of the very process of seeing . . . therefore involves a kind of fetishization of vision itself, a reassertion of the integrity of perception along the lines of sexual difference" (DD 140).[13] Moreover, this foregrounding will have an epistemological function in Doane's reading.

But here Doane's argument makes an interesting turn. For the above analysis concerns the *male* defense against castration anxiety when in the woman's film it is the woman who is made the subject of the gaze and for whom home and husband have an uncanny effect. How could women experience the uncanny if, as Doane assumes, castration cannot pose a threat to the woman's narcissism because she has nothing to lose?

In answering this question, Doane makes her most interesting gamble in explaining the tension between the ideological project of the gothic films and their potential representations of an authentic, feminine experience. In Doane's analysis, the anxiety of the female spectator devolves not from an experience of the uncanny but of the "abject" as defined by Julia Kristeva in *Powers of Horror*.[14] Anterior to castration, unmediated and unrepresentable by the forms of difference deriving from the phallus, female scopophilia is, in Doane's formula, "a drive without an object" (DD 141). In this respect, the paranoid anxiety of the gothic films returns to the problem of narcissism as a preoedipal fantasy devolving from the difficulties of separating from the mother's body. This anxious drive in the gothic heroines to find an identity separate from an absent yet all-powerful maternal imago is a barely disguised staple of the genre; Hitchcock's *Rebecca* (1940) is one particularly convincing example. But for Doane, the paranoia represented in the woman's film is not a deviation. Rather, it becomes a psychological mechanism proper to women as a necessary condition of "female" scopophilia:

Although neither Freud nor Lacan point this out, the etiology of paranoia suggests that it corresponds not to a pathological but to a "normal" psychical condition in the case of the female. For separation from the mother and the acknowledgment of difference as represented by the paternal signifier are, in any event, more difficult for the female subject than for the male. In other words, the female never fully resolves her Oedipal complex and is thus linked more strongly to the realm of the pre-Oedipal than the male. From an initial state of autoeroticism, both sexes locate the mother as their first object. Hence, the externalization or, more accurately, the very constitution of the object for the male subject is synonymous with sexual differentiation. Externalization for the female is merely an encounter with the same, and the girl-child experiences very early the failure and collapse of the opposition internal/external, subject/object. . . . In the Freudian formulation, the female subject does not institute a search to "refind" the object; she becomes that object. . . .

It is, therefore, not so much a question of the difficulty of feminine identity (although the identity proffered by the mirror in the Lacanian schema, illusory as it may be, is clearly more problematic for the female for whom boundaries must remain less well defined). The crucial consideration, instead, is that of access to subjectivity with all this entails of an access to language. What we are dealing with, then, is not really a loss of identity but a return to the locus of its unthinkability—psychosis—the preverbal, the space outside of language, a space which in psychoanalysis is, properly speaking, maternal. (DD 144–145)

What is at stake then is a repressed fear more powerful than that of castration—separation anxiety devolving from the maternal body. The repressed memory of the narcissistic, dyadic relation between mother and child inspires terror rather than solace as the threat of annihilation of subjectivity, overwhelmed by the fantasized maternal body. For Doane, the staging of this preoedipal fantasy accounts for the inability of the woman's films to sustain a coherent representation of female subjectivity within the Oedipal and phallocentric discursive forms of the classic cinema.

The attempted representation of female desire—and the association of that desire with representations of the preoedipal, madness, and paranoia—threatens a disintegration of the unity of the cinematic sign. "This undoing of the stability of the cinematic sign," writes Doane, "is fully compatible with the paranoid foreclosure of the paternal signifier, the third term which is alone capable of stabilizing and regularizing signification by enforcing the unity of the sign" (DD 152). Moreover, this threat inspires several mechanisms of "hysterical" compensation and recontainment that attempt to restore the "phallic" power of the camera. In her analyses of *Caught* and *Rebecca*, Doane provides the most complex argument concerning the relation between narcissism and paranoia in the woman's film. Narcissism is defined by attributing the agency of looking to the female protagonists but only in a specific context: their gaze must outline an image that they themselves wish to become. But in Doane's view, the films find this agency of projected desire intolerable. In every case the aggressivity of looking is turned against the heroines—control of point of view is displaced and returned to male figures in the films.[15] For Doane the represented activity of the female look is inherently unstable. It causes "narrative stress" and a "disturbance in the cinematic relay of the look," that "is often reduced or avoided entirely by means of the delegation of the detecting gaze to another male figure who is on the side of the law" (DD 135). More insidiously, the narrative logic of the paranoid gothics most often compensates for the assumed lack of castration anxiety in the female spectator through a hyperbolic representation of the husband as the punishing and castrating symbolic Father. In Doane's words, "The obsession with a potentially murderous fatherlike husband is thus a cover for a more intense fear concerning the annihilation of subjectivity" (DD 145).

The logic of Doane's book is complex but her conclusions are easily summarized. Just as Freud "absents the female spectator of theory" in his lecture on femininity, the woman's film chronicles "the emergence and disappearance of female subjectivity, the articulation of an 'I' which is subsequently negated. . . . It is as though each film adhered to the logic which characterizes the dreamwork—establishing the image of an absent woman as the delayed mirror image of a female spectator who is herself only virtual" (DD 174–175). There is no mistaking the consequences of this argument. Doubling the scenarios of the films with psychoanalytic theory itself, Doane understands female subjectivity to be unrepresentable, the locus of an impossibility.

In her conclusion, however, Doane wishes to put a utopian spin on these ideas, redeeming both the impossible female spectator and the genre of the woman's film itself. First, if Doane concludes that female subjectivity is only difficultly produced within a patriarchal and Oedipal discourse, she also takes great pains to emphasize the logic of this difficulty rather than its outcome. To be more precise, femaleness is difficult because in Doane's view it eludes the identifications that formulate a coherent (i.e. male) subjectivity. Similarly, what seventies film theory has identified as the ideological character of identification in figures of fetishism and voyeurism is not appropriate to women because in failing castration they also fail identification. For Doane the female spectator is "caught" as it were in a contradictory position of identification: she can either accept the image (and in doing so give up her subjectivity to become the image) or she repudiates it, rejecting it entirely. In Doane's view this situation in no way mirrors that of the male spectator. Like Sean Connery in *Marnie,* he is a "card carrying fetishist": "the male spectator does not have to choose between acceptance or rejection of the image; he can balance his belief and knowledge. Deprived of castration anxiety, the female spectator is also deprived of the possibility of fetishism of the reassuring 'I know, but even so. . . .'" (DD 169).

Doane is attempting to define an alternative to Mulvey's "transvestite spectator" as well as the dilemma posed by Silvia Bovenschen where the woman must "either betray her sex and identify with the masculine point of view, or, in a state of accepted passivity, she could be masochistic/narcissistic and identify with the object of masculine representation."[16] But is Doane's view so different? The consequences of this idea are paradoxical for an argument wishing to avoid essentialism, because Doane fully accepts castration as an ontological arbitrator of gender difference; as such it invokes the logic of the binary machine. Women and men are divided *essentially* by the stakes involved in castration anxiety and Doane frequently invokes Irigaray's motto: "nothing to lose." Here again is the problem of a biological prop—the penis—as the signifier of patriarchal authority and power, when what is at stake for all social beings is the delegation of that power which under the sign of the phallus takes the form of division and hierarchy. By wanting to preserve the specificity of the female subject as a different relation to castration, Doane implicitly evokes a psychoanalytic "ontology." In this respect, the figure of the phallus mediates difference in ways that are no less powerful than Freud's. In each case the division between subject and object is mapped across the opposition male/female. And following the logic of the binary machine, "male" and "female" are constructed as self-identical entities defined by their opposing relations to mechanisms of identification; for example maleness is to voyeurism and fetishism (identification as the management of distance) as femaleness is to narcissism and paranoia (the abolishing of distance as proximity). As discursive constructs, these "alternatives" demonstrate the ideological project of the woman's film as defining, delimiting, and perpetuating a certain conception of "feminine" identity as hysterical, narcissistic, or paranoid. As such they are justifiably abhorrent to feminist criticism. But Doane also wishes to account for the pleasure taken in these films by women. Is it simply masochistic or is there some alternative possibility recognizable in these films by women? In her response, Doane follows Irigaray and Kristeva, as well as Mulvey and Bovenschen, in associating femininity with negativity; what she has changed is reserving, for the woman only, the possibility of failing identification and of refusing the images offered by Hollywood cinema.

But there is one last problem that Doane faces in this account. She accepts, for example, that distinguishing between subject and object is intrinsic to the activity of theorizing as understood by Freud, and she consistently represents "distance" as an epistemological figure. Given her particular conception of the female subject, how can a critical activity be appropriated for the female spectator by feminist film theory? And to what extent can this critical activity be equated with the idea of feminine pleasure?

The answer to this question is presented in Doane's essay on "Film and the Masquerade," which strongly informs the conclusion to her book. In fact, the epistemological foundation of her arguments, and the possibilities of critical knowledge for the female spectators and feminist film theory she imagines, are regulated by this idea. I have already argued that Doane implicitly constructs an ontological distinction between "masculine" and "feminine" identifications according to psychoanalytic criteria. Her presentation of an idea of "femininity as masquerade" now implies an epistemological distinction based on her initial opposition of proximity and distance. In Doane's terms, knowledge becomes the property of men, or rather, a masculine subject-position, because of the management of distance and access to symbolization that develops in her reading of the mirror stage, voyeurism, and fetishism as foundational models of identification. But these are also models of unconscious identification that have been associated with illusionism in contemporary film theory. Furthermore, in "Film and the Masquerade" Doane suggests that "while the male is locked into sexual identity, the female can at least pretend that she is other—in fact, sexual mobility would seem to be a distinguishing feature of femininity in cultural construction" (FM 81). This mobility of the female subject-position derives from her failing of castration and, consequently, the stabilization of identity, the distinction between subject and object, and the mastery of objects provided by symbolization.

However, Doane does not wish to recuperate this mobility through the idea of "transvestite" or transsexual identifications. Instead, she turns to Joan Riviere's analysis of "intellectual" and professionally successful women who compensate for their theft of masculine activity by exaggerating the cultural accoutrements of femininity. According to Riviere, "Womanliness could be assumed and worn as a mask, both to hide the possession of masculinity and to avert the reprisals expected if she was found to possess it—much as a thief will turn out his pockets and ask to be searched to prove that he has not the stolen goods. The reader may now ask how I define womanliness or where I draw the line between genuine womanliness and the masquerade. My suggestion is not, however, that there is any such difference; whether radical or superficial, they are the same thing."[17] For Doane, then, masquerade is an appropriation and reidentification of "masculine" activity. She characterizes this activity as a "foregrounding" where the woman becomes a producing subject of discourse, and as "an acknowledgement that it is femininity itself which is constructed as mask—as the decorative layer which conceals a non-identity" (FM 81). In this manner, Doane appropriates for the masquerade the function of negation and the creation of critical distance. The masquerade strategically "doubles representation" and "hyperbolizes" the accoutrements of femininity. In fact, at one and the same time, it appears to represent reflexively the *constructedness* of femininity as well as to erode the safety of the male look:

> The masquerade's resistance to patriarchal positioning would therefore lie in its denial of the production of femininity as closeness, as presence-to-itself, as, precisely, imagistic. . . . [It] involves a realignment of femininity, the recovery, or more accurately, simulation, of the missing gap or distance. To masquerade is to manufacture a lack in the form of a certain distance between oneself and one's image. . . . By destabilising the image, the masquerade confounds this masculine structure of the look. It effects a defamiliarisation of female iconography. (FM 81–82)

Doane appears to be using the idea of the masquerade to develop a theory of reading, as a way of manufacturing "a distance from the image to generate a problematic within which the image is manipulable, producible, and readable by the woman" (FM 87). Similarly, in her readings of the woman's film, Doane gravitates between the critical positions of "symptomatic reading" and justifying the films as "progressive texts." The place of symptomatic reading is very clear in Doane's book. She articulately, and in many places brilliantly, demonstrates both the films' perpetuation of stereotypes that associate femininity with sympathy, closeness, over-identification, and pathos. Just as important, she reads the ideological project of the films through the contradictions that result from attempting to ascribe the activity of looking and desire to a position that patriarchy has a stake in limiting, controlling, and even suppressing.

However, defining the potentially progressive aspect of these films for female spectators is more difficult in the book. And here the function of the masquerade in the woman's film—as a reflexive presentation of the constructedness of femininity—has an important role to play. What Doane is most interested in redeeming in the films is a possibility that the pleasure that female audiences take in them is irreducible to their ideological functioning. For Doane textual pleasure is always the result of a complex relation between recognition and misrecognition, and of course, these are also the key terms of the logic of identification in her analysis. In this respect her point of view resembles that of Fredric Jameson in his important essay "Reification and Utopia in Mass Culture."[18] Jameson argues that mass cultural representations should not be understood simply as either the reified mouthpieces of ideology or the genuine expressions of popular aspirations; rather, it is always possible to read a dialectic between these two forces— of reified and utopian expression—in historically specific popular culture narratives. For Doane there is a utopian dimension inscribed in the woman's film as the authentic property of women: "It is not that women's genres have nothing to do with a marginalized female culture which organizes them as the property of women, but that something gets lost in the transition" (DD 180). But Doane's position differs in important ways from Jameson's. Where Jameson is interested in developing strategies for reading mass culture, Doane wants to define subject-positions that are proper to, indeed only "recognizable by," women. Moreover, these positions have a critical function as defined by the masquerade. In this respect, the dialectic between misrecognition and recognition defined by Doane becomes somewhat confusing. The terms seem no longer to be a function of identification and subjectivity, but rather a way of redefining relations between object and subject. In other words, Doane implies that pleasure for women audiences cannot be defined simply by illusionism or falsification. (If the ontogenesis of femaleness is not stabilized by identification in the same way as maleness, how can women be "taken in"?) Pleasure occurs only in the recognition of some residue of "authentic" female experience within the ideological definitions of femininity formulated within the woman's film. What is important for Doane is that these definitions are stylized in the films and that their credibility is subverted in strategic images or scenes:

> In the process of "respeaking" the woman's desire something slips through. Or more accurately, perhaps, a "respoken" femininity is subjected to a respeaking in its turn. Double mimesis renders void the initial mime or, at the very least, deprives it of its currency. There is a slippage between the two representations. . . . In the woman's film, the process of remirroring reduces the mirror effect of the cinema, it demonstrates that these are poses, postures, tropes—in short, that we are being subjected to a discourse on femininity. (DD 180–181)

It is necessary to emphasize that what Doane is describing is a position inscribed *within* the text of the woman's film itself; it is not theorized as a reading that attempts to produce knowledge about the films by reappropriating them in different critical contexts. The figure of the masquerade is evoked as an epistemological and potentially critical function that belongs to the text of the woman's film no less than to the psychological "construction" of femininity. In Doane's account the masquerade restores, within the text, the distance that the subject-positions attributable to women attempt to abolish. A panoply of tropes of defamiliarization are similarly presented—the woman's film stylizes femininity and makes it fantastic; miming, acting out, reenacting, a contradictory division between image and voice—to assure that there is something recognizable for women in the ideological figures of sight of the woman's film. Mimicry becomes a "political textual strategy" (DD 182). In short, Doane asserts that "The effectivity of masquerade lies precisely in its potential to manufacture a distance from the image, to generate a problematic within which the image is manipulable, producible, and readable by the woman" (FM 87).

Doane's particular use of psychoanalytic theory confuses the activities of identification and reading. Two observations might clarify this confusion. As she develops her argument concerning the masquerade, Doane evokes the entire rhetorical machinery of the discourse of political modernism. In its most progressive manifestations, the text of the woman's film is characterized by figures of defamiliarization, double mimesis, reenactment, interrogation of the image by the voice; in short, all the mechanisms of textual reflexivity that are assumed to manufacture a distanced and thus "critical" relation in the text and for the spectator. As a formal property of the sign and the text, distanciation works against "identification" to produce positions of critical reading within the text for women. Despite the acknowledged difficulties of defining the specificity of the woman's film, the masquerade as a critical figure requires an ontological justification. There must be figures that are "proper" only to the text of the woman's film, that are expressive of a genuine experience of femininity, and that will produce the tropes of defamiliarization proper to the masquerade in a way that is recognizable only by women. These figures are the representations of narcissism and paranoia, complexly described by Doane as eroding the Oedipal and phallic narrative paradigms of the Hollywood cinema. Recall again Doane's characterization of paranoia as a non-phallic economy inscribed within the more traditional mechanisms of suspense in the woman's film. In its foreclosure of the paternal signifier and corresponding return to the maternal, its destabilization of object and subject, and its foregrounding of epistemological agency in the female narrators, the gothic films literally disrupt the norms of Oedipal narratives, inspiring a hysterical and hyperbolic effort to contain or overturn the woman's narrational activity. And to the extent that Doane sees her work as a necessary prolegomenon for defining a feminist political modernism or an autonomous language of desire for women, these moments of disruption herald utopian possibilities for the feminist cinema to come.

There are many ways in which I have no argument with this analysis as an account of the ideological contradictions evident in many of the woman's films of the 1940s. But the figure of the masquerade presupposes a (self-) conscious activity as a defining property of the texts that is necessarily reproduced as a (self-)conscious activity of the female spectator. Paradoxically, psychoanalysis is the one theoretical discipline that radically dismantles any such appeal to a uniquely conscious, thetic activity. Similarly, Doane makes a great effort to characterize femininity as "unrepresentable," at least within a phallocentric paradigm of signification, and then attempts herself to represent "women" through psychoanalytic theory as a self-identical collective subject. Finally, there is a paradoxical relation between identity and distance in the way that the masquerade is characterized by Doane as a way of appropriating a position of reading for women.[19] Again, the figure of distance carries a definitive epistemological value for Doane. Moreover, this value is always defined by a certain interiority—it is producible within the text of the woman's film as a disjunction between signifier and signified, and image and voice, and it is potentially reproducible as a position that renders the image "manipulable, producible, and readable by the woman." This "mimetic" reproduction "in" the spectator of a position already defined within the formal space of the text characterizes the way in which all the figures of "Brechtian" distance invoked by the discourse of political modernism collapse into an identity theory of knowledge. As an epistemological figure, the masquerade is tautological. While required to manufacture distance in the text and in the spectator, it paradoxically serves to render them formally and functionally identical.

I will conclude by suggesting that there is another way of reading Freud. I suggested earlier that the "scandal" of Freud's invocation of Heine's "Fragen" in the lecture on femininity might be his pretense at having solved the riddle of identity *per se*. But a close reading of the opening pages of Freud's argument proves otherwise. Where the security of sexual identity is concerned, it is a text permeated with irony concerning the ability to decide or differentiate [*unterscheiden*].

Doane's version of sexual difference is ontogenetic if not essentialist. In her reading of psychoanalysis, woman's different relation to castration, and hence identification and symbolization, is meant to produce an ontological space for femininity to occupy. This is a curious account of the history of the subject. For individuals to undergo that liminal experience where sexual identity branches into masculinity and femininity, paradoxically, they must face the castration complex as already divided into male and female, which is why Doane relies so heavily on Montrelay and Irigaray. Equally curious is Doane's faith in the distinctiveness of masculine forms of identification as distance (voyeurism, fetishism) from the feminine as proximity (narcissism, paranoia). However, as Kaja Silverman has recently emphasized, the ontological, much less epistemological, security granted to "masculinity" by much of contemporary psychoanalytic film theory is fundamentally at odds with both Freud's and Lacan's version of the division of the subject.[20] For me, the primary question is: what is the logical nature of this division, and what are its consequences for a critique of patriarchal ideologies?

Undoubtedly, the construction of identity through a binary model of division and hierarchy is a powerful consequence of patriarchal ideology. Doane is frankly ambivalent as to whether Freud's psychoanalysis ultimately perpetuates or challenges this model. That indecision devolves, I believe, from the necessity of an *a priori* understanding of the experience of sexual identity as being ineluctably divided and opposed. What Freud's argument challenges is precisely this necessity, which is why Doane's reading in "Femininity and the Masquerade" is problematic. In fact, the notorious line from Freud's essay—"Auch Sie werden sich von diesem Grübeln nich ausgeschlossen haben, insoferne Sie Männer sind; von den Frauen unter Ihnen erwartet man es nicht, sie sind selbst dieses Rätsel" (Stud. 1: 544)—has been quoted more often and more radically out of context than Freud's apparent misappropriation of Heine.

Freud begins his lecture with a forceful interpellation—"Meine Damen und Herren!"—, but from this moment on the decisiveness of these two categories begins to shift and falter. The moment authorizing speech is difficult; Freud wrestles [*ringern*] with an internal difficulty [*einer inneren Schwierigkeit*] and is uncertain of the extent of his authority. In short, in turns of phrase no less exemplary of the work of the unconscious than Lacan's own rhetorical style, Freud undercuts his own position of speaking to the extent that it is based on the authority to ask and resolve questions of sexual being. The irony of Freud's comment, "from the women among you, one does not expect it—you are yourselves the riddle," is reserved, I believe, neither for "men" nor "women," but rather for those who require decisive answers to questions whose interest derives from the fact that they are undecidable; namely, "Was bedeutet der Mensch?" The target of Freud's irony here is emphatically the status of ontological questions. Further, Freud is more self-conscious than he is often credited for that the riddle of femininity is an imaginary projection of "man's" ontological doubts and in fact goes one better. The expectation of an *a priori* division between the sexes, which Freud casts into doubt from the first moments of his text, represents for Freud the impossible attempt to gain an ontological foundation whose security is unthreatened by difference and division. Psychoanalysis demonstrates that this foundation is destined to dissolve and shift beneath the constructions of identity. Like Heine, Freud considers the "questions" of identity to be oceanic, fluid, based on undecidability, and predisposed to the same outcome:

> Es murmeln die Wogen ihr ew'ges Gemurmel,
> Es weht der Wind, es fliehen die Wolken,
> Es blinken die Sterne gleichgültig und kalt,
> Und ein Narr wartet auf Antwort.[21]

While the foolish, young man anguishes and waits for an answer [*wartet auf Antwort*], from women one is not expected [*erwartet man es nicht*]. Could this be because through a lifelong study of the "riddle of femininity," Freud understood that gendered identity for either sex was not "one," that is, singular, selfsame, or isomorphic with the biological body?

Chapter 3
Reading Freud . . . Differently

Freud argues that there is no libido other than masculine. Meaning what? other than that a whole field, which is hardly negligible, is thereby ignored. This is the field of all those beings who take on the status of the woman— if, indeed, this being takes on anything whatsoever of her fate."
—Jacques Lacan, S XX: 75[1]

Freud's address to his audience in the lecture on "Femininity" is uncertain because for Freud sexual identity remained a lifelong psychological problem for individuals of either sex. The history of Freud's encounter with the "problem" of femininity—which is no less powerful in the case of the Wolf Man than it is in Dora—is in fact a confrontation with the ontological groundlessness of identity for every individual. The problem of sexual difference represents the attempt to gain a secure identity through division (masculine *or* feminine), an attempt that is usually doomed to failure. Freud never examined the historical and ideological consequences of this discovery. Nonetheless, he gained considerable insight into its "historical" nature.

In this respect, Doane rightly insists on examining how the female subject is constructed in theory. Or in other terms, what versions of the forms and processes of subjectivity are assumed by psychoanalysis? The difficulties of Freud's attributions of sexual difference are usually accounted for by examining contradictions and ideological biases in Freud's arguments. Undoubtedly, these contradictions and biases operate in powerful ways. However, I want to begin this chapter by examining how contemporary film theory, in its appropriation of Freud's work, constructs *its* version of subjectivity. How is Freud read by contemporary film theory and what versions of sexed identification and subjectivity are derived from this reading?

In the wake of Laura Mulvey's foundational work, feminist film theory has made the most important contribution to this question by fashioning an image of the female subject as *activity*—looking, desiring, identifying, and making meaning. One of the most interesting contributions to this theoretical effort is Linda Williams's "'Something Else Besides a Mother': *Stella Dallas* and the Maternal Melodrama."[2] Williams's arguments are similar to Doane's in that she examines how women might "recognize" in mass cultural artifacts a language appropriate to their experience under patriarchy and potentially speak to one another through that language. However, for Williams this activity of recognition cannot be represented by identification alone. Rather, she presents the possibility of a "female reading competence" with respect to melodrama and other "feminine" narrative forms. Williams's implicit distinction between identification and reading is an important one. However, her idea of reading competence does not derive from a sociological perspective like Stuart Hall's and thus is not comparable to the situation of a negotiated or oppositional reading. Instead Williams asserts that "melodramas also have reading positions structured into their text that demand a female reading competence. This competence derives from the different way women take on their identities under patriarchy and is a direct result of the social fact of female mothering" (SEB 8).

Several problems are already evident in Williams's argument. In her essay, female reading competence derives equally from a textual and a social positioning that is the construction of femininity according to psychoanalytic theory. One of the most important sources of Williams's analysis is Nancy Chodorow's *The Reproduction of Mothering: Psychoanalysis and the Sociology of Gender*.[3] Chodorow's book is, I believe, one of the most important contemporary rereadings of Freud, no less so for its critique and historical contextualization of Freud's thought than for its radical historicizing of the question of gender construction. But rather than appealing to Chodorow's historical arguments, Williams emphasizes instead how she might be used to explain the fundamental difference of femininity. Here Chodorow is placed with Williams's other theoretical sources, Luce Irigaray and Julia Kristeva, with interesting consequences. The common denominator between these three sources is an emphasis on the woman's preoedipal attachment to her mother as a formative experience of femininity. Because of the difficulty of breaking this powerful, narcissistic attachment, Williams represents female subjectivity as being intrinsically divided. Williams reads Chodorow and Irigaray as challenging standards of unity and autonomy that are traditionally associated with male subjectivity. In this respect, Williams writes that "Chodorow's analysis of the connectedness of the mother-daughter bond has pointed the way to a new value placed on the multiple and continuous female identity capable of fluidly shifting between the identity of mother and daughter" (SEB 9). Williams's discussion of Kristeva complicates this idea. Williams is disinclined to accept Irigaray's utopian solution of a space of language and desire that is formulated outside of patriarchy. Thus she turns to Kristeva for a sense of how femininity can position itself within the divisions of patriarchal language. Kristeva represents this division as an irreconcilable dialectic between two orders of language: the semiotic, as the maternal unrepresentable, and the symbolic as the paternal already-represented. Through Kristeva, Williams envisions feminine identification has always multiple, never singular, divided within itself, and contradictory.[4]

Williams asserts that this experience of division and contradiction also marks certain women's genres like the maternal melodrama. In her analysis of *Stella Dallas* (1937), Williams suggests that the succession of poses and masquerades staged by Stella, as well as the ironic division between the public point of view of Stella's behavior as distasteful or ridiculous, and the private point of view the audience shares of Stella's suffering motherhood, is isomorphic with this divided and contradictory subjectivity. Williams takes issue with critics who view the ending as abstracting Stella into an ideal of motherhood that resolves all the contradictions of femininity represented in the preceding scenes. Instead, she argues that

> although the final moment of the film "resolves" the contradiction of Stella's attempt to be a woman *and* a mother by eradicating both, the 108 minutes leading up to this moment present the heroic attempt to live out the contradiction. It seems likely, then, that a female spectator would be inclined to view even this ending as she has the rest of the film: from a variety of different subject positions. In other words, the female spectator tends to identify with contradiction itself—with contradictions located at the heart of the socially constructed roles of daughter, wife *and* mother—rather than with the single person of the mother. (SEB 17)

Williams characterizes this identification as a "double vision" typical of most female spectators. Moreover, this typicality derives from an ontogenetic argument bolstered by Williams's reading of Chodorow. Male identity is formulated by a linear sequence of differentiations from his original object of identification, the maternal imago. For the woman however this spatial sequence is dissolved into the copresence of a number of positions. Whereas Doane defines femininity as an over-identification that must be counteracted with a distance borrowed from masculinity as "masquerade," Williams sees femininity as having its own special form of distance: "I would argue instead that this manufacturing of distance, this female voyeurism-with-a-difference, is an aspect of *every* female spectator's gaze at the image of her like. For rather than adopting either the distance and mastery of the masculine voyeur or the over-identification of Doane's woman who loses herself in the image, the female spectator is in a constant state of juggling all positions at once" (SEB 19).

Williams continues this thought with the rather extraordinary claim, borrowed from Ruby Rich, that "women experience films much more dialectically than men."

> "Brecht once described the exile as the ultimate dialectician in that the exile lives the tension of two different cultures. That's precisely the sense in which the woman spectator is an equally inevitable dialectician." The female spectator's look is thus a dialectic of two (in themselves) inadequate and incomplete (sexually and socially) differentiated subject positions. Just as Julia Kristeva has

shown that it is the dialectic of a maternal body that is channeled and repressed into a single, univocal significance that makes it possible for women to be represented at all, so does a similar dialectic inform female spectatorship when a female point of view is genuinely inscribed in the text. (SEB 19–20)[5]

The premise of this passage is not only that female subjectivity is "inevitably" dialectical, but that its distinctiveness is defined by an epistemological character absent from male subjectivity. This is an extraordinary reversal of Doane's argument. Moreover, this epistemological experience derives from the female spectator's dialogic relation with a similar dialectic "genuinely inscribed in the text." Williams describes this dialectic as the relation between believing and knowing that Christian Metz adopts from Octave Mannoni in his representation of cinematic looking through the model of fetishism. Thus, whereas the spectator imagined by Metz chooses to believe in the cinematic illusion while knowing it to be an illusion, Williams suggests that when confronted by a film that "constructed its spectator in a female subject position locked into a primary identification with another female subject," the possibility of a radical feminist reading is generated (SEB 22). At the end of the film, while Stella stares through the window, choosing to believe in the happy spectacle of her daughter's marriage, Williams claims that the female spectator "knows" the artifice and suffering behind it. Because for Williams, the woman identifies with contradiction itself, unlike the male fetishist who displaces knowledge to maintain an imaginary belief, feminine identification involves a different form of disavowal: "It is both a *knowing* recognition of the limitation of woman's representation in patriarchal language and a contrary *belief* in the illusion of a pre-Oedipal space between women free of the mastery and control of the male look. The contradiction is as compelling for the woman as for the male fetishist, even more so because it is not based on the presence or absence of an anatomical organ, but on the dialectic of the woman's socially constructed position under patriarchy" (SEB 21). Reading becomes less a historical division between text and spectator that always makes it possible to create a new position of appropriation and reading, than a mirror between text and subject where an authentic experience is represented in sometimes distorted but always recognizable ways. All of which is to say that psychoanalysis becomes the story of the ontogenesis, in the sense of ontological development, of femininity.

Like Doane, what Williams really wishes to define is less a position of reading than a definitive way of dividing the woman's experience of texts from the man's by identifying textual processes and subject-positions that mirror one another as the collective property of women. Williams's analysis of *Stella Dallas* is extremely interesting in its description of how a Hollywood film can encode multiple and contradictory points of view within a single text. But according to Williams this experience of contradiction is only available to women as a product of their psychological development.

The theoretical dilemma posed by Williams's argument is clarified by examining how she addresses the problem of identification. There are two principal references to this concept in her essay, although the border between them is not often clear: the first is a properly psychoanalytic use of the term; the second, a construction of contemporary film theory. In psychoanalysis identification refers to processes where subjectivity and sexual identity model themselves through the incorporation of idealized images and relations from the outerworld. Though undoubtedly organized around a subject/object problematic, psychoanalytic theories of identification are strictly limited by the analysis of subjectivity. In Freud's few aesthetic writings, for example, analysis either treats the artwork as a phantasmatic projection of the artist's inner world (as in the study of a childhood memory of Leonardo da Vinci [1910c]) or produces a reflexive investigation of specific aesthetic affects ("The Uncanny" [1919h]). There are undoubtedly severe limitations to a classically Freudian aesthetic theory, but at least its methodological assumptions are relatively clear. The same cannot be said for how the problem of identification is treated by textual analysis in film theory. Properly speaking, textual analysis proceeds by the interpretive construction of a formal *object* with a view toward understanding problems of narrative structure, filmic signification, or diectic representation (the encoding of positions of subjectivity), all of which are important contributions to film theory. The problem occurs when *representations* of subjectivity are treated as subjective processes themselves, or when textual forms are considered as identical to subjective effects. Williams attempts to obviate this problem by treating the social construction of femininity and the narrative form of the maternal melodrama as separate yet isomorphic structures. Yet it is that very parallelism, designated as a "feminine reading competence," that allows female spectators to "recognize dialectically" the experience of their subjective construction under patriarchy. We are not so far from Doane after all.

The key questions here are how the problem of identification, especially sexual identification, is formulated by contemporary film theory, and whether or not this formulation imposes a logic of identity on psychoanalytic theory. Several related yet distinct questions must also be disentangled. The problem of identity first refers to the ideological construction of positions of subjectivity. Mulvey, Doane, and Williams all presume that sexual identity, construed in this sense, is exhaustively defined by the opposition of masculinity to femininity as distinct, selfsame, and irreconcilably opposed gender categories. From this binary schemata, positions of desire and knowledge are attributed to aspects of filmic signification and correlated with sexual identity. Here the arguments of Doane and Williams compliment one another in interesting ways. Doane sees positions of identification as intrinsically divided along gender lines. Voyeurism and fetishism belong to masculinity defined as "distance"; narcissism and paranoia belong to femininity defined as "proximity." Williams picks up on the "epistemological" associations of distance and extends the schema in a different way. Where critical "reading competence" is concerned, masculinity is associated with linearity, unity, and coherence, while femininity is marked by its fluidity, attention to contradiction, and capacity for dialectical thought.

According to this view, there are psychological and cognitive properties that belong only to women or only to men, and these properties are "reflected" in aesthetic texts in recognizable ways. Here the problem of identity refers to the form of the relation between subject and object.[6] In Williams's argument the social constructions of sexed subjectivity under patriarchy, and the positions of sexual identification represented in film texts, are identical in form. Through their supposed processes of identification, the films are presumed to reflect, if not repeat, the Oedipal, or as some would have it, the preoedipal story of identity. This position relies on an odd proprietary argument where aesthetic forms and structures of identification are divided between those that belong to men and those that belong to women, and where a socially constructed identity is always already guaranteed by a biologically gendered body. In this binary grid, neither a historical experience of race, class, nationality, nor deviant sexuality, much less an alternative critical position, will alter an experience of texts that only the sexed body can verify.

There are real risks in understanding the psychological development of individuals as linked tautologically with forms of cultural expression, especially when the dominant question is how one produces critical knowledge of mass culture. This is especially true for understanding the decisive and important contributions that critics like Mulvey, Doane, or Williams have made to these problems. In this manner, feminist film theory has often risked using psychoanalysis as an empirical science. I use the term "empirical" in a philosophical, not sociological, sense to refer to two tendencies. First there is the tendency to pose the work of criticism as the "rediscovery" of otherwise occluded elements of "authentic" feminine experience in both the texts of mass culture and feminist counter-culture. This experience is assumed *a priori* to be a property of the texts themselves, and not a critical construction of an informed reading, that simply waits for a proper gaze to illuminate and recognize it. The proper subject of this gaze is "the female spectator." The second tendency is to use psychoanalysis to recover an ontological ground for this subject. While refuting "essentialist" arguments with Freud or Lacan, feminist film theory has often invoked an "ontogenetic" conception of femaleness as, for example, an emphasis on preoedipality or a different relation to the castration complex. Both positions require that proper recognition of feminine identity be treated as the property of a recognizably female body. Ultimately, it matters little whether the self-identity of feminine experience is grounded in a real or imaginary body, for the ontological or "empirical" nature of the question derives from its phrasing as mutually exclusive pairs: male/female. What one gains by positing the singular specificity of "feminine" experience is achieved only at the cost of glossing over the variegate possibilities of hetero- and homosexual identities and pleasures, not to mention the multiple dimensions of subjectivity defined by class, race, and nationality.

Implicit in these arguments, and explicit in the work of Mary Ann Doane, is the criticism that Freud ignores or is unable to define the position of "femininity." In my view, quite the opposite is true; the difficulty of difference in Freud's writing lies elsewhere.

Freud's case histories and analyses of phantasy life repeatedly address the question of femininity. If Freud considered late in life that this question remained the "dark continent" for psychoanalysis, it wasn't for lack of trying to formulate it. The implicit conceit of Freud's statement is the pretense of having resolved the problem of *masculinity;* the difficulty from the point of view of his own discoveries is attempting to theorize subjectivity by dividing and separating these two terms. In contemporary film theory, the binary definition of sexual identity is too often characterized by the assumption that maleness can be associated with a sense of imaginary coherence and fullness of consciousness as opposed to the unrepresentability or negativity of femaleness. The former idea can be attributed to Jean-Louis Baudry's sketchy reading of Lacan and Freud (Metz presents a more complicated case); the latter idea derives from Kristeva's Hegelianizing of Lacan along lines of sexual difference. My point is that this logical schema is a product of film theory. It has produced a framework through which psychoanalytic theory is read and to which it is made to conform. To understand what psychoanalytic theory might still contribute to the study of sexual difference, especially in film and other artifacts of mass culture, the question of how the concept of difference is formulated in Freud's texts must be reconsidered.

If I were writing as a biographer and intellectual historian, I would explain Freud's paradoxical treatment of sexual difference in the following terms. Whenever Freud has recourse to the distinction between "masculinity" [*Männlichkeit*] and "femininity" [*Weiblichkeit*], he is caught between two contradictory "knowledges": on one hand, psychoanalysis' discovery that sexual identity is irreducible to anatomical or physiological definitions; on the other, Freud's belief in the norm of the nineteenth century, Western family where sexuality is defined as reproductive heterosexuality organized around the claims of patriarchal privilege. Here the structure of Freud's arguments and rhetorical style are themselves exemplary of a logic of disavowal as Freud's critics never tire of pointing out. Caught between knowledge and belief, Freud remained stubbornly blind to the ideological limits and consequences of his theoretical discoveries.

This critique is easily made and is now largely self-evident in Freud's writings. However, it has not yet contributed substantially to the issues that sympathetic critics want to foreground in Freud's texts; namely, the possible contributions of psychoanalysis to a theory of ideology and an alternative understanding of sexual difference. A redemptive reading of Freud's texts on sexual difference is confronted with great difficulties in this regard. Simply exposing contradictions in Freud's thought will not suffice. Rather, a redemptive reading must minutely engage and dissect the tangled lines of thought produced by the nearly 40 years of revision, rewriting, and autocritique as represented in Freud's treatment of the problem of sexual difference.

The set of terms Freud used to describe the problem of sexual identity— activity-passivity, masculinity-femininity, narcissism-anaclisis [*Aktivität-Passivität, Männlichkeit-Weiblichkeit, Narzißmus-Anlehnungs*] are notoriously mobile and non-linear, often coming together, dissolving, and recombining in dizzying constellations. In this respect, I want to propose a set of distinctions for charting the Freudian rhetoric of sexual difference. One way to begin is to ask whether Freud's treatment of the problems of "femininity" [*Weiblichkeit*] and "female sexuality" [*weibliche Sexualität*] can be rigorously distinguished?[7] Freud's crucial distinction between identification and object-choice is illuminating here. Freud most often outlines the question of female sexuality as a developmental schema leading to normative heterosexual object-choice and sexual behavior. The problem of infantile sexual development involves channeling a "polymorphous sexuality" through the Oedipus and castration complexes, thus coordinating a normative (hetero)-sexuality with a biologically defined body; in other words, for Freud this is the story of how little girls become women. Conversely, the concept of "femininity" is nowhere in Freud's work exclusive to the psychology of women, nor is "masculinity" exclusive to the psychology of men. Here Freud's treatment of the complexities of *identification* is focused on the detours, deviations, and divarications from "normal" sexual behaviors represented by the case histories, analyses of phantasy, and the theory of "perversions." Under the heading of object-choice, sexual identity is considered as a set of coherent positions, divided in two, and unified within themselves according to a binary conception of gendered character and behavior. With the problem of sexual identification, subjectivity is no longer unified, singular, nor capable of reduction to a biological body. However, since the problem of achieving a set of feminine identifications is crucial to Freud's theory of female sexuality, how can these two sets of separate yet indistinguishable questions be disentangled?

This question hearkens back to Freud's efforts in 1915 and 1930 to distinguish rigorously between the biological, sociological, and psychological definitions of masculinity and femininity. Freud's claims for the specificity of psychoanalysis devolved not only from the noncoincidence of biological and sexual identity, but also from the presumption that sexual identification could only be described by the logic of unconscious thought, which psychoanalysis alone was prepared to account for. For Freud, sociology mistakenly sees the "finished" individual as defined by sexual *opposition*. There are "men" and "women" indexed to a "normal" genital development; inbetween there are a variety of "deviant" sexual practices, activities, and identities, not the least of which is the complex and highly differentiated series of homosexual identities. Instead of accepting at face-value the two ends of this distinction, psychoanalysis discovered its specificity through the complexity, differentiation, and instability of the "inbetween." Where sociology saw either "men" or "women," and subsequent deviations from a norm, psychoanalysis saw a variety of fluctuating configurations in the ratios between masculine and feminine identifications within every individual. More simply put, the idea that there could be *a* "masculine" or *a* "feminine" identification, equatable in any direct sense with a "man" or a "woman" is incommensurable with Freud's theory of sexuality.

Freud insisted on this distinction because he wanted to preserve the autonomy and specificity of his psychological definitions of sexual identity. Nonetheless, he did not question the patriarchal norm of sexual division, nor did he easily recognize its power over other aspects of social life and labor. This problem has provoked many sympathetic critiques such as Nancy Chodorow's *The Reproduction of Mothering,* and has produced the potential for confusion in Freud's arguments. In my view, understanding the logic and the rhetoric of sexual difference in Freud requires imposing five sets of distinctions which, while a sympathetic reading might find them implicit in his thought, are nowhere clearly articulated. Briefly, these distinctions include: men-women, man/woman, male . . . female, active↔passive, and masculine:feminine. These five sets formulate different ways of categorizing the experience of gender under patriarchy; each is distinguished with its own particular logic of differentiation. While they interact in complex and contradictory ways, they must not be understood as forming any synthetic unity or totality. In this way, I want to emphasize the ways that psychoanalysis resists understanding gender as a monadic category. A brief digression working through these distinctions will clarify my subsequent arguments.

The starkest contrast is between the first two sets. The first set suggests commonsensically that men and women should be considered as concrete, historical beings living out—in singular if fragile and often conflicted and contradictory ways—the gender constructions they have chosen, accepted, or acquiesced to. The range of differentiation here is meant to be as extensive as possible to account for the resolutely individual ways that historically specific beings struggle with options and choices regarding social life, labor, and sexual practice. (It is given that the idea of "choices and options" is hierarchically defined and inequitably distributed under capitalism and patriarchy.) Where "men-women" describes a plethora of singular situations, the categorical "man/woman" wants to distribute every individual into two great masses defined by the sexual mythology of patriarchal culture. As the gender pattern designated by the binary machine, it is an ideological distinction and must be treated as such. This is the division of the sexes formulated according to the historical and semiotic practices that patriarchal culture uses to define gender and to hold individuals to a sexual division of labor. As such, it is a powerful (though nonetheless challengeable) discursive norm that replicates itself in legal, medical, economic, aesthetic, and political practices. In fact, it thoroughly informs the official and unofficial institutional legislations of private and public life. Within this great divide are located all the complex exchanges between the ideological and the political— the implicit and explicit coercions—that individuals confront in their daily existence as gendered beings.

The last three sets invoke categories regularly appealed to by Freud himself. "Male . . . female" refers to physiological and medical definitions of sexual dimorphism. While medical practice is no less permeated with ideological definitions than others, it nonetheless logically recognizes ranges of deviation (in the form of chromosomal damage, hormonal disturbances, and reproductive malfunctioning) if only to "correct" them. The point here is twofold and recognized by Freud as such: medical science can neither rigorously nor exclusively divide biological sex simply into two, nor can the enormous varieties of sexual identity and practice be traced back to a physiological origin. The set "active↔passive" is an original contribution of psychoanalysis. Freud used this distinction to describe the dynamic organization of the *Sexualtrieb,* or "sexual instinct," into distinct components characterized by polarity, reversibility, repression, and sublimation.[8] Freud vacillates constantly on the question of whether the qualities of activity and passivity are linked *a priori* to sexual differentiation. Nevertheless, he does often associate them with masculinity and femininity as used in a special, restricted sense. Here "masculine:feminine" represents a division *within* the subject as fluid patterns of sexed identification through which men and women attempt to choose "objects" and to formulate sexual identities within the historically given possibilities of gender construction. If men and women always live out their particular and individual sexualities in conflicted and contradictory ways, this implies that the fluidity of masculine and feminine identifications can never be contained by, or reconciled to, the ideological division of man/woman.

Undoubtedly, only the last three distinctions have any psychoanalytic specificity. Indeed one way of outlining Freud's theory of sexuality is to say that he traces the "originary" bisexual disposition of the *Sexualtrieb* (male

. . . female) as it is organized into components and vicissitudes (active↔passive), and finally channeled into masculine and feminine identifications. However, Freud's views on sexual difference are paradoxical: on one hand, his metapsychological writings treating the theory of sexuality tend to hypostatize these categories, organizing them in a linear sequence; on the other, his analytic case studies characterize them as a fundamentally non-linear and contradictory dynamic. Inhabiting this paradox, as we shall see, is the question of phylogeny, of "man's" archaic inheritance, to which all of Freud's contradictions concerning masculinity and femininity return.

These contradictions are best understood by tracing out the manifold ways that Freud associates the qualities of "activity and passivity" with "masculinity and femininity." The distinction between activity and passivity begins to appear in Freud's letters to Fliess as early as 1895 and 1896, but does not receive systematic elaboration until the *Three Essays on the Theory of Sexuality* (1905d). This distinction is central to the "dynamic" account of unconscious life, since it describes the formal qualities of the *Sexualtrieb* in the development of sexual identity. With respect to this dynamic, the *Sexualtrieb* takes a curious form. The expression of sexuality as a unified ineluctable drive in adulthood is characterized by Freud as deriving from a constellation of diverse infantile components. The apparent unity of this drive, as the genital aims and objects privileged by adult (hetero)sexuality, is derived from the organization of these components in particular compromises modulated by repression: "If such perversions admit of analysis, that is, if they can be taken to pieces, then they must be of a composite nature. This gives us a hint that perhaps the sexual instinct itself may be no simple thing, but put together from components which have come apart again in the perversions" (*Three Essays*, SE 7: 162). In a 1920 footnote, Freud adds that the origin of the perversions is a result of the unsuccessful formulation of Oedipal identifications. From here on, any discussion of the sexual drive is inseparable from an account of its "components" [*Triebkomponente*] or its organization into "partial drives" [*Partialtriebe*].

An exact listing of these components never appeared unambiguously in Freud's work, though "Instincts and their Vicissitudes" ["Triebe und Triebschicksale" (1915c)] provides a possible inventory with the pairs: sadism-masochism and voyeurism-exhibitionism [*Schaulust-Exhibition.*] The caution always invoked by Freud is that an understanding of these components is only available through analysis of the perversions, where they appear in singular and exaggerated forms.[9] Moreover, the theory of the drives undergoes a fundamental transformation with the publication of *Beyond the Pleasure Principle* (1920g) only five years later. However, the following ideas remain fundamental throughout Freud's writings. The sexual drive is situated on the border between the physiological and the psychical. Dedicated to the aim of "organ-pleasure," it is originally attached to the somatic sources organizing the erotogenic zones. This attachment in turn decides the phases of infantile sexual development—oral, anal, "phallic"—and through the autoerotic activity of childhood is associated with the scopic drive [*Schautrieb*]. On the psychical side, the drives may only be apprehended through their attachment to an idea or representation [*Vorstellung*]. This notion is crucial, for it is only through the organization of these "representations" in phantasy and other manifestations of psychic life that the structure of the drive and its components can be retroactively postulated. This is an activity of interpretation that only psychoanalysis can accomplish.

Freud's description of the particular "dynamic" of the partial drives is essential for understanding the ways he associates activity and passivity with masculinity and femininity. I have already introduced this idea in Chapter One by describing Freud's characterization of mental life as being governed by three "polarities" [*Polarität*]: active and passive, pleasure and unpleasure, and subject and object. The logical structure implied by the term "polarity" is unique. Freud remarks that in the development of neuroses the partial drives always emerge as contrasting pairs [*Gegensatzpaaren*], and suggests that both division and reversibility are fundamental to their organization: "Whenever we find in the unconscious an instinct of this sort [i.e., a "component"] which is capable of being paired off with an opposite one, this second instinct will regularly be found in operation as well. Every active perversion is thus accompanied by its passive counterpart . . . " (*Three Essays*, 167).

While components always form by splitting into contrasting pairs, the nature of the resulting opposition is strikingly complex and fluid. Of the four vicissitudes discussed by Freud in "Instincts and their Vicissitudes," two are characterized by reversibility. First, reversibility proper includes transformations of both the aims (e.g. the conversion of activity into passivity), and the content (e.g. the transformation of love into hate) of the drives. Second, and no less important, is the reversibility of subject and object so characteristic of, but not exclusive to, regression. Here the drives' targeting of an object reverts back on the subject. Freud understands the two forms of reversibility to be closely linked, as in the perverse formation where active sadism develops into passive masochism. However, the exchangeability of subject and object is equally found in more common phenomena such as autoeroticism and narcissism, where the subject takes itself as a sexual object, although the interactions and associations of the various components and their vicissitudes are here no less complex.[10] The idea of polarity therefore combines the qualities of differentiation with chiasmus, the inversion of complementary structures. In this respect, their "contrasting character" must be understood as incommensurable with the logic of binary oppositions.

Similarly, Freud's polarities are not dialectical forms, at least in the Hegelian sense of the term. The fluid oppositions and pairs that characterize the component forms of the drives are subject neither to synthesis nor to the formation of higher unities. While the partial drives are highly mobile with respect to transformations of their aims, objects, and dynamic forms, as well as their organization into complex structures, their basic character is indestructible. One example is the vicissitude of sublimation. Even though a component can be converted to a non-sexual aim, such as intellectual or artistic activity, the basic energy fueling that aim, asserts Freud, is still indisputably erotic.

The vicissitude of repression provides an even more convincing and complex example of the non-dialectical organization of the drives. Where discussion of the reversibility of the partial drives remains at the level of a dynamic description of their formal qualities, the vicissitude of repression—since it refers to the splitting of mental life into conscious and unconscious processes—requires a topographic explanation. In repression, what is foreclosed from consciousness is neither the drive itself nor its particular affects, but rather the representations [*Vorstellungen*] attached to it. In Freud's theories, repression is not only a neurotic mechanism; it is a fundamental property of mental life that represents the process of splitting so characteristic of the defensive strategies of the ego. As early as the *Studies on Hysteria* (1895d), Freud describes these drive-representations [*Triebrepräsentanz*] as "nuclei of crystallization," forming the basic contents of the unconscious. Moreover, the structure of foreclosure not only divides the system *Cs.* from *Uncs.*, it also fuels the compulsion to repeat. Thus these "instinctual ideas" never cease producing chains of associations governed by the primary processes; as such they are unruled by temporality, negation, or the principal of noncontradiction. In the conflicts between the sexual and ego-instincts, the basic structure and content of mental life builds up through the compromise formations where the ego attempts to arbitrate between the pleasure and reality principles, the inner and outer worlds. In sum, Freud writes that "The nucleus of the unconscious consists of instinctual representatives which seek to discharge their cathexis [*die ihre Besetzung abführen wollen*]; that is to say, it consists of wishful impulses. These instinctual impulses are co-ordinate with one another, exist side by side without being influenced by one another, and are exempt from mutual contradiction. When two wishful impulses whose aims must appear to us incompatible become simultaneously active, the two impulses do not diminish each other or cancel each other out [*oder heben einander auf*], but combine to form an intermediate aim" ("The Unconscious" [1915e], SE 14: 186; Stud. 3: 145).

These compromise formations are central to understanding Freud's accounts of how desire is organized in representation, as well his descriptions of the peculiarly complex architecture of phantasy life. As "formations of desire," in Jean-François Lyotard's apt phrase, they neither succeed each other in time nor cancel one another out in space. The accumulation of drive-representations are more like sedimentations. Freud himself describes them through geological and archaeological metaphors:

> We may split up the life of each instinct into a series of "thrusts," distinct from one another in the time of their occurrence but each homogeneous within its own period, whose relation to one another is comparable to that of successive eruptions of lava. We can then perhaps picture to ourselves that the earliest and most primitive instinct-eruption persists in an unchanged form and undergoes no development at all. The next "thrust" would then from the outset have undergone a change in form, being turned for instance, from active to passive, and it would then, with this new characteristic, be superimposed upon the earlier layer, and so on. So that, if we take a survey of the instinctual tendency from its beginning up to any given stopping point, the succession of "thrusts" which we have described would present the picture of a definite development of the instinct.
>
> The fact that, at the late period of development, the instinct in its primary form may be observed side by side with its (passive) opposite deserves to be distinguished by the highly appropriate name introduced by Bleuler: *ambivalence*.[11]

In his discussion of this passage, Lyotard also emphasizes that each phase in the development of a partial drive should be characterized by the peculiar, discontinuous coexistence in space—as well as simultaneity in time—which Freud imagines in *Civilization and its Discontents* (1930a) as the three archaeological ages of Rome together occupying its seven hills. "The space occupied by the formations of desire," writes Lyotard, "is not merely topological. What makes it impossible to represent is that it stands for the *atemporality* or *omnitemporality* of the primary process, in space. The primary process knows no such thing as negation. Whatever the drives produce last forever; an investment made by the unconscious is never liquidated. . . . Erasure is out of the question. Localizations accumulate, one on top of another" (FD 342).

What would it mean to characterize the drives as *either* "masculine" *or* "feminine" in this respect? Freud's distinction between the ego and sexual instincts illuminates this question. The latter derive from somatic sources defining the erotogenic zones, and are organized into "components" whose forms are governed by the distinction active↔passive. The former are concerned with self-preservation, and must find ways to compromise between the demands of the pleasure principle and the reality principle in the ego's practical relations with the outerworld. In adult life, the two are ultimately destined to conflict. The infantile aims of the sexual drive are "scattered" or "distracted" (Freud uses the term *verstreuen*). Pregenital sexuality is anarchic until it begins to coalesce genitally through autoerotic activity. To the ego-instincts is left the difficult task of channeling these drives, through the processes of identification and object-choice, towards heterosexual, reproductive goals. The conflict between the two classes of drives may be summarized by noting that the mobility and ambivalence of the active↔passive relation is scandalous from the point of view of the ego-instincts which, under the influence of the castration complex, attempt to reorganize it according to the distinction man/woman.

The complexity of this situation is recognized in Freud's important essay on narcissism (1914c), where sexual difference is examined by distinguishing between the anaclitic [*Anlehnungstypus*] and narcissistic types of object-choices. Anaclisis refers to the earliest object-choice and thus the earliest differentiation between the sexual and the ego-instincts; namely, the child's relation to its mother. Freud postulates that originally the two classes of drives are indistinguishable; the sensuality of sucking in the nursing infant, for example, is inseparable from a self-preservative need for nourishment. Only later will the sexual drive "components" achieve independent development by detaching themselves from these somatic sources. Narcissism refers to the subsequent stage of autoeroticism where the child takes itself as an sexual object.[12] Later, in "Some Psychical Consequences of the Anatomical Distinction between the Sexes" (1925j), Freud argues that the castration complex finally separates the two classes of drives, bringing them into a conflict that is only resolved by giving up these diverse and "non-productive" object-cathexes by replacing them with the branching identifications of the Oedipus complex.

Nonetheless, this process of division and branching—moving the subject away from autoerotic satisfaction and towards the finding of an external object—does not rest easily within the forking paths of masculine and feminine identifications. Even though Freud characterizes the anaclitic type as characteristic of men, while a reactivation and intensification of narcissism is characteristic of women, he refuses to rest easily with either a binary logic or a reduction of psychological arguments to biological gender:

> We have, however, not concluded that human beings are divided into two sharply differentiated groups, according as their object-choice conforms to the anaclitic or to the narcissistic type; we assume rather that both kinds of object-choice are open to each individual though they may show a preference for one or the other. We say that a human being has originally two sexual objects—itself and the woman who nurses it—and in doing so we are postulating a primary narcissism in everyone, which may in some cases manifest itself in a dominating fashion in their object-choice.
>
> A comparison of the male and female sexes then shows that there are fundamental differences between them in respect of their type of object-choice, although these differences are not of course universal. ("On Narcissism," SE 14: 88; trans. modified)

Indeed, Freud's repeated acknowledgment of these complex transactions in the formation of sexual identity led me, in the schema above, to describe the relation between masculine and feminine identifications as a ratio rather than a strict binary division.

This view is supported by Freud's statement that, as a general rule, the polarity of active-passive should not be confused with that of subject-object. In other words, the sexual dynamic of the pregenital period should not be conflated with the sexual division encouraged by the Oedipus complex and the identifications it exacts: "The antithesis [*Gegensatz*] active-passive coalesces later with the antithesis masculine-feminine, which, until this has taken place, has no psychological meaning. The coupling of activity with masculinity and of passivity with femininity meets us, indeed, as a biological fact; but it is by no means so invariably complete and exclusive as we are inclined to assume" ("Instincts," 131).

This statement, which seems so straightforward and supportive of a sympathetic reading of Freud, actually camouflages a stark equivocation. After all of Freud's efforts to divide psychoanalysis from biology, how can the association of masculinity with activity and femininity with passivity be construed in any way as a "biological fact"? This is especially true when read in the context of Freud's insistence, in the *Three Essays* and other writings, that the distinction between masculinity and femininity has no real psychological sense until after puberty. Here a complex problem of temporality and causality arises in Freud's history of the subject. For the production of sexual *difference*—as a process fraught with contradiction and internal complexity—seems nonetheless biologically predestined as a sexual *opposition* where masculinity and femininity appear to be incommensurable paths. Freud goes to great lengths to demonstrate that the psychological meaning of "masculinity" and "femininity" cannot be reduced to a unified structure of identity. Nonetheless, the problem still remains: from where do the meanings and values attached by Freud to the distinction between masculinity and femininity historically derive?

Part of the answer is ideological. Freud's views on sexual development are organized teleologically by the goal of reproductive heterosexuality, and this norm is universalized according to its biological function in the propagation of the species. Nancy Chodorow describes clearly and convincingly how Freud's arguments are delimited by patriarchal norms of heterosexuality and the sexual division of labor.[13] The coalescence of psychological meanings that Freud refers to indicates one thing: that male and female sexuality are defined as the "active" and "passive" parts in coitus. Brutely speaking, one acts or is acted upon, penetrates or is penetrated. Of course, the very terms "heterosexuality" and "the family" mean different things in different cultures and periods of history, and serve different ideological functions. But Freud's own conception is not necessarily recognized as a norm as much as a natural and universal function of sexuality. When Freud remarks that "anatomy is destiny," he assumes that sexual differentiation is meant only to serve biological reproduction. Thus the attachment of qualities of passivity and masochism to "femininity" by Freud, Helene Deutsch, and other classical Freudians serves a norm of reproductive sexuality that does not recognize its ideological functioning with respect to positions of womanhood and motherhood.

Coming to grips with these problems in depth means confronting Freud's theories on their own terms especially with respect to his arguments concerning bisexuality and the legacy of "man's archaic heritage." In this respect, the hypothesis concerning the bisexual disposition of human sexuality is a curious idea, marked by a fascinating ambivalence in Freud's thought. On one hand, his adherence to this idea demonstrates his insistence on the non-teleological orientation of object-choice and gender identification. Here anatomy is not destiny. The biological constitution of the subject cannot predetermine either its sexuality or gender. As he explains in " 'A Child is being Beaten,' " this was the basis of Freud's objection to Fliess's version of bisexuality, which explains the motive force of repression as a conflict between two sexual characters: "The dominant sex of the person . . . has repressed the mental representation of the subordinated sex into the unconscious. Therefore the nucleus of the unconscious (that is to say, the repressed) is in each human being that side of him which belongs to the opposite sex. . . . [With] men, what is unconscious and repressed can be brought down to feminine instinctual impulses; and conversely with women" (SE 17: 200–201). Freud summarily rejects this position for unproblematically identifying a person's sexuality with their genital sex. Nor is it a far leap to associate this idea with Ernest Jones and Karen Horney's hypotheses concerning complementary libidinal economies in men and women.

Freud's contrasting position on bisexuality can be summed up in the following statement: "In the last resort we can only see that both in male and female individuals masculine as well as feminine instinctual impulses [Triebregungen] are found, and that each can equally well undergo repression and so become unconscious" ("Child," 202). Freud's distinctive difference from Fliess hinges on the term Triebregung. Where Fliess's theory devolves from the idea of a congenital division and complementarity, Freud's version of bisexuality is dynamic and transactional. Laplanche and Pontalis point out that Freud most often reserves Regung or impulse to connote internal movement, in fact, to designate the specific form of drive activity.[14] In the context of Freud's analysis of beating phantasies, to which I will turn in the next chapter, what is at stake is understanding the development of specific positions for the sexuality of men and women through complex permutations of masculine and feminine identifications.

However, even if an originary, congenital division of the sexes is definitively rejected, and the reversibility and fluidity of masculine and feminine identifications in each individual is accepted as given (as I believe it should be), on what basis are these terms to be distinguished? Here the debates concerning the castration complex and the phallic phase of infantile sexuality reassert their centrality. When Freud insists that the motive forces of repression should not be "sexualized," he is reaffirming his commitment to the idea that sexual identity does not have a physiological origin. Yet, for Freud, the Oedipus complex is the nucleus of the neuroses not because of the cultural interdictions it imposes—which could be addressed critically in historical and materialist terms—but because "man's archaic heritage [*die archaische Erbschaft des Menschen*] forms the nucleus of the unconscious mind . . . ." ("Child," 203–204). Although Freud uses the more neutral *Menschen* or humanity, this thesis proves to be the Charybdis that continually pulls Freud's theories of sexual difference toward an androcentric conception of the unconscious.

This is the fundamental problem that must be overcome in Freud's theory of sexual difference, and to which all the contradictory interpretations of Freud's arguments bear witness. Despite its complexities, the theory of the drives, and the account of sexual difference that accompanies it, is relatively straightforward until the following hypothesis arises: that the libido is "masculine." The paradox is apparent: how can the premise of a disposition to bisexuality in all individuals be reconciled to the singularity of a "masculine" libido? One of Freud's most unambiguous statements of this idea is found in the *Three Essays* in the section on "The Differentiation Between Men and Women." Curiously, this is precisely the point where the first footnote on distinguishing between the biological, sociological, and psychological definitions of masculine and feminine appears in 1915:

> The auto-erotic activity of the erotogenic zones is, however, the same in both sexes, and owing to this uniformity there is no possibility of a distinction between the two sexes such as arises after puberty. So far as the auto-erotic and masturbatory manifestations of sexuality are concerned, we might lay it down that the sexuality of little girls is of a wholly masculine character. Indeed, if we were able to give a more definite connotation to the concepts of "masculine" and "feminine," it would even be possible to maintain that libido is invariably and necessarily of a masculine nature, whether it occurs in men or in women and irrespectively of whether its object is a man or a woman. [The 1915 note appears here.]
>
> Since I have become acquainted with the notion of bisexuality I have regarded it as the decisive factor, and without taking bisexuality into account I think it would scarcely be possible to arrive at an understanding of the sexual manifestations that are actually to be observed in men and women. (*Three Essays*, 219–220)

Freud's commitment to the theory of bisexuality is ambivalent, complex, and permeates all his hypotheses concerning sexual difference, up to and including his insistence on the centrality of the castration complex. For example, in 1905 the section on "Bisexuality" in the *Three Essays* appears as Freud's most definitive and least ambiguous statement concerning the irreducibility of psychological definitions of gender to the biological (141–144). Even within the domain of biological science, Freud warns, the strict definition of gender by mutually exclusive terms can be undecidable, and not only in special cases such as the various forms of hermaphrodism. By the same token, even if the libido is no longer *purely* physical, nevertheless, as the energy fueling the "component instincts," it must have its somatic origins. In "On the Sexual Theories of Children" (1908c) Freud argues that the initial stage of infantile sexual theories, which is supposed to precede sex differentiation, begins with a peculiar universalizing hypothesis: that all creatures are endowed with a penis, and that subsequently, children begin their theorizing of sexuality on the evidence of presence or absence of the penis. It is remarkable that Freud so quickly makes such global claims, since he has already admitted that he can present no evidence from the point of view of little girls.[15]

This observation motivates Freud's attestation of the universality of the castration complex and inspires further interesting claims. From the standpoint of biology, Freud asserts that the infantile penis and clitoris are fundamentally homologous such that the latter "behaves in fact during childhood like a real and genuine penis . . ." ("Sexual Theories," SE 9: 217). The nature of this behavior is telling: ". . . that it becomes the seat of excitations which leads to its being touched, that its excitability gives the little girl's sexual activity a masculine character and that a wave of repression in the years of puberty is needed in order for this masculine sexuality to be discarded and the woman to emerge" ("Sexual Theories," 217).

By the 1920s, Freud's ideas undergo a fundamental, if not yet decisive, shift that eventually provides Lacan with the textual evidence for his arguments concerning the "signification of the phallus" and the place of the Name-of-the-Father in Oedipal conflict.[16] The theorization of the phallic phase in infantile sexual development, and consequently the primacy of the phallus for both biological sexes, is a product of Freud's essay on "The Infantile Genital Organization of the Libido" (1923e), where the universal presence of the penis is extended by children to "all other living beings, humans and animals" (SE 19: 142). Of greater interest is Freud's assertion of the intense activity concentrated on the male genitals: a drive that is at once intensely active, autoerotic, and epistemological. Epistemophilia, curiosity, and the desire to know, are thus attached to this activity that eventually eroticizes both seeing and hearing, giving them the status of partial drives. Moreover, this confluence of drive components will be a major factor contributing to the organization of the phantasy of the "primal scene," as the imagined witnessing or overhearing of parental coitus. In Freud, then, the meaning of the phallus is drawn from a huge narcissistic investment in the infant's body that takes the form of an active autoeroticism. This axiomatic linking of "maleness" with "activity" is simply speaking an onanistic autoeroticism. Autoerotic activity, and especially masturbation, play fundamental roles in Freud's theories of sexuality and phantasy life. But Freud's assertion of gender difference here, where theoretically sexual difference should play no part, yields many perplexing questions. Why is autoeroticism fundamentally a "masculine" behavior? In a period where gender is supposed to be so ineffable, why does the criterion of the "genuine and real penis" establish the standard for a "symmetrical" behavior that renders boys and girls as physiologically equivalent while paradoxically serving later to differentiate psychologically between them? For Freud, a requisite for female sexual maturation is an effort of repression where women must renounce this "activity of a male character." Why is there no similar accounting of the difficulties of the male renunciation of onanism as a "non-productive" sexual activity? And why is vaginal satisfaction linked so fundamentally to a renunciation of autoeroticism and sexual "activity"?

These contradictions are not irresolvable, even within the letter of Freud's theories as his Lacanian defenders have pointed out. What seems insurmountable is dividing the sense of "active" from "masculinity" in the definition of the libido.[17] Though no right can be claimed here to question Freud's clinical evidence, it is striking that it seems only on the basis of sexual "activity" that autoeroticism is granted a "masculine" character whose proof requires the morphological equivalence of the genitals on the model of the penis. Unlike Lacan 25 years later, Freud refuses to understand that the various ideological and cultural values which the phallus comes to represent are retroactively postulated in the wake of the castration complex. The phase of intense autoeroticism and narcissism that paves the way for the castration complex is no doubt fundamental. Why Freud should characterize this activity as "masculine" in direct contradiction to his assertions that the term can as yet have no psychological signification means only one thing: that for Freud the signification of the phallus is neither social nor historical. Indeed in "The Dissolution of the Oedipus Complex" (1924d) Freud suggests that the Oedipus complex might arise and decline according to a temporal schedule laid down by heredity. Although Freud anticipates the discoveries of genetic coding and hormonal cues, the biology of sexual development is not necessarily the issue here. Rather, this idea is the product of the anthropological works, such as *Totem and Taboo*, with their suggestion of a linear and irreversible continuum through which the history of the subject is destined to pass as its phylogenetic inheritance.

This idea inhabits all of Freud's fundamental writings from *The Interpretation of Dreams* (1900a) to the *Outline of Psychoanalysis* (1940a [1938]). It comprises, in fact, Freud's views on the history of the subject as an androcentric idealism that any materialist theory hoping to incorporate Freud has to confront. Freud acknowledged that his ideas on phylogenesis were speculative, and that analysis should not invoke them until all ontogenetic evidence had been exhausted. Nevertheless, one often finds that the phylogenetic argument is invoked at precisely those places in a given argument where no other material evidence is forthcoming. (The case history of the Wolf Man provides many striking examples.)

Although Freud is speculating to Fliess on the possibility of "endopsychic myths" as early as 1897 (Letter 28), his most concentrated work on phylogenesis occurs between 1910 and 1914. This is the period covering the writing and publication of *Totem and Taboo* and the analysis of Sergei Pankeiev, the "Wolf Man." Briefly, the first thesis of *Totem and Taboo* derives from a peculiar doubling where the psychic lives of neurotics are presented as recapitulating the obsessions of "primitive savages." Freud's "vision" (as he calls it in "An Autobiographical Study" [1925d]) involves a primal event in the history of humanity, marking nothing less than its emergence from the primal horde to take the path of civilization. In Freud's origin myth, a group of tribal sons rebel against the primal father for monopolizing the women of the tribe by killing and then consuming him. In order to expiate their guilt and maintain unity among the rival brothers, they vow only to mate outside the tribe and to commemorate their crime regularly with a totem meal to prevent its repetition. Freud condenses his most cherished ideas into this myth: the experience of an unconscious sense of guilt, Oedipal struggle with the father, as well as the incest prohibition and incorporation of the Law as the foundation of symbolic behavior and civilized life.

It is obvious that women figure nowhere in this myth except as objects of desire, tokens of power, and signifiers of guilt and transgression. However, there is more at stake than symptomatic analysis. Throughout his life, Freud sees this endopsychic myth as a deep structure, transmitted across generations and underlying the forms of mental life. In the *The Interpretation of Dreams* (1900a), the latent content of dreams is understood as deriving from two prehistories, that of the individual as well as his "primal symbolic inheritance." Through the case study of the Wolf Man, the origin of primal phantasies (of castration, the primal scene, and seduction), as well as children's "instinctual" knowledge of genital sexuality, are all understood as patterned on phylogenetic memory-traces to which the child refers when its own experience fails to answer the perplexing questions of sexual difference. Even more crucial is the "universal" experience of castration and the Oedipus complex as "a phenomenon which is determined and laid down by heredity and which is bound to pass away according to programme when the next pre-ordained phase of development sets in. This being so, it is of no great importance what the occasions are which allow this to happen, or, indeed, whether such cases can be discovered at all" ("The Dissolution of the Oedipus Complex," SE 19: 174). In *The Ego and the Id* (1923b), this archaic inheritance is understood as the nucleus of the id, determining the figure of the father as the focus of the child's first identifications and the kernel of the super-ego as the agent of a social sense and moral restraint. Here Freud states that "the male sex seems to have taken the lead in all these moral acquisitions; and they seem to have been transmitted to women by cross-inheritance" (SE 19: 37).

Here at last is the key, unlikely as it seems, to understanding why for Freud mental life is so dominated by masculinity and why an "originarily bisexual disposition" has now become androcentric. Women have only a marginal role in the story of civilized man and femininity has no place, as it were, in either sexuality or unconscious life. This is why for Freud the little girl's sexuality is so dominated by "masculine" behavior, why she is destined to confront the law of the Father, and through the imposition of that law to be returned to a "passivity" that guarantees the propagation of the species. However, this law does not derive from social and historical forces; rather, it is the product of a universalizing *Kultur* that reaches across time. Freud's (ontogenetic) history of the subject is regulated by a teleological unfolding within an eternal and universal schema foreordained by a phylogenetic prehistory where the place of women is unquestionably foreclosed. This is a fundamental problem in Freud's writings on sexual difference. The teleological force of his phylogenetic arguments continually appears—literally and figuratively a return of the repressed—to undercut those aspects that are more conducive to the ideological analysis of sexual difference. It is striking, as Luce Irigaray so clearly points out, that Freud cannot grant a form—a narcissistic becoming—to femininity.[18] The vaginal apparatus which must eventually regulate her sexual identity is formless, absence, a passive receptacle. All the difficulties of difference represented in the case histories and analyses of phantasy life, then, are representative of an individual's specific struggle which unfolds from within, not a historical situation which he or she encounters.

Women nonetheless exist, and they powerfully exist, in ways that defy the privilege of phallic power. This was true even in Freud's time, a fact to which many of his female patients gave eloquent testimony. I have dwelt at length on these themes because they are so often ignored in contemporary writing on Freud. Moreover, Freud's suspect historical views must be confronted if any credence is to be given to a redemptive reading of his theories from the standpoint of a historical materialism sensitive to the demands of contemporary feminism. By the same token, it is only against these ideas that the importance of Lacan's innovations concerning the place of the Symbolic order in the subject's confrontation with the "paternal metaphor" can be measured. If, as Freud asserts in "The Sexual Theories of Children," the sight of the penis inspires desire of possession on the part of the little girl, it is not the "thing" itself that structures this desire, but all of the power, authority, and command possessed historically by the Name-of-the-Father in patriarchal culture, which appears to be the designated heritage of the little boy. Lacan, of course, never really applied these categories to a historical or ideological analysis. Nancy Chodorow, however, pays careful attention to psychoanalysis' symbolizations of anatomy and the connotations of social power invested in them. Her discussion of the notorious concept of "penis envy" as a narcissistic desire is instructive. According to Chodorow, the phallus "is a symbol of power or omnipotence, whether you have one as a sexual organ (as a male) or as a sexual object (as her mother 'possesses' her father's). A girl wants it for the powers which it symbolizes and the freedom it promises from her previous sense of [preoedipal] dependence, and not because it is inherently and obviously better to be masculine . . ." (ROM 123).[19]

Chodorow does not take issue with the hypothesis that sexual difference and identity are formulated from the perception of genital difference by children, and indeed, by parents' attributions of gender according to criteria of genital difference. Instead, her theory focuses resolutely on the conscious and unconscious symbolizations of genital difference perpetuated historically in the social drama of the family. Rather than a conception of presence and lack (whose investment in metaphysical conceptions of identity is extraordinary), Chodorow understands these attributions as the relation between two "positivities."[20] Similarly, Chodorow does not question the phenomenon of penis envy in girls and the role it plays in Oedipal and postoedipal genesis of gender. However, she does emphasize the network of authority and resistance organized through this particular and complex desire, including: independence from the mother; defense against an active, incestuous desire for the father; and finally, symbolization of the social privileges and empowerment of the father and males in general, which is communicated consciously or unconsciously by the parents.

How fundamentally different is this argument from Lacan's own important formulations concerning the Name-of-the-Father? In its attention to the network of significations attaching the claims of activity, empowerment, and authority to the paternal signifier, the arguments are compatible in important ways.[21] One of Lacan's major achievements was to emphasize that where psychoanalysis is concerned, only the symbolic functions of the phallus have any meaning. And here commentators have far too quickly attributed the scandal of Freud (universalizing of the imaginary penis and concomitant biological justification) to Lacan as well. For what the phallus signifies is what, under patriarchal culture, one imagines the Father has and everyone else wants: command of language and the satisfaction of desire, power, authority, all communicated by the paternal metaphor. If Lacan's comments on femininity seem problematic in ways that Freud's are not, his analysis of the perpetuation of patriarchal authority through the symbolization of language and desire is nonetheless fundamental. An important difference, however, is that Chodorow's conception is not based on a dialectic of presence and absence where sexual difference is organized around castration in the same terms of negativity, foundational lack, and "unrepresentability."[22] What is challenged here, I believe, is not the relation of lack-in-being to desire and its representations, to adopt momentarily Lacan's own terms. Rather, the "fact" of castration is understood as a positive and material symbolization of sexual difference—not its "origin"—that carries a particular and powerful ideological charge.

At the same time, Chodorow ignores, as Jacqueline Rose has pointed out in her contribution to the volume on *Feminine Sexuality,* that what is most fundamental to Lacan's account of the signification of the phallus is that subjectivity, especially sexual subjectivity, is only possible at the price of internal division. In Rose's view, Lacan's arguments present less a theory of the subject than a radically antihumanist critique of any notion of identity that constructs itself on notions of selfsameness and non-contradiction. For Rose, this division suggests a critique of Saussure's definition of the sign— itself understood as a divided yet integral body—with important ramifications for an account of sexual difference. On one hand, in her view Lacan insists on the relation of signification to the symbolic law which fixes meaning and "subjects" individuals in language; on the other, he rewrites Saussure's model of the sign such that the signifier is always outrunning the signified. "Sexuality," Rose rightly insists, "is placed on both of these dimensions at once. The difficulty is to hold these two emphases together—sexuality in the symbolic (an ordering), sexuality as that which constantly fails" (FS 43). Indeed this is the "difficulty" of difference. The problem is how to describe the logic of the unconscious as a force that simultaneously supports and undermines the relation of sexuality to its historical and cultural representations.

Rose also asserts that when Lacan restores primacy to the signifier, he replaces Saussure's insistence on the arbitrary nature of the sign with the argument that "sexual difference is a legislative divide" that "creates and reproduces" the categories of signification (FS 41). The importance of Lacan's version of the castration complex resides not only in his account of how the subject's desire and sexual identity are forged simultaneously in submission to the symbolic law; his insistence on the fragile, mistimed, and contingent nature of this event also mocks any effort to fix sexual identity as descending from a unique originary moment. Examples would include the

Ernest Jones and Karen Horney's essentialism and Freud's own phylogenetic theories, as well as contemporary theory's efforts to define preoedipality as a utopian space of non-patriarchal language and desire. Rose insists correctly that what the phallus signifies is the subject's subordination to a cultural order, still dominated by the demands of patriarchy, that predates it. In this manner, Freud and Lacan's critics have "failed to see that the concept of the phallus in Freud's account of human sexuality was part of his awareness of the problematic, if not impossible, nature of sexual identity itself. They answered it, therefore, by reference to a pre-given sexual difference aimed at securing that identity for both sexes. In doing so, they lost sight of Freud's sense that sexual difference is constructed at a price and that it involves subjection to a law which exceeds any natural or biological division. The concept of the phallus stands for that subjection, and for the way in which women are very precisely implicated in its process" (FS 28).

That the division of the sexes, which the meaning of the phallus mediates, is central to the hierarchization of power in the fact of language itself, is without question Lacan's most important discovery. In his lecture on "The Agency of the Letter," this inspires Lacan to replace Saussure's illustration of the arbitrary relation of signifier to signified—a drawing of a tree juxtaposed with the word "arbre"—with the following image:

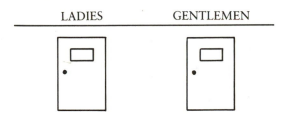

Lacan uses this image to introduce one of his famous jokes, in fact a "childhood memory" produced by "the person most worthy of his trust": "A train arrives at a station. A little boy and a little girl, brother and sister, are seated in a compartment face to face next to the window through which the buildings along the station platform can be seen passing as the train pulls to a stop. 'Look,' says the brother, 'we're at Ladies!'; 'Idiot!' replies his sister, 'Can't you see we're at Gentlemen' (E 152).

There are many fascinating dimensions to this parable. Lacan is invoking Freud's own story of sexual difference of course, but he gives the itinerary his own special twist. The boy and girl are placed as mirror images to one another, a state of unbroken narcissistic bliss until they are faced with the signs of sexual difference. From this time forward, they will only see one another as unequally opposed antagonists. "For these children," writes Lacan, "Ladies and Gentlemen will be henceforth two countries towards which each of their souls will strive on divergent wings, and between which a truce will be the more impossible since they are actually the same country and neither can compromise on its own superiority without detracting from the glory of the other" (E 152).

Lacan's appeal to "Ladies and Gentlemen" recalls Freud's opening address to his imaginary audience in the lecture on femininity. And like Freud, Lacan is at pains to emphasize the ontological insecurity to which the subject's recognition of place falls prey. What is in question here is the insatiability of desire and the entropic character of the drives with respect to the (self-) representations of identity, "a purely animal Dissension," in Lacan's terms, "to the unbridled power of ideological warfare, relentless for families, a torment to the Gods" (E 152). But Lacan is too faithful to Freud in portraying this journey teleologically. Not only are the children ferried by train, an inexcusable phallic symbol, they are also carried, unwittingly and ineluctably, towards their destination.

It is striking enough that this is one train that always arrives on schedule at its only stop without detours, derailings, or other sidetracks; more striking still that Lacan evades explaining why the joke is funny. In their introductions to *Feminine Sexuality,* both Juliet Mitchell and Jacqueline Rose evoke this moment from Lacan's writings as evidence that the theory of bisexuality in Freud is meaningful only when understood retroactively as a choice that every individual confronts when living out the scenarios of the Oedipus and castration complexes. In her contribution, Juliet Mitchell emphasizes that "Sexual difference can only be the consequence of a division; without this division it would cease to exist. But it must exist because no human being can become a subject outside the division into two sexes. One must take up a position as either a man or a woman" (FS 6). The formula of "either/or"—sign par excellence of the binary machine—thus appears again in the text of Lacan and his most ardent supporters. For the disposition of the drive is to be one or the other; the teleology, while not singular, cannot be more than two.

I prefer to contrast Lacan's bathroom joke with a scene from Terry Jones's film *Personal Services* (1987).[23] Midway through the film, the character Dolly (played to perfection by Danny Schiller and accepted by all, including the audience, as a woman) is discovered in the ladies room to possess a penis. When her friend Christine exclaims gleefully, "Dolly, you've got a willy!," Dolly responds, "It's nothing to be proud of." That the scene takes place in the ladies room of a church as Christine's sister weds a policeman, is not insignificant. Chaos ensues when the groom's mother stumbles onto this scene. Yet despite the protestations of the wedding party that Dolly is in the "wrong place," she matter of factly replies, "But I *am* a woman." Neither transvestism nor masquerade is the issue here, though these strategies of difference are amply celebrated in the film. With the exception of this single scene, for all the characters in the film Dolly simply "is" a woman because this is what she has chosen to be. Towards the end of the film, just before order is restored to Christine's "disorderly house" by the agents of State power, Christine sorts out her friends and clients for a celebratory photograph of "women only." In the terms of the film, "women" turn out to be anyone who refuses or holds in disregard the unitary demands of phallic sexuality, including gays, lesbians, transsexuals, transvestites, and a retired wing commander who flew 207 combat missions wearing a bra and panties. Although uneven as a film and certainly no great political document, *Personal Services* is a rather exuberant celebration of difference and deviation in its myriad erosions of phallic identity and sexuality.

My point here is that the train of phallic sexuality (unlike the letter in Lacan's seminar on Poe) rarely arrives at its destination and that its tracks fork more than once. I am challenging here neither Lacan's emphasis on the role of the paternal metaphor, nor that of the division of the subject in language through the symbolizations of sexual difference, all of which I take to be fundamental to contemporary psychoanalytic thought. Moreover, as the opening quote of this chapter testifies, Lacan is quite perceptive concerning the erosions of sexual identity to which psychoanalysis bears witness. However, like the character Dolly in Terry Jones's film, Lacan's bathroom joke is funny because of its matter of fact inversion of place: the little passengers on Lacan's Oedipal train each arrive at the wrong destination. Lacan could have followed Freud's own train story in "The Uncanny," but instead finds it out of place, misrecognizing misrecognition. If this story is a parable of the role of bisexuality in Freud's story of sexual difference, then Lacan, like Freud, would seem to fall back on teleological arguments. While Freud refuses to attribute determination or cause to the domain of biology (whether in the form of genital dominance or phylogenetic inheritance), he nonetheless continually finds echoes of both in his theory of sexuality.[24] The forking path toward two leading zones is organized by a single phallic phase; the division into two sexual functions, the "active" and "passive" part in coitus, derive from the "cultural goal" of reproductive sexuality as a necessary species function.

In Freud's theory of sexuality, the Oedipus complex is a universal norm which is not only centered around patriarchal privilege derived from the prohibition on incest; it has also determined that the survival of the species requires division of the sexes into two. Here a "naturalist" hypothesis, which has no grounds in nature, is mustered tautologically to shore up a set of fundamentally historical and ideological values. All of Freud's writings are informed by this normative view of heterosexuality in its patriarchal forms, which dominates because nature and species survival demand it. By the same token, if Freud's views are consistently paradoxical in the widest sense of the term, it is because the entire theoretical edifice of psychoanalysis derives not from the presumed norm, but from the multiple and variegate fascinations of its failures. What happens, then, when the paths of deviance are followed?

Chapter 4
Metamorphoses

Phantasy is the support of desire; it is not the object that is the support of desire. The subject sustains itself as desiring in relation to an ever more complex signifying ensemble. This is apparent enough in the form of the scenario it assumes, in which the subject, more or less recognizable, is somewhere, split, divided, generally double, in its relation to the object, which usually does not show its true face either.
—Jacques Lacan, S XI: 185 trans. modified

The Sexuality of Tiresias

In the Oedipal mythologies of contemporary film theory, the figure of Tiresias is all but forgotten. The Sphinx has been most often invoked as the emblematic figure of sexual difference, from the enigmatic and fatal other of Romanticism to her redemption by contemporary feminist writers from Montrelay to Mulvey. Tiresias, however, is a different figure altogether. Unlike the myth of the primordial androgyne attributed to Aristophanes—the originary bisexual being forever divided from itself—or Hermaphroditus who, merged with the nymph Salmacis, became neither man nor woman, Tiresias embodies more than any other mythological character the undecidability and mutability of sexual identification. The best known version of this story is found in Book III of Ovid's *Metamorphoses*. Tiresias is asked to settle a wager between Jove and Juno concerning whether men or women have the greater pleasure in sex, since he knows well the "two extremes of Venus' subtle arts."[1] Born a man, Tiresias was changed into a woman after striking two "love-joined serpents"; he was restored after seven autumns by striking them again during their act of love. Deciding on the part of Jove, Tiresias is blinded by the vengeful Juno but compensated by Jove with the gift of prophecy. More interesting is the version attributed to Sostratus of Alexandria. Born a girl, and alternately blessed and cursed by the gods, Tiresias lives for seven generations and suffers seven metamorphoses. S/he suffers the wrath of Apollo, Hera, Poseidon, and Aphrodite, lives and loves as girl, a boy, and as a young woman bears a son afflicted by strabism. She is further changed into an ugly man, a mature woman, suffers an attempted rape, becomes an old man, loses and regains the gift of prophecy, is transformed again as an old woman, and having her beauty restored, is changed by Aphrodite into a mouse. What fascinates in this tale, according to Luc

Brisson, is the diversity and mutability of Tiresias's sexual transformations.[2] Her original name unknown, she lives out seven generations, experiencing numerous sexual roles and identities as an emblem of undecidability.

Tiresias is the image of sexual metamorphosis—an uncanny figure who shifts sex, experiences *jouissance* across difference, and elicits the rancor of the gods. How different the reasoned mythology of psychoanalysis would be if she had a greater place in the Oedipal story. When I first began work on "the difficulty of difference" in 1981, I pursued Janet Bergstrom's suggestion that ". . . it is now possible and absolutely necessary to complicate the question of identification as it functions in the classical film, first of all in terms of the realization that spectators are able to take multiple identificatory positions, whether successively or simultaneously."[3] Bergstrom's response and my own was motivated by Raymond Bellour's argument that female spectators could only identify against their sex with respect to the Oedipal scenarios of most Hollywood films. Since that time there has been no dearth of essays examining the possible mobility of identification, beginning with Laura Mulvey's account of "transsex" identification in female spectators. In films centered on conflicts of feminine identity such as *Stella Dallas* (1937) or *Duel in the Sun* (1946), Mulvey envisions the possibility of the female spectator as split, through a narcissistic identification with the female protagonist, between a passive femininity and a regressive, active masculinity. As I described in the last chapter, Linda Williams understands this oscillation to be fundamental to female spectatorship as the ability to hold simultaneously multiple and contradictory positions of identification as opposed to the supposed unity, linearity, and coherence of male spectatorship. In *Alice Doesn't,* Teresa De Lauretis explains with greater complexity the possible mobility and oscillation of feminine identification as a process. I highly value each of these essays as important contributions to feminist film theory. Still they have not yet adequately addressed the problem of sexual *difference,* at least in the sense that Janet Bergstrom calls for. For each argument assumes, implicitly or explicitly, that film theory has resolved the question of masculine identification, that masculine and feminine identifications are decisively aligned with male and female spectators, and that the position of the female spectator can be defined ontogenetically in opposition to that of the male.

Each of these essays responds in important ways to the desire of contemporary film theory to formulate a theory of the subject through Freudian and Lacanian psychoanalysis. This desire, however, is paradoxical. For contrary to contemporary film theory's emphasis, psychoanalysis is not a theory of the subject, at least in the usual philosophical sense of the term. Juliet Mitchell's account of Lacan's antihumanisim succinctly describes the import of this idea. In contrast to the various forms of object relations analysis, which emphasize the ego's deviations and return to "norms" of self-identity and coherence, Mitchell writes that "Lacan takes the opposite perspective:

the analysand's unconscious reveals a fragmented subject of shifting and uncertain sexual identity. To be human is to be subjected to a law which decentres and divides: sexuality is created in a division, the subject is split; but an ideological world conceals this from the conscious subject who is supposed to feel whole and certain of a sexual identity."[4]

Jacqueline Rose also insists that Lacan's writings do not suggest a theory of the subject; rather they present a critique of the subject as incommensurable with any notion of self-identity, unity, or coherence. This is why Lacan increasingly referred to the meaning of the phallus as a fraud or fiction even while insisting that it superintends the divisions where subjectivity, sexuality, language, and culture are articulated. As integral positions, masculinity and femininity are phantasies of a unified and unthreatened subjectivity. From Lacan's point of view any theory proposing the autonomy or self-identity of *the* woman or *the* man would be understood as caught explicitly in a phallic phantasy of identity. In Rose's account,

> Sexuality belongs in this area of instability played out in the register of demand and desire, each sex coming to stand, mythically and exclusively, for that which could satisfy and complete the other. It is when the categories "male" and "female" are seen to represent an absolute and complementary division that they fall prey to a mystification in which the difficulty of sexuality instantly disappears: "to disguise this gap by relying on the virtue of the 'genital' to resolve it through the maturation of tenderness . . ., however piously intended, is nonetheless a fraud' (MP 81). Lacan therefore, argued that psychoanalysis should not try to produce "male" and "female" as complimentary entities, sure of each other and of their own identity, but should expose the fantasy on which this notion rests." (FS 33)[5]

In Lacan's view, the form of sexual binarism itself is the greatest fiction, regardless of its theoretical derivation: biological essentialism, ego psychology's theories of development and nurturing, the emphasis on preoedipal fusion with the mother, or even Freud's own phylogenetic and anthropological speculations. If psychoanalysis understands the development of sexual identity as an experience of division and loss, then any attempt to associate subjectivity with criteria of unity, coherence, or mastery, especially as one side of a binary equation, is meaningless. (The same is not true for ideological representations of sexual difference, which heavily invest in such dualisms.) From the perspective of psychoanalysis' understanding of sexual identity, the goal is to understand the range of scenarios that describe the different experiences of division and loss where sexual positions are constructed.

Jacqueline Rose also insists that Lacan's rereading of the concept of bisexuality must be substituted for Freud's. Thus bisexuality would not mean "an undifferentiated sexual nature prior to symbolic difference (Freud's earlier sense), but the availability to all subjects of both positions in relation to that of difference itself" (FS 49). This does not mean that there is "no difference" between men and women. Nor does Rose underestimate the power of the symbolic—historically dominated by patriarchal and phallocentric forms— to divide Man from Woman in a binary grid where the latter must represent lack for the former. The point is that this is a division in language that rarely if ever adequately anchors the imaginary identifications of men and women as sexual beings. If Lacan suggests that "Woman is excluded by the nature of words," this means neither that women are excluded from speech nor that femininity is a sign of a repressed but articulate being that might return as the ruin of representation. Rather, the nature of phallic division is that of a phantasy whose very insistence and repetitiveness is an indication of the impossibility of its finding an adequate or convincing representation in the symbolic. Therefore, Rose emphasizes that "For Lacan, men and women are only ever in language . . . . All speaking beings must line themselves up on one side or the other of this division, *but anyone can cross over and inscribe themselves on the opposite side from that to which they are anatomically destined* [my emphasis]. It is, we could say, an either/or situation, but one whose fantasmatic nature was endlessly reiterated by Lacan: 'these are not positions able to satisfy us, so much so that we can state the unconscious to be defined by the fact that it has a much clearer idea of what is going on than the truth that man is not woman' (S XXI, 6 p. 9)" (FS 49).

In this context, I have argued that the problem of feminine identification is of much greater theoretical interest than the question of female spectatorship, which despite its important political implications will always come to grief through the dualisms it must posit. In the early version of my work on "the difficulty of difference," I implied that I had no alternative theory to offer. Through an account of Freud's essay "'A Child is being Beaten'. A Contribution to the Study of the Origin of Sexual Perversions" (1919e), I simply tried to demonstrate the possibility of a theory of sexual difference based on complex and mobile transactions between feminine and masculine identifications within given gender positions. There has been no lack of commentary on this important essay, though much of it has been blind (indeed as blind as Freud) to the more radical implications of Freud's discoveries. There are, however, two rare exceptions: Jean-François Lyotard's *Discours, figure* and Kaja Silverman's essay on "Masochism and Male Subjectivity."[6] Both works focus on the utopian function of phantasy. In this respect, I would like to readdress Freud's essay, as well as my earlier account, by rereading them from a perspective where the relationship between Oedipus and the architecture of phantasy life is understood as an explicitly ideological struggle. Here the Oedipus complex will be understood as the Maginot line of patriarchal culture and the discursive structure of phantasy as a site of resistance and revolt.

The importance of Freud's study of infantile beating phantasies in his *oeuvre* cannot be overestimated. Jean Nassif argues that it has larger significance than a discussion of one genre of phantasy. It sheds light on the structure of phantasy itself, and above all on one of the three forms of primal phantasy (castration, seduction, and the primal scene). "It is therefore not a question of an individual neurosis," writes Nassif, "but the metaphorical presentation of a fundamental phantasm; under the circumstances, as we shall see farther on, a castration phantasy whose function is to narrate the origin of sexual difference."[7] Through the peculiarly complex logic of phantasy, the child finds an uneasy compromise between the expression of desire and its division in the Symbolic order as required by the logic of Oedipus. Similarly, this essay represents a turning point in Freud's assessment of the problem of sexual identification as well as the role of the Oedipus and castration complexes in the genesis of phantasy. This shift is the product of Freud's analysis of Sergei Pankeiev, the "Wolf Man." All of Freud's writings of this period are informed by the tension I discussed in the last chapter between phylogeny and ontogeny; or more precisely, a teleological argument representing an ideology of universal sexual division on one hand, and on the other, the polarity of the drives representing a logic of difference. Here the fragility and mutability of sexual identification in each individual is informed by a series of transactions between masculine and feminine identifications. The interest of Freud's analysis of masochistic phantasy derives neither from recognizing his blindness to this contradiction at the heart of his argument nor from overcoming it. Rather, I will try to locate in the contradiction itself the utopian function of phantasy life.

The inspiration of Freud's paper is a commonly uttered phantasy: "a child is being beaten. . . ." As his analysis proceeds he unearths an increasingly elaborate scenario that underlies and structures this simple utterance, revealing a system of desire where, to return to Bergstrom's phrase, the subject "has taken up multiple identification positions, whether successively or simultaneously." Thus, Freud's analysis is important for several reasons. Freud demonstrates that phantasy life unfolds *across* positions of sexual difference. As such, he examines the structural foundations that regulate the enunciation of phantasy and the accretion of discourse to a variety of aims and objects organized by the drives. Moreover, of the six examples of this phantasy that Freud uncovered and analyzed, four came from women and only two from men. Although Freud had no reason to doubt the commonality of this phantasy, for once the masculine example is taken to be the minority one. More importantly, while Freud attempts to draw a distinct division between the sexes in the genealogy of the scenarios he describes, sexual difference is nonetheless understood as being *constructed* in language as a process of division and loss. It does not devolve *a priori* from genital sex nor can it be understood as the teleological unfolding of a predetermined sexual division.

Rather, sexual differentiation is a historical and contingent process. The function of identification in these scenarios is shown to be variable and diverse, setting up a number of coexisting yet contradictory subject-positions. This entails the production of a circuit of identifications, materially inscribed in the subject's discourse, where transactions between masculine and feminine positions are both variable and necessary.

The manifest content of the phantasy, regardless of the accepted gender of its author is: "A child is being beaten on its naked bottom . . ." Freud then isolates three distinct stages of the phantasy, two of which are conscious, the third unconscious. Each stage is differentiated according to whether the subject is genitally male or female. (Each version of the phantasy and its stratifications are summarized in Tables One and Two.)[8] Freud claims that the "male" version of the phantasy derives from an "inverted" (that is, homosexual) Oedipal situation and that the feminine version derives from "normal" Oedipal relations. In either case the objective of the phantasy is genital arousal and onanistic gratification.

As to the infantile origins of the phantasy, there are three basic factors in common between the beating phantasies of men and women. First, the phantasy represents a "perversion" in the form of the exaggerated development of a single drive-component, sadism, as well as a premature struggle towards the choosing of an object. Second, the phantasy is the product of the "phallic" phase of sexual development that prepares the way for Oedipal conflict and the castration complex. In the first stage of the phantasy, the differentiation between active-sadistic and passive-masochistic, on one hand, and masculine or feminine identification on the other, is not clear; this is central problem and conflict that the phantasy desires to articulate and resolve.

Table 1.

Female version:
"normal" Oedipal attitude

I (cs): "My father is beating the other child [whom I hate . . .]"

II (uncs): "I am [being beaten / loved (genitally)] by my father . . ."

III (cs): "My [authority figure] is beating the [anonymous boy] . . . "

Male version:
"inverted" or homosexual Oedipal attitude

I (cs): ?

II (ucs): "I am [being beaten / loved (genitally)] by my father . . . "

III (cs): "I am being beaten by my mother . . ."

Table 2.

	Agent	Victim	Place of subject	Drive "content"	Meaning in terms of pleasure
I	adult, father	child masc. or fem.	spectator	sadistic	genital arousal
II	father	subject	victim	masochistic	genital arousal
III	adult	male children	spectator	masochistic w/ overlay of sadism	genital arousal
I	?	?	?	?	?
II	father	subject	victim	masochistic	genital arousal
III	mother	subject	victim	masochistic	genital arousal

By the same token, the phallic phase involves the renunciation of an intensely active autoeroticism for a heterosexual object-choice. All the "scattered" aims of the partial drives must be regrouped and directed through the binary division of reproductive sexuality and heterosexual object-choice. This requires both boys and girls to identify with the authority of the Name-of-the-Father with unequal consequences. The polymorphous, unrestrained sexuality of the child confronts a social authority demanding that sexual division be represented by only two choices, and thus legislates who gains what rights of sexual identity by deciding what their bodies may signify. The phantasy is therefore the product of an explicitly ideological struggle between desire and the Law that is never resolved. Rather, the very architecture of phantasy is an unconscious evasion of the demands of patriarchal law. This paradoxical role of phantasy will prove useful in defining its utopian function as well as its interest for a theory of ideological criticism.

Third, the phallic phase is characterized by a special form of incestuous object-choice: the desire to be loved by the Father, and especially to have one's narcissism unconditionally supported by his love. Neither the boy nor the girl will achieve what they desire; nevertheless, what they receive will be different. Ultimately, the desire of the child is not to be loved literally, but to accede to all the attributes, privilege, and authority that patriarchal culture ideally and imaginarily confers on the paternal metaphor. This is why Lyotard insists that the invariability of the agent of the beating phantasy "is not based on an individual, the real father, but on a kind of imaginary archetype who can be readily identified by the rod [*verge*] he has and the one with which he beats the child. This doubling of the phantasized penis is adequate proof that the imaginary roles are anchored, not in the father's *person*, but in the symbolic function of the phallus" (FD 338). Both men and women are doomed in Freud's account to have this childhood narcissism demolished, inspiring Lacan's formula that no one possesses the phallus and that castration is a fraud and a fiction. For the phallus signifies nothing except the hierarchical organization of power according to patriarchal culture; and castration means nothing except the cultural violence that enforces submission to that authority.

The formulation of the Oedipus complex in this essay is fascinating because in a theory marked by sequence, linearity, and contiguity, there arises the possibility of division, divigation, and forking paths. The fundamental choice—as described later in "The Dissolution of the Oedipus Complex" (1924d)—is not necessarily between a male or female gender identity, but rather, between an active or passive sexual relation with the father. Either the father must be supplanted in an incestuous desire for the mother, or the child substitutes itself for the mother to attract the desire of the father. In other words, for both boys and girls there is a double-bind between an incestuous or a homosexual object-choice. As Freud's detailed analysis of phantasy life demonstrates, these choices are open to either sex and the castration complex decides the consequences. In "normal" development, the child's narcissistic interest in preserving the integrity of its body prevails over the attempted parental object-choice, and this object-cathexis is replaced by two identifications: on one hand, the introjection of paternal authority forms the kernel of the super-ego, and on the other a narcissistic identification with the parent of the same genital sex is formulated. Identification, then, has a very special role here. The renunciation of an active object-choice with respect to the parents "desexualizes and sublimates" these libidinal trends, reinvesting them in parental imagos. In sum, the Oedipus complex is a cultural agency and an ideological machine whose product is women and men, each failing and searching out compromises, in their particular ways, with the idealized norm of Woman/Man. Little wonder, then, that phantasy life, so closely tied to the Oedipal situation, organizes scenarios of crisis, renunciation, and the problem of identity.

In the first, conscious strata of the phantasy, Freud has only identified a "female" version; he is unable to verify a parallel first stage for the male patient. The first articulation of the phantasy is:

I (conscious)

male: ?

female: "My father is beating the other child [whom I hate,
         therefore he loves only me . . .]

The point of view of this first formulation is objective and observational, and the gender of the object of the beating phantasy is undetermined. While the aim of phantasy seems *sadistic,* there is no constant relation between either the sex of the phantasizer or that of the beaten child. Sexual difference has yet to be represented clearly, as predicted by Freud in the *Three Essays on Sexuality.* "Not clearly sexual," quips Freud, "not in itself sadistic, but yet the stuff from which both will later come. . ." (SE 17: 187). Neither does the phantasy articulate a feminine or masculine identification, yet it provides the stuff from which both will later come. The phantasy is not clearly sadistic because the child itself does not phantasize carrying out the beating; instead, she begins to identify with the activity of the father.

Six years later, in "Some Psychical Consequences of the Anatomical Distinction Between the Sexes" (1925j), Freud reflects again on the first stage of the beating phantasy, characterizing it as a "relic of the phallic phase" (SE 19: 254). In this account the phantasy originates in an intense autoeroticism that conflicts with an incestuous desire for the father. Freud views the "peculiar rigidity" of this stage as giving expression to a jealousy motivated by penis-envy, but I believe a simpler and more apposite interpretation is possible. If indeed the phantasy is a "confession of masturbation" as Freud insists, perhaps it represents an attempt to find a compromise between autoerotic desire and its prohibition by inscribing an identification with the paternal imago within the circularity of autoerotic activity. Lyotard argues that the phantasy is generated by a "deeply buried trauma . . . the established fact of castration" (FD 337). In other words, the phantasy represents, repeats, and reworks a prohibition that has already been carried out against the girl's "activity," and in this respect models itself on a structure of disavowal where the child divides herself imaginarily between the three roles: onlooker, agent, and victim. In this manner, the child distributes herself in phantasy across three positions, successively occupying those places where Oedipal desire can be most strongly fulfilled without enjoining the father's punishment on her bodily narcissism. In Lyotard's account,

> The desire to be the phallus (the denial of castration) and the desire to have it (the incestuous desire of the father's desire) are the producers (in the theatrical sense) of phantasy I. The first allows the subject to come on to the scene in the role of the father, the second leads up to the subject's entrance in the role of the

child being beaten (II). Both are fixated on the action of *beating*. But what counts is that the phantasizing subject is not herself represented. She is not on the stage and loses herself among the spectators. She is therefore at once behind the scenes, prompting her father, and in the audience clapping. When the female patient succeeds in verbalizing this phase, she casts herself in the role of spectator. (FD 349; trans. modified)

In other words, in the originary strata of the phantasy the girl witnesses the carrying out of the paternal prohibition, she accepts it and rejoices *(jouit)* in it, but disavows that it has any claim on her. Across her own body she stages onanistically the activity of the father and the passivity of the "other" child, and by projecting herself into the space of the spectator [*Schaulustiger*], she combines satisfaction of the scopic and genital drives. Finally, the terms of disavowal are complex even if they derive from the same motivation, that is, identification with the father. The girl not only identifies with the father's "sexual" activity, she also places herself in the space of his imagined look— an all-seeing, punishing gaze. All of which is to say that she betrays and usurps at every level the law of the Father—she appropriates for herself and her own pleasure his imagined activity and his look as representatives of the phallus she is supposed to renounce—as paradoxical proof that his interdictions are being carried out.

This situation changes dramatically in the transition to the next stage. This transition is motivated by the development of an incestuous attitude towards the father who is executing the phantasy. The child thinks, "Because my father is beating the other child, he loves only me . . . ," and this thinking represents an attempt to take the father as a sexual object. From the standpoint of a genital organization dominated by patriarchal authority, such an incestuous solution is clearly untenable. Therefore, love for the father is subordinated to the development of a sense of guilt that distributes the libidinal economy of the phantasy according to its sadistic and masochistic forms. The figuration of the beating phantasy thus formulates a condensation that exploits this relationship by uniting a sense of guilt with sexual love: *"It is not only the punishment for the forbidden genital relation,"* writes Freud, *"but also the regressive substitute for that relation. . . ."* ("Child," 189).

This introduces the second stage of the phantasy:

II (unconscious)

male: "I am $\left[\begin{array}{l}\text{being beaten} \\ \text{loved (genitally)}\end{array}\right]$ by my father . . ."

female: "I am $\left[\begin{array}{l}\text{being beaten} \\ \text{loved (genitally)}\end{array}\right]$ by my father . . ."

The phantasy is the same for girls and boys; in both cases its form is masochistic and the subject introduces her/himself into the phantasy as the subject of enunciation as well as the object of the phantasized activity. Both phantasies clearly rely on a transaction between the libidinal economies of identification and object-choice. For the little girl, being loved by her father represents an incestuous object-choice; for little boy, a choice that is both incestuous and homosexual. The transition to the second stage of the phantasy also formulates a feminine identification for both sexes as a passive sexual desire for the father. On this basis, Freud divides the two versions of the phantasy between a "normal" female and "inverted" male version. This ambiguous relationship, which is clearly present in both cases, motivates a factor of repression that functions in three ways. First, it renders unconscious the consequences of the developing genital organization ("I am loved by my father . . ."). Second, it compels this organization to regress to the earlier sadistic-anal phase (the imagined beating). Third, this regression turns the sadistic attitude back around upon the subject's own self, substituting sadism for masochism, active for passive aims, or in other words, redirecting the libidinal economy of the phantasy from other to ego. Repression reverses the transgressive term (loved), which is transformed through identification with patriarchal authority as "being beaten"—a gratification of the desire without the admitting of an incestuous relation.

Before proceeding, the blank spot in Freud's analysis—the missing first stage of the "male" phantasy—requires commentary. Freud never explains why he believes the first strata of the male version of the phantasy to be potentially conscious, nor does he investigate the possibility that there could be a repressed, unconscious primary strata requiring analytical reconstruction. By the same token, he is not surprised when his male patient can bring the second stage of the phantasy to conscious memory while his female patients cannot. This does not prevent him, of course, from constructing an unconscious second stage for the female version of the phantasy. This ellipsis is extraordinary, considering Freud's efforts to find symmetries between the two versions of the phantasy wherever possible. In trying to explain the attenuation of repression with respect to the second stage on the part of the single male patient discussed, and thus its accessibility to analysis, Freud suggests that "one more reversal has to take place than in the case of a girl, namely the substitution of passivity for activity, and this additional degree of distortion may save the phantasy from having to remain unconscious as a result of repression" ("Child," 190). This retroactive postulation derives from Freud's difficult relation to the theory of bisexuality, examined in the last chapter. The boy's situation is complicated because Freud assumes that, unlike the girl, he begins from a position of originary *activity*. At the starting gate, as it were, Freud's view aligns maleness-activity-masculinity, on one hand, and femaleness-passivity-femininity, on the other, even though his own material gives striking evidence of the autoerotic activity of the little girl. Freud must be presuming the originary linking of the libido to "masculinity" as the product of "man's" archaic inheritance: the development of infantile sexuality being governed by the ontogenetic recapitulation of a phylogenetic experience of incest and repression. Moreover, this is not a simple synonym for the activity of the drives. Freud has unwittingly put himself in the following paradoxical position: either the theory of bisexuality is accurate, in which case the little girl "begins" under the dominance of a constitutional passivity, or else her autoeroticism is incomprehensible.

On the contrary, I have tried to emphasize the power of the girl's active autoeroticism from the very beginning of her sexual life, an idea that derives considerable support from Freud's own account of the originary strata of the "female" phantasy. This involves renouncing Freud's phylogenetic arguments in favor of an emphasis on the originary autoerotic and narcissistic activity in children of either genital sex. In this case, what if a first stage for boys is imagined that is identical in form to the female phantasy, yet different in having submitted to a primal repression that Freud will identify in the *second* stage of the female phantasy? If this were true, what the boy would have failed to accomplish is an identification with the father's activity that enables the mechanism of disavowal wherein the girl distributes herself among the roles of onlooker, agent, and victim. Instead, the boy might have emphasized his homosexual desire for the father by identifying with the "other" child, thus intensifying his passive, anal eroticism. Simply put, where the girl identifies with the activity of the father, the boy identifies with the passivity of the other child; the girl gravitates towards a "masculine" identification, the boy towards a "feminine" one. Both scenarios are intolerable from the standpoint of Oedipal authority. However, this might explain both the nature of the regressive split between being beaten and genital love in the second stage of the phantasy, as well as the different stages of repression in boys and girls. What is being prohibited in both cases is an incestuous desire for the father, and in the case of the boy there is an enjoinment against a desire that is both incestuous and homosexual.[9]

Nevertheless, the situation of the female version of the phantasy remains more concrete. In spite of the proximity of beating and loving that takes place in stages I and II of the phantasy, the profound structural difference between them should be stressed. The splitting of the ego characterized by disavowal in stage I is not topographical; the phantasmic narration remains entirely capable of conscious expression. The song of stage I ("My father is beating the other child . . . therefore he loves only me") is sung as a canon; stage II is the superimposition of discordant motifs, neither of which the child can hear even if the song is played across its body. As Lyotard explains, "Phase I not only bears witness to a demand addressed to the father (to have the phallus), it also attests to an identification with him (to be the phallus).

The regression would thus derive its significance not from the strength of the complex, but from its weakness" (FD 340).

Therefore, the transgression represented by an incestuous object-choice motivates more than regression. In the passage from stage I to II, the girl inscribes herself in the first-person at the price of renouncing an active identification with the father in exchange for an incestuous passive position in relation to him. In this manner, the sadistic-anal component of stage I is transformed into what Freud will later call "moral masochism" as the product of a developing sense of guilt. Nonetheless, this reversal from sadism to masochism and activity to passivity preserves its sexual content by figuring the beating as a regressive substitute for genital love. Conserving and intensifying an incestuous desire, Freud calls this compromise the essence of masochism. The transition between stage II and III, then, requires the onslaught of an inexorable repression, an *Urverdrängung*, that commits the phantasy to the unconscious.

The nature of this unconscious placement is worth remarking upon. Phantasy II is foreclosed from consciousness because it brooks no coherent verbalization nor visual representation. Both require a position based on separation in space: the patterned differences of speech (distinguishing signifier from signified, I from you, here from there); the distance of the gaze carving out a space of the scene and a perspective from which to view it. Repression abolishes these positions, consigning the drive-representatives to the unconscious whose effects are only apprehended through its distortions and disturbances of verbal and visual coherence. "We know what is meant by an *unconscious* imaginal presentation," writes Lyotard, *"the subject does not see itself seeing.* . . . The representation is an oneric one. . . . The subject's presence in the dramatic action goes hand and hand with her loss of the power to produce meaning verbally . . . .: what presents itself without a double is that which cannot signify itself. . . ."(FD 349; trans. modified).[10] Disavowal, allowing the subject to split herself between the space of onlooker and victim while denying she is both at once, is not an adequate defense against her incestuous desire. Thus Lyotard describes stages I and III as organizing a perspectival space where the visual coherence and pleasure of the phantasmic scene are made possible by the forms of division characterizing preconscious thought. By inscribing herself in the displaced position of the gaze, which trenches a protective divide between seer and scene, the girl camouflages a transgressive desire while maintaining the unity of a point of view. This compartmentalization of contradiction through a splitting of the ego, which allows the subject to maintain a fictional sense of coherence and self-identity through a process of negation [*Verneinung*], is unknown to the unconscious. If the patient cannot give coherent expression to the incestuous desire figured in stage II of the phantasy, this is because the qualities of negation, non-contradiction, and patterned differences that allow the subject to represent itself are absent from the unconscious. Lyotard writes that the space of phantasy II

> envelops the subject, who cannot get it within her sights. This envelopment must not be conceived of as a spatial inherency within a montage in three-dimensional space. It is rather a matter of the coexistence of mutually exclusive points of view. . . . [this implies] an exploded subject, incapable of locating herself, and a non-place, where something may take place: I am being beaten by my father. This shattering of the subject and of the scene is the equivalent, in the representative order, of regression in the order of the drives. If it is true that the latter does not involve a withdrawal of investment from one bodily zone (genital) to another (anal), but a new investment that adds itself to its predecessors, the thing-presentation (in II) should simultaneously fulfill the incestuous desire, its interdiction, the sadistic drive and the superimposition of the conglomeration (*Zusammentreffen*) of this cluster of impulsions in the masochistic setting. The subject must be able to recognize herself in the father and in the child; in the beating position and in the position of being beaten. She explodes, and with her the contours, the outlines, the plastic writing. It is the unseen visible. (FD 351; trans. modified)

In the regression from I to II, the girl accepts the classically "feminine" position—passivity and masochism—only by succumbing entirely to a transgressive, incestuous desire. This position can only be realized in the space of the unconscious, which, ruled by the pleasure principle and ungoverned by the principle of noncontradiction, can render an incestuous desire (genital love) and its punishment (beating) as equivalent.

The repressed (unconscious) phantasy of the male and female patients is the same. The transition to the third, conscious stage begins to differentiate the content and the structure of the phantasy by submitting the subjects in question to a social authority demanding that their desires be articulated differently. The third stage of the phantasy is tabulated as follows:

III (conscious)

male: "I am being beaten by my mother . . ."

female: "My [authority figure] is beating the [anonymous boy] . . ."

In the third stage of the phantasy, the structural positions are profoundly distinguished by sexual difference. The girl retains the figure of the father in a disguised form as the agent of the beating while transforming the figure and sex of the phantasized victim. Through repression, the masochistic and passive structure of strata II is transformed producing a particularly complex scenario. In this respect, the interplay between repression and regression is particularly important for the female version of the phantasy. Regression actually changes the organization of the drives, transforming activity as passivity, sadism as masochism, and vice versa. In contrast, the topographic split characteristic of repression only effects the symbolic form of the scenario: the girl changes gender, singular becomes plural, first person becomes third, and the original agent of the beating is disguised. The form of the scenario is transfigured from top to bottom but its libidinal organization remains constant. As Freud notes, its form is sadistic but it satisfies a masochistic desire. In this manner, stage III of the phantasy finds a compromise between the strata that lie beneath it while simultaneously giving them expression.

In contrast, the boy preserves himself as the imagined victim while changing the figure and sex of the agent, thus maintaining a passive ("feminine") attitude while relinquishing a homosexual object-choice. The masochistic form of the scenario is retained along with its genital significance. However, even though the only change in the scenario involves the substitution of the mother for the father, this apparently simple variation has complex consequences. For the little boy the transition to the third stage is motivated by the need to avoid both a homosexual object-choice and an incestuous genital relation. This inspires a paradoxical identification that preserves an incestuous desire for the father by trading places with the mother. Through this maternal identification, the boy usurps the mother's "femininity" while investing her with the phallic activity formerly attributed to the father. This is a textbook example of regression: giving up an object-cathexis (the genital love demanded from the father) by replacing it with an identification (with the mother), and transforming the drive-content by recoiling from the phallic phase to the earlier anal phase. The function of subjectivity in the phantasy is shifted from the feminine to the masculine position, and the figure and sex of the agent of the phantasy are changed as the father is displaced for the mother (although Freud cautions that the figure of the mother nevertheless retains residual masculine and phallic attributes). The question of incest is also avoided by maintaining a masochistic libidinal economy where the relation of genital sex is transformed into its regressive substitute—the beating phantasy. Owing to the lesser quota of repression, a transsex identification is carried out completely on the figure of the agent of the phantasy (unlike the girl), and incompletely in its subject, motivating a strategic splitting of ego: the boy does not imagine himself consciously as a woman, yet reverses his attribution of masculine and feminine attributes to the victim and agent of the phantasy. Nevertheless, regression to the sadistic-anal phase effects both versions in the same way: "... in both sexes the masochistic phantasy of being beaten by the father, though not the passive phantasy of being loved by him, lives on in the unconscious after repression has taken place" ("Child," 199–200). Repression only incompletely achieves its objectives. The girl has not freed herself Oedipally from the figure of her father. The boy, attempting to evade homosexuality, "nevertheless feels like a woman in his conscious phantasies, and endows the women who are beating him with masculine attributes and characteristics" ("Child," 200).

Though there are clear parallels with the situation of the boy, for the little girl the outcome is somewhat different. The transition to the third stage is also motivated by the need to avoid an incestuous relation. However, her solution requires carrying through completely her identification with the father. Here the two situations diverge. First, the boy's relationship to his phantasy is *active* in the sense that he is a participant identified in the phantasy, although it is passive in the context of its masochistic aims. Unlike the boy's subjective participation in the phantasy, the girl's scenario is marked by the objective "voyeuristic" position characterizing the first stage of her phantasy. The girl's relationship to this scenario is passive only in the sense that she produces it as a spectator to the phantasized event. Moreover, the third stage resembles the first in every way except that the object of the beating is now generally derived from the class of boys and the one who administers the beatings is now derived from the class of male authority figures in the girl's life.

Two consequences of the third stage must be accounted for here: the first involves the displacement of the phantasy from the familial scene; the second the overdetermination of the male gender in the phantasy. The first consequence is easily attributed to a distortion of the mise-en-scène caused by regression. The second, however, is rendered more disturbing by Freud's claim that in taking up this spectatorial position the little girl refuses her genital sex. In other words, the figures in the phantasy are boys because the little girl wishes to identify herself in the position from which she has been excluded. Freud suggests that this phantasy provides masochistic gratification by taking a sadistic form. But I believe that it is possible to go farther in a way that substantively challenges my earlier analysis. Freud deemphasizes the fact that the three stages of desire do not cancel one another out and that the three strata of phantasy are simultaneous and co-present in their expression and organization of the drives. Moreover, unlike the male version, the third strata of the female version is neither clearly nor simply masochistic. Split between two desires, an extraordinary situation is produced where the structure of disavowal characterizing the first stage is recapitulated and intensified by the division of mental life motivated by repression in the third. The phantasy is once again *sadistic* in a specific sense: it overdetermines the sadistic component attached to voyeurism. Note for a moment how some of the most cherished axioms of psychoanalytic film theory fall to ruins. In both the pregenital and postoedipal phases of feminine sexuality, the desire of the little girl has a powerful relation to components that are simultaneously active, sadistic, and voyeuristic. The subjective structure of her gaze inspires a powerful relation to desire.

This does not mean, however, that there is "no difference" between the construction of men and women in this respect, nor that the woman entirely escapes a process attempting to submit her to a phallic division and hierarchization of power. Nonetheless, the particularly complex structure of "female" phantasy provides striking insights to the psychology of spectatorship as well as the structural relation of phantasy to narrative forms. The female patients in Freud's analysis produce themselves not just as voyeuristic onlookers, but as members of a (male) audience. Part of the structure of desire in the phantasy is that it is imagined as shared—a collective experience organized around a singular spectacle. Freud also insists that the third strata represents the formulaic expression of a generative matrix. Not only does it creatively produce "an elaborate superstructure of daydreams" ("Child," 190), it is also triggered by, and elaborated through, the private experience of popular narrative forms; for example, the *bibliothèque rose* of adolescent literature. As opposed to the "male" version, which as Silverman points out deliriously produces masochism as a perversion proper, there is no evidence that the female subjects engage in sexually masochistic behavior. Their only "failing" with respect to patriarchal expectations is to have an extraordinary narrative creativity whose aim is autoerotic gratification. Lastly, appealing simply to masochism as an alternative theory of spectatorship, as some critics have suggested, is unsatisfactory in my view. What must be stressed in Freud's essay is the structural complexity and fluidity of spectatorial activity, which may combine different mechanisms of defense (disavowal and repression) with intricate transactions between activity—passivity, sadism—masochism, and masculine or feminine identifications in both men and women.

However, one last "complication" in the case of girls must be explained. Unlike boys, they accomplish a transex identification between the second and third stages of the phantasy that, according to Freud, attenuates its erotic charge. In the symbolic structure of the third scenario, the objects of beating are always boys, regardless of the sex of the phantasizer. Freud remarks that "When [the female patients] turn away from their incestuous love for their father, with its genital significance, they easily abandon their feminine role. They spur their 'masculinity complex' . . . into activity, and from that time forward only want to be boys. For that reason, the whipping boys who represent them are boys too. In both the cases of day-dreaming— one of which almost rose to the level of the work of art—the heroes were always young men; indeed women used not to come into these creations at all, and only made their first appearance after many years, and then in minor parts" ("Child," 191). Here Freud notes, without making a point of it, that the patients also produced themselves as subjects in the phantasy as boys.

This undoubtedly represents a phallic identification with the Oedipal privilege accorded to boys which is not simple, for it also draws its power from
the pregenital phase where the sadistic and voyeuristic components were
exercised without the price of a repressive phallic division.

Kaja Silverman has also commented on the complex symbolic structure
of the girls' third scenario, where gender transgression seems so strongly
marked, but in a different way that I find convincing. For her the last stage
of the phantasy represents three transgressive desires: "that it be boys rather
than girls who be loved/disciplined in this way; to the desire to be a boy
while being so treated by the father; and, finally, to the desire to occupy a
male subject-position in some general sense, but one under the sign of
femininity rather than masculinity" (MMS 48). The last formula is provocative and intriguing. Silverman understands immediately that Freud's reading
of this transformation as an "extinction" of the girl's sexuality is a misprision
that turns a blind eye to the ideological question at stake: "what might it
mean, apart from simple disguise, for a female subject to represent herself
in phantasy as a group of passive boys?" (MMS 49). Freud refuses to
recognize both the voyeuristic content of the phantasy and its erotic charge.
More importantly, he does not account for the complex set of identifications
attached to this position. In stage III, the girl is divided in her position as
Schaulustiger between an identification with the boys who are beaten/loved
by the father's representative and an identification with the onlooker. In this
manner, the desire narrated in phantasy coalesces around a particularly
utopian situation. Silverman notes how the idea of deviance is usually articulated through a binary grid which manages it: when a male doesn't identify
with a male position, he is supposed to identify with the female and vice
versa. "The beating phantasy, however, attests to the desire for imaginary
variations that fall outside the scope of the Freudian model, and whose
complexities work to cancel out masculinity altogether" (MMS 50). In
Silverman's explanation, these variations include an unthinkable identification with (passive) male homosexuality as well as a displacement of masculinity within the libidinal space of the look. The masculinity, aggression, and
sadism culturally associated with voyeurism are invested elsewhere, namely,
in the punishing figure of the father. The position of the spectator in the
phantasy is less the site of a controlling gaze than a heavily defended erotic
vantage point that conserves the investment of desire in looking, while
attempting to reconfigure it as a desiring gaze that places masculinity under
erasure. In phantasy, the female patients identify with boys only in the sense
that they represent a "feminine" position. At the same time, they distance
themselves from problem of "maleness or femaleness" in Freud's sense
("a male genital organisation or a castrated condition"), thus enjoying the
father's love without submitting bodily to his authority. Is this the utopia of
an active desire, based on feminine autoeroticism, that is regained by subvert-

ing the phallic division that represses it? The answer to this question must be withheld until the next chapter. First, the relation between utopia and the expression of desire must be clarified.

Phantasy and Utopia

In English, the word "fantasy" connotes escape from or reconciliation to the status quo. Kaja Silverman and Jean-François Lyotard, through brilliant and original readings of Freud's work on masochism, have a very different emphasis. Phantasy becomes a site that erodes proper meaning, undermines opposition with difference, resists patriarchal authority, and thus presents a utopian remodeling of desire. The role of phantasy is not to reconcile desire to the law, which is of course the most concise expression of the logic of Oedipus. Rather, the logic of phantasy derives from the simultaneous and paradoxical expression of desire and its interdiction. The utopia expressed in phantasy life, regardless of the sexual identification of the subject, is for a sexual world ungoverned by the constraints of phallic desire.

In "Masochism and Male Subjectivity," Silverman's stated object is the study of non-phallic male subjectivity. Her analysis examines the idea that "male subjectivity is far more heterogeneous and divided than our theoretical models seem to suggest; it cannot be adequately summarized by invoking either the phallus, or the more flexible concept of bisexuality" (MMS 62–63). I have argued that the same is true for female subjectivity which is far too often described either under the signs of negativity and lack or as the dialectical reversal of those values. Referring to Freud's paper on "The Economic Problem of Masochism" (1924c), Silverman describes how "moral" masochism, the internalized feeling of guilt which operates more or less in every individual, is forcefully characterized by internal division and the oscillation between distinct positions of identification. Silverman describes this oscillation as an impossible position deriving from the contradictory demands formulated with respect to the father's desire. In boys, the mechanism for overcoming an incestuous and homosexual desire for the father, so poignantly deployed in the second stage of infantile beating phantasies, is to achieve an identification with his symbolic place and position. In the technical language of psychoanalysis, the boy must transform object-libido into narcissistic libido, or object-love into ego-love. However, the interdiction of this desire requires a topographical division exacted through repression. Part of his identification with the paternal imago then splits off to form the super-ego. The severity of this internalized symbolic father, his omniscience and his despotic power of observation and punishment, are internalized in the following form: you must aspire to be like me in every way, but you can only share in a small portion of my power. Thus love for the father is transformed as self-love, but only on the condition that it is formulated as a passive relation to the super-ego. The ego's subordination to the super-ego, which generates unconscious feelings of guilt, is precisely the "moral" masochism described by Freud. As Silverman describes, "The 'ordinary' male subject oscillates endlessly between the mutually exclusive commands of the (male) ego-ideal and the super-ego, wanting both to love the father and to be the father, but prevented from doing either" (MMS 41). This fundamental division within the subject casts moral masochism "as a kind of chamber play for two in which the same actor plays both parts" and "where psychic differentiation makes it possible for the subject to function both as the one who punishes and the one who is punished" (MMS 42).

Reading Freud with Theodor Reik, and through her emphasis on the complexities of the positive and negative versions of the Oedipus complex in individuals of both sexes, Silverman also emphasizes the transactional nature of masculinity and femininity in every individual. As importantly, from the beginning of her essay Silverman associates the theory of "perversions" with a potentially utopian function, an erosion of the laws of nature and nations: "perversion turns aside from both biology and the social order, and it does so through the improper deployment or negation of the binarisms upon which each regime depends—binarisms that reinforce each other in the case of gender, if not class. The 'truth' or 'right' which is thus subverted is the principle of hierarchy" (MMS 31). For Silverman, masochistic phantasy is driven by a "heterocosmic" impulse: the utopian desire to remake the cultural order by turning the division, negativity, and loss of castration into an erosion of phallic values. Only in this respect is the logic of Oedipus central to the theory of phantasy. "The concept of perversion," writes Silverman, "is . . . unthinkable apart from the Oedipus complex, since it derives all its meaning and force from its relation to that structuring moment and the premium it places upon genital sexuality. It is in fact something of a misnomer to characterize infantile sexuality as 'polymorphously perverse' since sexuality only becomes perverse at the point where it constitutes either a retreat from Oedipal structuration, or a transgressive acting out of its dictates" (MMS 32). Thus the "revolutionary" aspect of perversion is not only sexual; it tends to elude or erode the divisions of language and identity, and the hierarchies of power, regulated by the paternal signifier. The paternal signifier demands the articulation of sexuality as division; it is the peculiar function of phantasy to transform division as reversal and chiasmus. In this respect, the polarity and reversibility of the drives always conflicts with the restrictive and dualistic logic of Oedipus.

By the same token, the mobility of the drives fuels the transpositions of sexual identification that take place in phantasy. This is exemplified by the paradox of "feminine" masochism as a particularly male pathology. Its most formulaic expression is found in stage III of the "child is being beaten phantasy: "I am being beaten by my mother." As I described above, in order to avoid a homosexual object choice, in phantasy the boy positions the mother in place of the father, identifying himself with her "passive femininity." But just as "feminine" masochism has little to do with the pathology of women, the "femininity" defined here has less to do with the behavior of actual women than with the imaginary place assigned to femininity in the phantasy of sexual division exacted and superintended by the paternal signifier; namely castration, giving birth, or taking the passive part in coitus. Here the fluid and unstable boundaries of sexual identity—where the maternal imago replaces the paternal yet retains phallic attributes, and the boy retains his masculinity yet "feels like a woman" in phantasy—testify to the power and flexibility of mechanisms of disavowal. This concept should be dissociated from film theory's false identification of disavowal only with fetishism, and should be rethought as a mechanism of defense taking many forms in the psychology of both women and men. In its most general sense, disavowal enables the holding of contradictory beliefs in virtue of divisions in the ego exacted through repression. In the divaricating and stratified identifications of the beating phantasy, for example, the boy knows that he is not a girl, yet chooses to identify himself with their phantasized passivity. Alternatively, the girl knows that she is not a boy, yet chooses to place herself surreptitiously among them to revel in their witnessing of a phantasized activity. These are two very different forms of disavowal and two different forms of positioning one's self in the passive role in phantasy. Both powerfully demonstrate that disavowal is not simply a defense mechanism. Rather, it represents a utopian drive to imagine scenarios where the subject occupies a position or positions other that those dictated by Oedipal sexuality. In this manner, Gilles Deleuze writes that "disavowal should perhaps be understood as the point of departure of an operation that consists neither in negating nor even destroying, but rather in radically contesting the validity of that which is: it suspends belief in and neutralizes the given in such a way that a new horizon opens up beyond the given and in place of it . . . "[11] In sum, the emphasis on femininity in men patients derives from their identification with the mother, and, consequently, an elevation of the maternal ideal at the expense of the paternal. As Silverman puts it, "in inviting the mother to beat and/or dominate him, [the male masochist] transfers power and authority from the father to her, remakes the symbolic order, and 'ruins' his own paternal legacy" (MMS 57). And if, as Freud asserts, the phantasy implies a feminine attitude without a homosexual object-choice, then it "effects another revolution of sorts, and one whose consequences may be even more socially transforming than eroticism between men—it constitutes a 'feminine' yet heterosexual male subject" (MMS 57).

A more extreme version of this scenario is played out in the "Moloch" phantasy, described by one of Theodor Reik's patients as necessary to his sexual potency.[12] Silverman cites and analyzes this phantasy in depth, but I will restrict myself to two observations. First, while the patient is the author of the phantasy, he also visualizes himself within its narrative as one of a group of athletic young men waiting to be sacrificed to a pagan god. In this respect the structure of the scenario parallels that of stage III in Freud's description of the beating phantasy. However, in the Moloch narrative the subject projects himself into the phantasy both as witness to the sacrifice and the penultimate victim; he produces the scenario in his mind's eye, and as an actor within it projects himself as a passive spectator. The nature of the sacrifice is telling. After a high priest examines the genitals of the victim, carefully certifying their size and weight as acceptable to the god, they are removed with a sharp cut which is timed to the orgasm produced by the phantasy. Behind this imaginary renunciation of genital sexuality is the relinquishing of a desire for the father's love, or perhaps more precisely, the recurrent desire to abolish the desire for the father's love. As Silverman emphasizes, the male masochist will not be reconciled to the symbolic order nor to the paternal ideal; this is the second point. He prefers to place his sexual subjectivity on the side of ritual self-immolation, a reduction to zero. He enacts and reenacts the scenario of castration and the execution of the law of the father in order to demolish it, even if he expects to be extinguished along with it. Yet, at the same time he extracts the greatest *jouissance* from it. "His sexuality," Silverman notes, "must be seen to be entirely under the sway of the death drive, devoid of any possible productivity or use value" (MMS 58). I will reemphasize the importance of the death drive in a moment. However, what is excruciating and fascinating in this phantasy is its visceral, demonstrative expression of what is behind "feminine" identification for the masochistic male subject—he achieves *jouissance* by identifying with painful evisceration, and places himself as next in line for the symbolic excision of his masculinity. However, what is stake in this scenario of castration is less an identification with "womanhood," as Freud would seem to think, than a ritualized renunciation of paternal power and privilege. "The stipulation that each victim must conform to the phallic ideal," writes Silverman, "means that what is really being defaced or disfigured in this phantasy is the paternal imago, and that what is cut-off and thrown away is the phallic legacy . . . . In this phantasy nothing is salvaged, and nothing is redeemed. It is a narrative of the darkest negativity and loss" (MMS 53).

Reik's male masochist assumes the passive position of "femininity" in his erotic life—demonstratively being castrated—as well as in the structure of his ego as represented by the narcissistic formula "I see myself seeing myself." Both of these positions, of course, are evaded in the forms of disavowal adopted by Freud's female patients. Where the divisions of the female version of the beating phantasy represent a transgression of active and voyeuristic "masculine" positions, enjoying them without submitting to them, the male version enjoys "femininity" by magnifying those aspects that erode the phallic ideal. Both positions are transsexual while neither is homosexual in the sense of a simple inversion of the norms of reproductive heterosexuality. Both examples represent versions of phantasy life that either evade or displace normative heterosexuality in the effort to dream a position undefined by phallic desire. Alternatively, it is important to reemphasize that the "perversions" of phantasy life are intimately attached to the powers they desire to undermine; this is part and parcel of the repetitiousness and circularity of phantasy life. To fashion a world of desire by remaking and disordering castration scenarios that foreclose the paternal legacy, the masochist must nonetheless continually reinvoke the logic of Oedipus. As Silverman puts it, "by projecting a cruel or imperious authority before whom he abases himself, the masochist only acts out in an exaggerated, anthropomorphic and hence disruptive way the process whereby subjects are culturally spoken. . . . The crucial question to ask here is whether the heterocosmic impulse exhausts itself altogether in the boudoir, or whether the 'play' spills over into social intercourse as well, contaminating the proprieties of gender, class, and race" (MMS 55).

Silverman brilliantly accounts for the power of phantasy to formulate deviant subjectivities that resist patriarchal authority and phallic sexuality. However, where Silverman focuses on the structure of perversion as a limit case of desiring subjectivity, I am more interested in the general question of the potentially utopian function of phantasy, regardless of its adopted forms. In this respect, masochism should not necessarily be elevated to the site of utopian subjectivity as Silverman herself points out. Freud and Reik's examples are extreme cases exemplifying the complexity and variety of sexual identification. Fundamental here is the idea that sexual difference is based on transactions between, and erosions of, the culturally given norms of femininity and masculinity, and that the evasion of the law of the father is more the norm than the deviation in phantasy life. The scenarios of negativity and loss that Silverman so beautifully describes in the male masochist inform, in ways different in kind and degree, all forms of phantasy life.

Attracted by other questions, Silverman has little to say about the repetitiveness of phantasy life. From my point of view, however, what is most striking about the representation of desire—from the most private phantasies to the most public narratives—is the force of recurrence, linked by Freud fundamentally to the death drive. In the domain of mass culture, the phenomenon of genres gives the most eloquent evidence of this fact. While the repetitiveness of genres is undoubtedly sustained by their economic function within the culture industry, this neither explains the pleasure derived from them nor their striking ideological ambivalence, that is, their potential for both supporting and challenging the status quo.[13] I suggested earlier in this book that the peculiar logic of repetition in mass cultural narratives itself provides a cue for ideological criticism. If the simplest definition of ideology is to say that it attempts to provide imaginary solutions for specific social dilemmas and conflicts, then the fact of repetition itself is testimony to the inherently contradictory and irresolvable nature of the desires historically represented in mass cultural forms.

Psychoanalysis is not equipped conceptually to address those problems best posed and resolved by a historical and materialist criticism; namely, the historical specificity of contradiction. Alternatively, if the historical expression of desire remains of central interest to ideological criticism, then perhaps psychoanalysis can clarify the deeper narrative matrices that fuel contradictions. (In particular I am thinking of how the textual analyses of Raymond Bellour and Thierry Kuntzel, while based on single films, are meant to demonstrate the force of primal phantasy—for example, castration or the primal scene—in the general narrative structure of classical films.) Just as the quotidian residues of thought, perception, and memory are adapted by dreams to represent more fundamental conflicts in the history of the subject, perhaps an examination of the relation between phantasy and narrative, regardless of its manifest content, will provide insight to, in Fredric Jameson's apposite phrase, the "political unconscious" of mass society.

In this respect, Jean-François Lyotard's interest in masochistic phantasy differs from Kaja Silverman's. In his reading of Freud's essays of the 1920s—including "'A Child is being Beaten,'" *Beyond the Pleasure Principle,* and "The Economic Problem of Masochism"—Lyotard develops an idea that Silverman leaves aside; namely, the controversial function of the death drive in the forms of organization and recurrence in phantasy. In Lyotard's reading, Freud's late essays on masochism are less concerned with the study of "perversions" than with fundamental insights to the economy of the drives with respect to representation. For Lyotard, Freud's last revision of the theory of the drives as the struggle between Eros and Thanatos provides the key for understanding the utopian function of phantasy as an erosion of the systematic expression of phallic desire. Here the repetition compulsion materializes where the drive for unity represented by Eros struggles vainly against the entropic force of the death drive.

It is unclear from Silverman's essay how the heterocosmic impulse of phantasy might inform mass cultural as opposed to private narratives, and what the consequences of this impulse might be for textual analysis and ideological criticism. Alternatively, in *Discours, figure* one of Lyotard's main objectives is to explain how the structure of phantasy generally informs aesthetic expression. Lyotard develops the terms figure-image, figure-form, and figure-matrix to represent a scale from the most manifest to the most deeply unconscious articulations of phantasy. The figure-image is visceral; it belongs to the visible and the expressible as a literal representation in the form of a picture, theme, or motif. The figure-form is the underlying, often unapprehended, support of this image. Lyotard calls it "the Gestalt of a configuration, the architecture of a painting, the scenography of a performance . . ." (FD 333). In the close analysis of film, one might call it the textual *system,* in the same sense that the systemic aspects of a *langue* are the invisible background against which the intelligibility of any utterance is measured. Like a *langue,* then, the figure-form is in principle analyzable as a patterned system of differences or set of oppositions that bestows identity on a text by ordering and unifying its formal elements from the smallest to largest units of structure.

The figure-matrix, however, is of a different order altogether. As a generative matrix, it is embedded in the deepest processes of unconscious thought—the phantasy materials created by primary repression—and thus cannot be apprehended consciously. One might believe that the atemporality of the primary processes and the discontinuous intervals produced by the drive-representatives in phantasy would warrant understanding the matrix as a structure, thus supporting Lacan's idea that the unconscious is structured like a language. But Lyotard insists that the two poles represented by matrix and structure, phantasy and discourse, or the primary and secondary processes, are strictly incommensurable. "What the matrix and structure have in common," writes Lyotard,

> is that both are invisible and synchronic. But these two characteristics derive in their turn from qualities that are diametrically opposed to each other. A structure's invisibility is that of a system, which is a virtual but intelligible entity. Its intelligibility manifests itself precisely in the observing of formal rules, the rules of logic that define the properties of a system in general, internal rules governing transformation. . . . Negativeness [in the sense of a meaning supported by patterned oppositions and the principle of non-contradiction] has an essential function here. The unconscious, on the other hand, does not recognize negation; it does not know what contradiction is. The matrix does not consist in a series of fixed oppositions, and whatever "propositions" [*"énoncés"*] might be attributed to it—combining the aim (to beat), the source (the anal zone), and the object (the father) of the drive in one sentence—are themselves condensed into a formula-product—"A child is being beaten"—whose apparent coherence conceals the fact that the life of the psyche contains a multitude of "sentences" that are mutually exclusive, that cannot possibly coexist. . . .
>
> If therefore the matrix is invisible, it is not because it belongs to the realm of the intelligible. It is because it occupies a space that remains on the far side of the intelligible, that is diametrically opposed to the rule of opposition and completely under the control of *difference.* . . . But we can already grasp that this property of unconscious space (a property it shares with the libidinal body)—its capacity to contain several places in one place, to form a bloc out of what cannot possibly coexist—is the secret of the figural, which transgresses the intervals that constitute discourse and the distances that constitute representation. Word-presentations and thing-presentations spring from the matrix and inherit their deviancy from it. (FD 343–344; trans. modified)

For Lyotard, to assert that there is desire in representation is equivalent to acknowledging that the architecture of form or system that renders the latter intelligible is sustained by and against a force that continually threatens that intelligibility. The very idea of a textual *system*, then, may be an obstacle to understanding the expression of desire in mass cultural forms. "To make [the matrix] intelligible by reducing it to a schema," writes Lyotard, "would be to make its immersion in the unconscious unintelligible. The figure-matrix attests to the fact that is the 'other' of discourse and intelligibility that is at issue. To situate it within a textual space, especially a schematic one, would be to imagine it as an arché, to entertain in its place a double phantasy: first of all that of an origin and secondly that of an expressible origin" (FD 333).

Lyotard's argument can be clarified by comparing his formulation of the figure-matrix with the place of primal phantasy in Freud's thought. Both represent a (non-)place where every desiring representation originates, without themselves being apprehendable as an origin. The most concrete example of this paradox is the place of the primal scene—the witnessing of parental coitus—in the case history of the Wolf Man. In his analysis, Freud describes an astounding variety of figure-images in the Wolf Man's phantasy life—the figure five, the erect ears of the dream wolves, the closing wings of the butterfly, the hallucination of the semi-detached finger—all of which derive from a figure-form in the shape of a "V." Behind this schema Freud discerns the phantom shape of a *coitus a tergo,* witnessed by the Wolf Man from his crib, that retroactively [*Nachträglich*] confirms the possibility of castration through the unconscious memory of the father's disappearing penis. It is important to emphasize that even if the primal scene functions as an historical origin for the Wolf Man's phantasy life, nevertheless it cannot be historically confirmed. Like the second stage of the infantile beating phantasy, it has been formulated through primary repression; radically unconscious, it can only be reconstructed after the fact in the structure of its repetitions in symptoms and phantasy life.[14] This otherness of the figure-matrix under-scores the fundamental difference of the primary processes with respect to the more quotidian forms of language and representation, whose systematic nature, deriving from the coherence of a *langue,* is continually eroded by the eruption of unconscious thought.

This special logic of repetition and difference is fundamental to Lyotard's analysis. For in the drive of repetition one apprehends both the form of a system attempting to give intelligible expression to unconscious thought and the forces of disorder that doom those attempts, thus spurring forward the process of recurrence. This is equivalent, in Lyotard's view, to Freud's description of Eros as the drive to build ever higher unities out of a fundamen-tally disunifying force—the death drive. In his attempt to define the utopian potential of phantasy, the most important question that Lyotard asks is how can phantasy be form and transgression at the same time? Lyotard insists on the fundamentally disordering, entropic, and transgressive nature of phantasy—its alienness with respect to discursive systems and its erosion of binary oppositions. By the same token, the narrative support of phantasy is not formless incoherence. He calls its a "repetitive configuration" or matrix whose regularity—while it derives neither from the structure of the phantasy's representamens, its discursive constructions, its affects, nor its narrative contents—nonetheless underlies them all like a "(silent) language."

Lyotard writes that "the 'form' we are dealing with in the phantasy is not a proper one. It is certainly a form in which desire remains engaged—*form in the grip of transgression*—but is also, potentially at least, *the transgression of form*" (FD 354). This striking chiasmus derives from Lyotard's reading of Freud's revision of the theory of the drives in *Beyond the Pleasure Principle*. If phantasy has a form, it is neither unary nor selfsame, nor can it be constrained by criteria of unity, closure, or systematic expression. At the risk of reducing a very complex argument, I'll reiterate that Lyotard's formula is designed to express the conflict of forces between Eros and the death drive and the forms of repetition they generate. In this respect, "form" represents Eros in its function of giving representation to sexuality, and more importantly, its drive to bind, cohere, and build ever higher unities. In contrast, the death drive is not negativity, but rather an entropic force—erosion, dis-integration, and reduction to zero. The former tends toward unity and order, the latter towards defusion and entropy. Lyotard represents the two drives with the numerical operators $(+ \ -)$. There is a risk in using these values, however, since they imply positivity and negativity in an argument where Lyotard takes extraordinary pains to demonstrate the absence of negation and the non-dialectical logic of the primary processes. It would be more accurate, then, to represent them by $(1,0)$, and I will reconsider Lyotard's argument through these operators.

For Lyotard, the matrix of phantasy is generated through its forms of repetition—a game of rhythm and intervals—where word and thing-presentations blossom according to strictly composed scenarios. Thus in "a child is being beaten" the basic formula is $(1,0 \ 1,0 \ 1,0)$. This is the rhythm of connection, interruption, and reconnection represented by the contact of the father's hand or rod with the child's naked bottom. This scansion has a distinct meaning with respect to the pleasure-principle; it produces *jouissance,* in this context safely translated as orgasm, as the difference between a charge and discharge of cathexis. However, if for Lyotard quanta of *jouissance* are organized in this manner, it would not be through their investment in a representamen—as, for example, in the bundling of binary groups where a computer translates letters and figures into a numerically manipulable code—although the contents of the phantasy could be described in this matter. Rather, *jouissance* is produced in the spacing of intervals, a form of hesitation which Silverman describes as the (pleasurably) agonizing suspense of masochistic phantasy. In phantasy, *jouissance* cannot be represented by a letter or a figure, but only in the intervals of the special form of repetition and difference blossoming from the struggle between Eros and the death drive. Once again transposing Lyotard's schema: "absolute difference would be death, in so far as it is irreversible: the $(1,0)$ which the resurgence of desire in its $(0,1)$ form . . . cannot annul. That is how $(1,0,1)$ the dialectic thinks it can put death into language, "pocketing" it and mastering it. But the truth is that there is no process but rather a cycle $(1,0,1,0,1,0 \ldots n)$ without end. Absolute difference would be $(1,0)$" (FD 355).

In this manner, Lyotard follows Freud's argument in *Beyond the Pleasure Principle*, examining the subtle and complex ways that the death drive invaginates, in Derrida's apposite metaphor, the relation between Eros and representation. In Freud's original schema, he opposed the pleasure-principle—as a means of keeping psychical energy constant by binding it—to a principle of inertia seeking total discharge. After 1920, following my digital metaphor, Freud argues that the drive toward identity (1) represented by Eros can neither bind desire to representation, nor build higher and more complex schema from this binding, without enlisting the absolute difference (0) of the death drive. Both elements are required for any "coding" of desire. This is none other than the fable of the *fort/da* game, which Lyotard examines at great length in these terms. However, if phantasy is a machine for producing *jouissance*, its utopian potential derives from the fact that *jouissance* is neither representation nor death, but something that oscillates between them:

> . . . like death, at the same time that it discharges tension, it brings obscurity: the annihilation of representation, and the annihilation of words: silence . . . . If it is taken in the absolute sense, difference "must" come to terms with life, with the survival of the system. *Jouissance* stops short of death, it is a compromise between Nirvana and the constancy principle. If the "letter" of desire were merely a letter, death would be excluded from it and for that very reason desire would be *readable* because it would literally be contained within the stable networks of meaning and representation. That "letter" would at least be a proper form, a configuration capable of remaining constant amid the flow of events. But the order of desire is not the order of the secondary process. It is that order overthrown by a disorderly force. Beyond the pleasure principle, what Freud is surely trying to conceptualize is "the eternal return of the same," as it manifests itself in the child's game, in the symptom, in the transference, but what he is trying to get at is not the *same*, but the *return*. What strikes him is not the *law* of repetition, but recurrence. . . .
> It is not the same which returns, neither is it a discourse that unfurls. It is a configuration that does not succeed in liberating itself sufficiently to form a predicative identity in a sentence or in an assertive statement. (FD 355–357)

Desire, then, even if expressed in the law of the letter, will not be reconciled to the letter of the Law. If what Lacan means by the symbolic is how the child comes to terms with sexual difference through the acquisition of "discourse" in the largest sense of the term, then the forms of the Oedipus complex and the matrices of phantasy are revealed in their actual agonistic relation. The uncanny recurrence of phantasy always represents an attempt to restage the Oedipal drama of desire and identity, to rewrite it and to have it conclude differently. Moreover, the inherent fragility of sexual identity devolves from this relation. Oedipus and the castration complex attempt to divide and conquer, imposing sexual division on desire, structured oppositions in language, and the "proper" forms of sexuality on the subject. But this process of division, and the unities subsequently constructed through binary opposition, must continually enlist the force of the drives, and so are undone by them. "To take the drive for a binding force," writes Lyotard, "would be worse than to take the unconscious for a language and to make the Id (Ça) talk. Because after all, there is some liaison in the unconscious—a phantasmic and formal liaison, Eros. But the unconscious is not what it is (i.e., unknowable), except in so far as the liaison separates, comes undone, and it is here that the death drive reveals itself . . . . Now we understand that the principle of figurality which is also the principle of unbinding . . . is the death drive: 'the absolute of anti-synthesis': Utopia."[15]

This idea must have severe consequences for how the reigning theories of textual analysis and narration in the cinema have appropriated psychoanalytic theory. In particular, the concept of enunciation has been used to describe the forms of pleasure and identification organized for the spectator by the textual systems of given films. These arguments have all been formulated through the terms of identity where the proper forms of the text find themselves completed in the (sexual) self-identity of the spectator, a logic utterly at odds with that of phantasy. If Lyotard is taken at his word, this approach would be fundamentally unfaithful to the nature of the primary processes. Moreover, textual analyses organized through terms of system and identity tend to pose the problem of ideology as a teleological force, fully realizing itself in the forms of the text and in the spectator's apprehension of those forms. A *critical* reading, in the best sense of the word, would be organized otherwise. It would watch and listen, with the floating attention of the analyst, for silences, equivocations, evasions, denials, and contradictions. It would understand the recurrences of form not as a desire fulfilled in signs, but as the dream of unfulfilled desire; repetition not as a drive toward ending, but towards new beginnings. Rather than understanding the text as completing itself in the spectator, the encounter between text and reader would be understood as a historical dice-throw, a contingent event, the possibility for renewing terms of meaning, identity, and desire. What is needed, then, is not a theory of spectatorship based on identification; rather, we must imagine the activity of reading as difference.

Chapter 5
The Difference of Reading

*As for knowing who signs the mise-en-scène, psychoanalysts should no
longer decide by relying solely on the resources of their science, nor even
on those of myth. They must also become philosophers.*[1]

The "novelistic" structure of Freud's case histories and analyses of phantasy is often remarked upon. By the same token, using the model of phantasy
to examine the relation between narrative structure and desire is one of the
most compelling points of exchange between psychoanalysis and film theory.
According to Jean Laplanche and J.-B. Pontalis, what characterizes all types
of phantasy "is their mixing in various degrees of the *structural* and the
imaginary. It is in this sense that Freud always chose the daydream as a
model of phantasy—this sort of serial melodrama [*roman feuilleton*], at the
same time stereotypical and infinitely variable, that the subject produces and
narrates for itself in waking moments."[2] Following Laplanche and Pontalis,
I want to examine in *Céline et Julie vont en bateau* (Jacques Rivette, 1974),
the narrative relation between the structure of phantasy, phantasies of the
origin of identity [*Familienroman*], and primal phantasies [*Urphantasien*].
Few would question that *Céline et Julie* is a film "about" phantasy, narrative,
and spectatorship. However, my interest in the film does not derive from its
"reflexive" presentation of these themes, thus implying epistemological values articulated by the film and absent from more "classical" narratives.
Whatever critical knowledge the film may yield will blossom in the context
of a reading, a differential appropriation of the film, and it is very much the
stakes of reading that I have in mind here. Despite the great pleasure that
working through this film offers, I invoke *Céline et Julie* not to interpret
it—clarifying its themes or saying what it means in its stead—but as an
opportunity for examining how the theoretical arguments I have presented
so far may be put to work by textual analysis.

There is another problem at stake based on the following question: in
what ways can the specificity of Freud's analyses of phantasy suggest a theory
of reading? And can this idea of reading serve as a critique of the existing
paradigms for discussing spectatorship, especially in relation to the problem
of sexual difference? These questions are complicated by the fact that Freud's
published work itself offers two different images of interpretation. More-

over, these models diverge on the problem of the analysis of phantasy, above all in Freud's attempts to explain the temporal and causal relation of the *Urszene,* or primal scene, to the production of phantasy and the history of the subject. In Chapters Three and Four I contrasted two different vectors in Freud's thought: on one hand, a teleological orientation and a logic of binary division where the theory of phylogeny informs Freud's ideas on bisexuality and the acquisition of sexual identity through the Oedipus and castration complexes; on the other, his intricate understanding of the nondialectical organization of the drives, and after 1920, an increasing emphasis on their entropic character. These vectors represent two forms of reading and rational explanation that exist side by side in Freud's thought. As I will explain in a moment, both are represented in the narrative system of *Céline et Julie,* which is itself two films characterized by two different forms of repetition. My point, then, is not that Freud's writings are falsified by contradiction. On the contrary, his views after 1920 comprise the most replete account of the specific logic of contradiction that generates the complex architecture of phantasy, where one activity of mental life never ceases organizing, systematizing, and building higher unities against an equally powerful force of disintegration.

Most fundamental in Freud's speculations concerning conflicts between Eros and the death drive is the idea that desire only finds expression in the compromise between incommensurable orders of thought. Alternatively, Freud's most basic miscalculation involved mistaking the historical and social nature of these conflicts. As an agent of Eros, the binary logic of Oedipus is not an archaic memory. Rather, it is a historically defined regulatory apparatus whose efforts to bolster the subject within the reigning norms of self-identity and hierarchies of power issue from the attempt to construct order out of the disorderly force of the drives. This is not a process that emerges from within the subject according to genetic program; it is a cultural drama where the subject is caught up, initially within the mise-en-scène of the family, then increasingly in its encounter with mutually supporting educational, religious, political, economic, and aesthetic practices. The role of criticism here is to articulate the potentially utopian function of phantasy. I argued in the last chapter that the "narrative" structure of phantasy is fundamentally paradoxical—the simultaneous expression and prohibition of desire. An impossible process, the nature and forms of repetition in phantasy represent an expressly ideological conflict in the attempt to represent a mostly inchoate desire that is utopian in the sense of its effort to dream possibilities of identity, sexuality, and pleasure unconstrained by norms of phallic division. A larger and more concrete account of the potentially utopian function of mass culture is beyond the scope of this study. However, I do not believe that the psychoanalytic approach I have adopted here excludes the diverse traditions of cultural criticism represented by Ernst

Bloch, Georg Lukàcs, Walter Benjamin, Theodor Adorno, and Herbert Mar-
cuse among others. If indeed the pleasures of narrative, and especially film
narrative, derive from ideological ambivalences whose form originates in the
peculiar logic of phantasy, then the forms of reading offered by psychoanalysis have much to offer to a criticism sensitive to the diverse, if often inchoate
and contradictory desires for a different society articulated in mass culture.

However, as I mentioned above, Freud's models of explanation and read-
ing are neither simple nor unified. This is exemplified by his attempts to
describe the temporal system of the Wolf Man's phantasy life and the theoretical place of the primal scene there.[3] This problem returns obsessively in
Freud's writings of this period, including "Remembering, Repeating, and
Working-Through" (1914g), "A Case of Paranoia running counter to the
Psycho-Analytical Theory of the Disease" (1915f), and the *Introductory
Lectures on Psycho-Analysis* (1916–1917 [1915–1917]). Freud never stops
attempting to ascribe the force of the primal scene to an historical real, an
indisputable originary moment that verifies, in a *coup de théâtre,* the repressed truth of phantasy scenarios. This model of explanation and proof
repeats itself in three of the major Freudian ideas of this period: the theory
of seduction; Freud's complex ambivalence as to whether the Wolf Man's
symptoms and phantasies devolved from the activation of actual memory
traces—the witnessing of parental coitus; and finally and most insistently,
the phylogenetic explanation where the originary moment of *Urphantasien*
or primal phantasies becomes a function of prehistoric memory. Without
doubt, all three hypotheses demonstrate the conformity of Freud's narratives
to a spatiotemporal logic predicated on a specific relation to truth and a
belief in the rational foundations of mental life.

Between phylogenesis and ontogenesis, the history of the subject poses a
fundamental problem of not only time and causality, but also the fixing of
self-identity as the integral difference between an outside and inside. If it is
equally unlikely, Freud speculates, that the Wolf Man could have witnessed
or understood either parental or animal coitus, deferring understanding of
those events to a later more sexually mature date, then the primal scene must
refer to a "species" memory that is radically anterior to, yet resides "within,"
the subject: an inheritance of the struggle between the primal father and his
sons as the prototype for Oedipal conflict. This is, of course, the problematic
of masculine identity and the struggle for patriarchal authority staged in
Totem and Taboo (1912–1913) that I criticized in Chapter Three.

Freud's appeal to phylogenesis conforms to a teleological conception of
history and narrative that is explicitly Aristotelian. This idea is best understood by referring, not without a certain disingenuousness, to one of Aristotle's own examples in the *Poetics,* Sophocles's *Oedipus Rex.* In Sophocles's
Oedipus, the past/present division of the plot, and the form of reading
and narrative explanation it presumes, are conceived as a point moving

continuously through a linear continuum towards the full disclosure of truth. But the forward movement of Oedipus's investigation is only driven by an equal and opposite plunge into history as the manifestation of the past's originary force in the present. The development of the narrative system is understood as the repetition or replication of an event foreordained in the prehistoric past that unfolds ineluctably in the present. In this manner, Aristotle's Oedipal narrative rehearses the transcendental redemption of the masculine subject as a rational monad—a point moving along a linear and irreversible continuum. In sum, the plot of *Oedipus* is based on a specific kind of repetition: linear in that the forward thrust of the narrative must repeat, in a certain sequence, the precipitating events of the past; teleological in its restoration of temporally disjunct fragments into a continuous whole, equivalent to the reintegrated memory of the male protagonist.[4]

Such ancient notions live undiminished in contemporary narrative forms, including and especially the cinema. In film, of course, the linear unfolding of (past) time is strictly measured by the passage of the filmstrip through the projector at 24 frames per second. This rationalization of time and perception, which fundamentally "underwrites" the forms of reading presumed by cinematic technology, must have serious consequences for textual analysis. More pertinent to my argument here is that the structure of the Oedipal plot is the prototype for most plots of investigation (including the Hollywood model of the "cure" presented by the popular version of psychoanalysis presented in films of the 1940s and 1950s).[5] This pattern is exemplified in the first hermeneutic path introduced in *Céline et Julie*, which differs little from the montage organization of early melodrama. In the opening segment of the film, a simple ABA pattern of alternation is set up—first by the structure of Julie's look, which conjures forth the image of Céline and the curiosity it inspires [figure 1], then by the structure of pursued and pursuer formulated both by parallel montage and a system of entries and exits within a single frame [figures 2 and 3].[6] Moreover, this segment unfolds in a relatively uninterrupted pattern of spatial and temporal succession and contiguity where the duration of the plot is approximately equal to the presentation-time of the film. This path, however, will soon begin to branch, divaricate, and stray from its linear course, interrupted not only by the sense of play and narcissistic desire exchanged between the female protagonists, but also by the uncanny repetition of an "other film" within the space of the first.

If the phylogenetic explanation, which is especially characteristic of Freud's general theory, is caught up in an ideology of scientific rationality and in the distribution of past/present distinctions along a linear and teleological continuum, Freud's close analyses of specific phantasy scenarios reveal a different temporal patterning and a different strategy of reading. Here I am thinking not only of the Wolf Man analysis and other essays mentioned before, but also the important study "'A Child is being Beaten'" (1919e). I argued in the last chapter that the problem of *femininity* is central to the genesis of phantasy scenarios, even if the patient, like the Wolf Man, is male gendered. Just as important, memory-repetition does not occur along a linear and irreversible continuum, but as multiple reinscriptions and transactions between disjunct historical strata where the subject is divided within itself. (As early as 1896 Freud writes to Fliess: "As you know, I am working on the assumption that our psychical mechanism has come into being by a process of stratification—the material present in the form of memory-traces being subjected from time to time to a re-arrangement in accordance with fresh circumstances—to a *re-transcription*," "Letter 52," 11/2/96, SE 1: 233.) Later, the repetition characterizing the stratifications and displacements of the Wolf Man's scenarios are described as *Nachträglichkeit*, or retroactive understanding.

These, then, are the two poles of Freud's indecision concerning the generation of phantasy and the originary, traumatic moment of the primal scene. In his original presentation of primal phantasy, the genesis of identity develops according to a linear schema where the ontogenetic truth of the subject unfolds along the continuum foreordained by its phylogenetic prehistory. Alternatively, in the analyses of phantasy life, the system and subject of these scenarios are characterized by difference, dispersion, and the impossibility of assigning the truth of desire to the punctual certainty of any originary moment, including that of the primal scene.

In *The Ego and the Id* (1923b), Freud departs from the origin myth of primal phantasy and poses his most replete version of Oedipus. The Oedipal relation now permits a radically new understanding of the temporality of phantasy scenes with respect to the genesis of subjectivity, the articulation of desire, and the narration/figuration of the problem of sexual difference and sexual identity. From this period on, the difference between the phylogenetic and ontogenetic explanations is no longer clear-cut, either along the lines of temporal causality or in ascribing the genealogy of the subject's desire to the repetition of an anterior and originary moment. Freud's model of the acquisition of sexual identity through the logic of the Oedipus complex, as the new "phylogenetic" explanation, can and has been understood, time and again, as repeating the patriarchal privilege and hierarchization of gender order implicit in the "prehistoric" theory. I do not necessarily wish to reconvene that debate here, for another often ignored emphasis is possible. If Freud's *general* theory of sexuality leads him to an impasse on the problem of female sexual identity, the clinical papers and the specificity of his analyses of phantasy establish a running dialectic with that theory as the insistence of the problem of a femininity whose recognition is refused. From the moment that the Oedipal explanation is proposed, Freud's two "theories" are marked by an undecidability that turns the linear causality of the earlier model into the incessant twisting of a moebius strip. On one hand, the theorization of the Oedipus complex attempts to establish a double track for the subject, a fork in the road to identity where the child must irreversibly choose either the route to maleness or femaleness. On the other, Freud's reading of the specificity of the structure of phantasy life confounds this formula of either/or. The road to a fixed and unambiguous sexual identity branches and turns on itself incessantly. It is full of traps, detours, and labyrinthine constructions. The formulation of a gendered identity is fragile and subject to constant crisis and revision. In the constructions of phantasy life, the logic of Oedipus, if still teleological, is no longer Aristotelian. It requires a different form of reading.

As I argued in the last chapter, the best example of this logic is Freud's remarkable analysis of the phantasy "'A Child is being Beaten'." In this essay the structure of phantasy is described as a series of conflicts articulated in three areas: the expression and repression of desire; the vacillation of the subject between identification and object-choice in its relations with both its father and mother (revealing a continual hesitation between "masculinity" and "femininity"); and the eventual (though not final) fixing of desire through the resolution of the castration complex. The origin of phantasy devolves from a fundamental structural splitting that yields a series of coexisting, mutually determining, yet non-reconcilable narrative spaces. In each stage of the "child is being beaten" phantasy, the teleological yet unconscious demands of the Oedipal logic repeat themselves all the more insistently to the extent that they are deviated, fragmented, and repressed according to the compromise formations of phantasy life. On the Oedipal track, the more the subject is asked to choose an identity, the more it is undecidably split in phantasy between masculinity and femininity. This idea is foreshadowed in Freud's essay on hysterical phantasies and bisexuality (1908a), where hysterical phantasy is defined structurally by the co-presence of masculine and feminine choices. But lest we forget, from a social and cultural viewpoint, the choices are not equal.

All of these ideas are brought together in Laplanche and Pontalis's remarkable commentary on Freud's analysis of a case of female paranoia (1915f). Lying with her lover, towards whom she has ambivalent feelings, the woman reports being frightened by a "click." After the fact [*nachträglich*], she believes herself to have been observed and photographed in a compromising way. Freud discovers in this paranoia the insistence of *der Belauschungsphantasie* where the woman reproduces, without understanding, the occluded memory of the primal scene: being awakened by and overhearing the sexual intercourse of the parents. The uncanniness of the situation devolves not only from the hallucinated repetition of an unconscious memory in the woman's present sexual life, but in the splitting of her identification as witness *and* participant across the two scenes—the paranoia of being observed descending from the unconscious memory of observation. Within Freud's use of the term "*Belauschung*," or eavesdropping—translated in their commentary as "*l'entendu*" (heard, understood)—Laplanche and Pontalis unravel two motifs: "The first considers the sensorium in question: the overheard, when it interrupts, fractures the continuity of an undifferentiated perceptual field and at the same time signifies (as a noise waited for and perceived in the night), calling forth and positioning the subject" (FO 50–51).

Both awakened and called forth as subject, the eavesdropping child, with its scopophilic and epistemophilic drives, becomes the prototype of spectatorial activity. As such, in phantasy the subject is always split between two mutually present yet incommensurable scenes, conscious and unconscious. This idea is echoed in *Céline et Julie's* parable of spectatorship. While the film begins by imagining a space organized by the active exchange of looks based on the playful narcissism of its female protagonists, it now branches and divides again with more severe consequences. Returning from her first trip to the mysterious house with the unlikely address of 7 bis, rue du Nadir aux Pommes, Julie attends Céline's magic act at a Montmartre cabaret. While watching Céline's performance (with a small but vocal male audience), Julie is called forth as the spectator of two "scenes" that are temporally co-present but spatially incommensurable—one conscious, the other "unconscious." The pattern of alternation that began the film in Julie's gaze as a succession of shots within an homogeneous, diegetic space is now replaced by the irruption of an unconscious memory that literally fragments a spatially continuous organization of sight [Figure 4]. Céline's previous (spoken) paranoid fabulation—involving a job as a nanny, a threatened child, and the competition of a blond and a brunette for the man of the house—takes on a perceptual reality. This other story bursts into the "first" film as visual scenes that insistently repeat themselves, producing terror and anxiety without submitting themselves to the reassuring organization of conscious memory. At this moment, the narrative logic of *Céline et Julie* splits into two mutually exclusive yet parallel spaces where, like the paranoid woman in Freud's case, Julie and Céline are produced simultaneously as auditors of *and* participants in an uncanny scenario. Within this other film, they are projected as the forbidding nurse, Miss Terre Angèle, their original identities forgotten; as spectators, they are able to produce these scenes, visually and sonorally, without understanding or controlling them.[7]

But the "overheard," Laplanche and Pontalis insist, is also a pre-constituted narrative of a special type:

the stories or legends of parents, grandparents, and ancestors—the family story, this spoken or secret discourse that pre-dates the subject who must nonetheless locate itself there. These "little noises" (or any other discrete sensory element able to serve an indexical function) are valorized to the extent that they serve to recall retroactively this "discourse."

Both in their content and in their *theme* (primal scene, castration, seduction . . .), primal phantasies also inspire this retroactive postulation: *they refer to origins.* Like myth, they pretend to offer the child a representation of and a "solution" to its most perplexing enigmas. They dramatize, as moments of emergence or as the origin of history, what appears to the subject as a "reality" requiring an explanation or a theory. (FO 51)

For Laplanche and Pontalis, phantasy is always generated as a chiasmic structure where the uncanny repetition of primal phantasy stages the origin of phantasy life as an incessant return to phantasies of origin. Moreover, this origin myth is no longer a species memory, but a narrative and semiotic memory specific to the history of the subject within the material, social context of the Family. It is interesting then that the "other film," the occluded memory that Céline and Julie appear to share, should represent so precisely the tragic fate of femininity within the family story. Referring to Henry James, Jacques Rivette calls this film "the house of fiction." It is an uncanny, parallel fictional world whose ineluctable presence patterns the chain of seeming coincidences that are threaded through Céline and Julie's encounter. The other film is in fact a melodrama and a *Familenroman,* drawn from Henry James's story, "The Old House," and play, "A Romance of Certain Old Clothes." More importantly for my argument, the parallel films perfectly reproduce the structural relation of chiasmus, described by Laplanche and Pontalis, between the two polarities of phantasy life—the unconscious and originary force of primal phantasy, and the conscious fabulation of daydream:

A play of images: the daydream uses indiscriminately the glimmerings of daily life; but it also draws upon the primal phantasy whose *dramatis personae* are emblematic of the players in this family legend that is mutilated, confused, and badly understood. As structure, the Oedipal relation is easily read in primal phantasy; but this is also true in the daydream where analysis always rediscovers repetitive and clichéd scenarios within the variability of fabulation. . . .

At the pole of the daydream, the scenario is essentially given in first person; the place of the subject is clearly marked and invariable. Its organization is stabilized by the secondary processes and buoyed by the "ego": the subject, one would say, *lives* its phantasy. Inversely, the pole of primal phantasy is characterized by an absence of subjectivization combined ineluctably with the presence of the subject in the scene. . . . (FO 62)

These two polarities of phantasy easily find homologues in the text of *Céline et Julie vont en bateau* and are structurally similar to the placement of the "two films."[8] On one hand, there is the film where Julie conjures up the image of Céline like Alice whose reverie produces the White Rabbit. I loosely refer to it as the plot of investigation because its hide and seek parody of the detective film is characterized by a spatial linearity and sequentiality familiar to that genre. This plot reproduces Céline's doubtful fabulation of pursuit and of nefarious goings-on at the old house at 7 bis, rue du Nadir aux Pommes. Likewise, it comprises Julie and Céline's efforts to sort out the narrative chaos of the House of Fiction, first using the entire technology of textual analysis [figure 5]—charts, diagrams, simulacral reproduction, visual citation and reediting with the broken bits of candy—but finally resorting to magic.

On the other hand, if Céline and Julie see themselves in the House of Fiction, it is only at the cost of relinquishing their subjectivity to the predetermined role of the suspicious nurse, "Miss Terre Angèle." Moreover, unlike the improvisational and ludic character of the "first" film with its sense of self-conscious play, and despite its seemingly arbitrary and fragmentary construction, the Oedipal plot in the House of Fiction is characterized by a demonic circularity and teleological force. This overdetermination of the Oedipal situation is exposed by the guessing game with candies: "Tu peux perdre," says Sophie to Madlyn, "mais tu gagnes toujours." In fact there is no choice: you could win, but you always lose. The House of Fiction with its insidious, Oedipal plot is thus situated structurally in the film as a primal phantasy. And its presence is all the more threatening because of its relation to Freud's own "dark continent": the problem of female sexual identity. This incessant melodrama is based on competition between women for the place of the absent mother. A desire for the desire of the Father, it is a special hierarchical relation to the only male of the family as source of authority, wealth, and the satisfaction of desire. In this respect, the other film pushes to extremes the potentially paranoid relations of the primal phantasy, where the (female) child is subject to a peculiar aggressivity it cannot comprehend— the sexual competition of adults, whose conflicts are played out across demands for the child's attention and where every gesture carries a sexual charge and potential threat of death. In the eternal recurrence of this melodrama, Madlyn is the utopian figure of a possible female identity destroyed by the insistence of the Oedipal plot; and in the same moment, the figure of a possible cinematic writing, based on montage and fragmentation, which is consumed by the structural demands of the investigative narrative organization of the first film. Paradoxically, the more Céline and Julie restore this melodrama to its "proper" narrative sequence, the more they realize it must be strategically disarticulated, its eternal return interrupted by relinquishing their position as spectators and adopting a different relation to the text.

However, this play of division and exchange between the two films is ill-served by describing a simple opposition between linearity and circularity, for example, or between the loss and acquisition of memory. Like Freud's reading of "a child is being beaten," where the conscious and unconscious poles of phantasy never cease to interpenetrate one another, the relation between the two films is best described as one of chiasmus. For the terror of the memory of the other film as primal phantasy resides in the discovery that unlike a detective plot or Hollywood's version of the cure, the death of the female subject and the trauma it inspires is not safely lost to the narrative past—it ceaselessly and multiply inscribes itself in the first film. In *Céline et Julie vont en bateau,* this multiple reinscription occurs first of all as a *mémoire involontaire,* conjured either by magic or by the consuming of candies but also according to a series of mysterious coincidences. First, if the basic story of the House of Fiction is introduced by Céline's (apparently) imaginary and paranoid narrative, it has an uncanny resemblance to a memory invoked by Julie's nanny of "the child who used to live next door. . . ." Second, a picture of the house is produced unexplained from Julie's trunk. The film also suggests unclear parallels between Céline and Julie's dolls, toys, and other childhood memorabilia and the characters and events of the other film. Finally, and most disturbingly, if the plot of the House of Fiction assures the demise of a possible female subjectivity, this telos repeats itself in the potential destinies of Julie and Céline: for the former, an autonomous subjectivity may be lost in marriage to the returning childhood sweetheart, Guilou; for the latter, lost in a career of dubious "magic," performing as erotic spectacle for the male gaze. Most sinister, however, are the two signifiers that cross most freely between the two films—the red hand and the candies. The red hand is first the emblem of Julie and Céline's "telepathy": during their initial encounter in the library of magic, the film intercuts Julie's distracted fingerprinting in red ink with Céline's outlining of her hand in red pen on the page of a children's book [figure 6]. It is also the visceral trace of the other film on the body of the first. When Julie and Céline each "return" for the first time from the old house, their shoulder is marked by Camille's bloody palm [figure 7]. Finally, the candy is the gateway between the two films; its consumption assures the serial continuation of the uncanny narrative. Both are emblems of Madlyn's death, doubly assured by Sophie and Camille [figure 8].

This intertwining of parallel narratives reveals an obsession with the problem of time in Rivette's films. The unique achievement of Rivette's work derives from his attempt to redefine the conditions of cinematic pleasure and spectatorship through a strategic exploration of problems of narrative time in two ways. First, all of Rivette's films experiment with temporal structuring according to the possibilities of *montage* (of editing, of establishing specific relations between shots, between sequences, and in fact blocks of sequences; but more abstractly, the combination of signifying elements and their dispersion through the cinematic text). Second, Rivette's experiments with films of non-standard length (at 760 minutes, *Out 1: Noli Me Tangere* [1971] dwarfs *Céline et Julie's* mere 192 minutes) reveal his interest in the problem of *duration:* the spectator's experience of time in relation to the film projection. Rivette uses extended duration to cut loose the spectator's synchronization with the linear and ineluctable forward movement of the plot and the determination of time by the filmstrip. Pleasure is defined here as "floating attention" and as multiplying the possible forms of the spectator's attentiveness to the text: "This pleasure, or—why not?—," says Rivette, "this *jouissance* of the spectator's . . . can tend more in the direction of . . . let's not say work—which is a large word that has been much abused (and one mustn't confuse the work of the spectator or of the signifier with other forms of work)—but this pleasure in fact passes through certain stages, certain periods, which can equally well be attentiveness, perplexity, irritation, or even boredom."[9] In this manner, Rivette has attempted to formulate "a cinema of monumentality and signification," of spectacle and semiotic density irreducible to a univocal and linear sense. Similar to Maurice Blanchot's experiments in fiction, Rivette's concern with time proposes what might be called an ethics of reading for the cinema.

Blanchot opposes his ethics of reading to a conditioned response that one might call *spectating.* In his novel *Death Sentence* [*l'Arret de mort*], this opposition is rendered through figures of boundary and of watching from a distance: scenarios of voyeurism, no doubt, that discomfort the reader with their specular, distanced, non-tactile, and non-sensuous relation to the text. But I am thinking in particular of a passage from his essay "The Narrative Voice" where Blanchot questions the ideal of aesthetic uninvolvement. Blanchot criticizes Flaubert, and indeed Henry James, because in their fictions,

what is narrated has aesthetic value only in so far as the interest it arouses is uninvolved. Uninvolvement—the basis category of aesthetic judgment since Kant or even since Aristotle—implies that the aesthetic process, if it aims at arousing a justifiable interest, must never derive from personal involvement. Uninvolved interest. Therefore the author must take and valiantly keep his distance so that the reader or the spectator may stay at an equal distance. Classical drama remains the perfect model: the narrator has no other function than as prologue. The play is enacted in the background since the beginning of time and almost without him. *He does not narrate, he shows; and the reader does not read but looks, attends, taking part without participating.*[10]

Compare this passage to Rivette's description of the "ideal viewer," who in fact resembles the ideal reader imagined by Blanchot: "the 'ideal' viewer is one who agrees to enter the fiction: it's the least one can demand of a spectator. . . . This ideal spectator should gradually begin to realize . . . that the ficton is in fact a trap, that it's full of cracks and completely artificial, in every sense of the word, and has only been a vehicle."[11]

The problem, then, is aesthetic distance and of transforming the management of distance that stages pleasurable looking. This is very different from the Brechtian problematic one usually finds in contemporary film theory. Céline and Julie must abolish the distance in space and time which situates them between the two films as spectators or onlookers, and which effaces their identity by projecting them into the mise-en-scène of the House of Fiction as an other—the nurse, Miss Terre Angèle. No doubt this is a complex joke where cinematic identification is considered as a "forgetting of one's place." Alternatively, they will have to project themselves into the fiction as performers-in-the-text rather than spectators of it. In another Freudian metaphor, they must interrupt the repetition of this fiction in order to work through it.

I am referring, of course, to Freud's essay on analytic technique, "Remembering, Repeating, and Working-Through" (1914g), written at about the same time as the Wolf Man case history.[12] Several suggestive passages deserve commentary with respect to the problem of memory and repetition as represented in the narrative system of *Céline et Julie vont en bateau.*

One of the fascinating distinctions in Freud's essay is the relation between memory and forgetting. First of all, Freud writes that "The forgetting of impressions, scenes, events, nearly always reduces itself to a 'dissociation' [*Absperrung*] of them" (RRW 367). This Absperrung or dissociation of consciousness is equivalent to the peculiar splitting of phantasy life, and in its disintegration of proper forms it recalls the entropic force of the death drive. However, for Freud forgetting is only a particular form of memory. For the repression of material, which divides conscious and unconscious processes, also fuels the compulsion to repeat. Forgetting generates memory in the form of repetition—as the compromise formations of phantasy life (the serial narrative aspect remarked upon by Laplanche and Pontalis) and in the symptomatology of lapsi, parapraxes, and screen memories. Secondly, Freud remarks that ". . . 'forgetting' consists mostly of a falling away of the links between various ideas, a failure to draw conclusions, an isolating of certain memories" (RRW 368).

So far, the equation of dissociation with the absence of causal links departs not in the least from the Aristotelian conception of narrative and narrative interpretation. It perfectly describes the linear distribution of time along a clear past/present axis, as well as the Formalist model of reading where the strategic disordering of plot elements are predestined to be restored to a story sense of linear causality. But the conception of time in *Céline et Julie vont en bateau,* and the kind of splitting characteristic of the relations developed between its parallel films, involve a different representation of memory. In explaining the strange ratio between memory and forgetting, Freud continues by remarking that

the patient *remembers* nothing of what is forgotten and repressed, but that he expresses it in *action*. He reproduces it not in his memory but in his behaviour; he repeats *it, without of course knowing that he is repeating it*. . . . *(RRW 369)*
  The patient reproduces instead of remembering, and he reproduces according to the conditions of the resistance; we may now ask what it is exactly that he reproduces or expresses in action. (RRW 371)

In *Céline et Julie vont en bateau,* the quality of repetition as reproduction perfectly describes the system of chiasmus in the film as a whole. This is a specific transactional relation between the two films that, moving vertically rather than horizontally, refuses to recognize the temporality of Aristotelian logic. Without being understood as such the circularity of the Oedipal plot never ceases to inscribe its effects and leave its traces—in short, to reproduce itself in "forgotten" ways—in the first film. Among the most important examples are: the coincidence of Céline and Julie's shared memory, phantasy life, and childhood recollections; and the telos of the female subject—haunted by Madlyn's death in the House of Fiction and reproducing itself in Julie's betrothal and Céline's commodification as spectacle. Most importantly, repetition and forgetting is not an attribute of character psychology in the film. What has fallen away in forgetting is the link between the two films and its representation of the relation between narrative form, phantasy, and the genesis of gendered subjectivity. And to the extent that this dissociation derives from Oedipal divisions, it finds itself doubly inscribed—between the conscious and unconscious strata interior to phantasy, and in the representation of the structure of phantasy interior to the text of the film—but without the quality of knowledge. So far it is a game of mirrors; repetition without difference.

This is not a fortunate situation for the film's representations of female spectatorship. In the image of interpretation set up by the plot of investigation, Julie and Céline only mimic, if parodically, a masculine and voyeuristic model of spectating: they simply wish to reassemble the fragmented images of the Oedipal plot into a coherent story, and to satisfy a desire to know through a mastery of sense from the safety of distance that can not be transgressed. Similarly, the narrative function of the candies figures a particularly ambivalent relation to the pleasures of narrative. For what produces the scenes of fascination as a *séance permanente* also extinguishes life, encouraging the slow death of the female subject.

Happily, in *Céline et Julie vont en bateau* neither the restoration of memory nor the recovery of narrative sense from the fragmented primal phantasy is ultimately at stake. The film draws to a close by recognizing the links between the two films and overcoming the dissociation that splits the film topographically. Moreover, this action is staged as the utopian redemption of an autonomous female identity and desire ungoverned by phallic division that is threatened by the uncanny repetition of the Oedipal situation. As Céline and Julie relinquish their place as *spectators* in order to become *performers* of the text, instead of observing its serial repetition at a distance ("looking, attending, taking part without participating"), they fulfill the obligation of "working-through." This process begins with the exchange of roles where Céline then Julie interrupt each other's "Oedipal" destinies, and follows through with their intercession in the Oedipal plot of the other film [figures 9, 10 and 11]. In short, by exchanging identities, and by crossing between the two films, "they agree to enter the fiction."

In "Remembering, Repeating, and Working-Through," Freud insists on distinguishing between the interpretive method in psychoanalysis and its origins in Breuer's cathartic method and the use of hypnosis. In simply requiring the patient to repeat dissociated material under hypnosis, Breuer's method differs little from the first image of interpretation offered in *Céline et Julie*—the *mémoire involontaire* induced by the poisoned candies. How, then, might the film be read as "working through" the history of interpretation that Freud presents for the psychoanalytic movement?

Freud's second theory of reading, which is also the second image of interpretation in *Céline et Julie,* derives from the following point: If the quality of dissociation defines memory as unconscious repetition, interpretation is not necessarily the restoration of memory, the recovery of a lost infantile history, nor an anchoring of present identity in a finished past. Freud is unambiguous on this point. The simple naming of a resistance accomplishes nothing in overcoming the dynamics of repetition and forgetting. Rather, what counts is mapping the *pattern* of resistances and analyzing forms of repetition as they appear in the narrative figures produced in the structure of phantasy. The existence of the primal scene is no longer as important as reading the structure of its effects. The historical status of memory becomes less important for Freud when, in the temporal dislocation between the primal scene and its subsequent repetitions in phantasy life, the pattern of representations becomes indistinguishable from screen-memory and other imaginary constructs. Likewise, it is not an actual memory that Céline and Julie attempt to reconstruct through their initial desire to see and interpret, but rather a historical and cultural relation: the genealogy of narrative form and desire in Oedipus as a *cultural* figure, a historical montage of narratives through which the subject is required to ask and answer questions of sexual identity and sexual difference. Primal phantasy is constructed here as a purely imaginary referent. And being a historical construction, and not an unalterable event, *Céline et Julie vont en bateau* stages the utopian possibility of re-writing it, of interrupting its demonic repetition and re-inscribing it differently. Reading as working-through marks an insistence that the reality of narrated desire devolves neither simply from this imaginary referent nor from its symbolic figuration. Rather, it restores a sense of the economy of exchange and transaction, or the system of chiasmus, that paradoxically links and dissociates the two poles of phantasy life where phantasy and narrative forget their origins in questions of sexual identity and sexual difference. Working-through is finally to interrupt this uncanny repetition by tracing its caricature in the physiognomy of resistances. The will to read derives from the desire to exorcise this uncanny force—whose terror resides in its anonymity and omnipresence—to give it a name, and to account for its intangible origins.

Céline et Julie is a fiction about the recovery of an experience of text and of reading that has been occulted by the formal demands of the Oedipal and Aristotelian plots and the logic of interpretation derived from them. As such, its narrative trajectory stages a parable of reading that desires to transform spectators of the narrative into performers of the text. Céline and Julie, along with the viewer, must reach the point where there is really something at stake in the House of Fiction, which requires that they no longer stand outside of it or enter it in a somnambulistic state, passively identifying with the fiction and floating in channels preordained by the ordering of the plot. They must enter the House of Fiction for the last time as performers who can spy out the ghosts in the attic, disturb the "destiny" of the plot, open the narrative to a freer circulation of meaning, and finally, to rescue the possibility of a different kind of narrative and a different sort of reading. The utopian dimension of *Céline et Julie,* and its continuing interest for contemporary film theory, resides in the following possibilities: to rewrite the narrative past and to alter its destiny as the redemption of occluded potentialities of sexual identity and narrative pleasure.

In conclusion, I am struck with how these comments made by Rivette six years before the film was produced seem to take up directly the ideal of reading represented in *Céline et Julie:*

> . . . a film must be, if not an ordeal, at least an experience, something which makes the film transform the viewer, who has undergone something through the film, who is no longer the same after having seen the film . . .; the film must make his habits of thought go off their beaten tracks: so that it can't be seen with impunity. . . . That's another sort of fascination, which is not contradicted by the intellectual tension [required], but on the contrary is connected to it— actually very similar to the great amount of work we sometimes do in a dream in order to follow it. But fantasy is not necessarily fascination; it can have lots of dimensions.[13]

But as the last frames of *Céline et Julie vont en bateau* slip through the projector, there is one last twisting of the moebius strip. The tautological circularity of fascination and terror will begin yet again [figure 12]. For the film can only *dramatize* the utopian trajectory that makes readers of spectators, and can only stage allegorically the genealogy where narrative forms reproduce, in the form of forgetting, the agonizing questions of sexual difference. If that last repetition reinscribes the film after the fact in the difference of reading, it can only do so as invoked by a viewer who has learned to see and understand the utopian face of narrative.

Figure 1a

Figure 1b

Figure 1c

Figure 1d

Figure 1e

Figure 1f

Figure 2a

Figure 2b

Figure 3

Figure 4a

Figure 4b

Figure 4c

Figure 4d

Figure 4e

Figure 4f

Figure 4g

Figure 4h

Figure 4i

Figure 5

Figure 6a

Figure 6b

Figure 7a

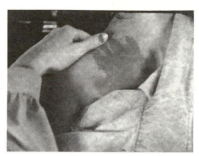

Figure 7b

Figure 8

Figure 9

Figure 10a

Figure 10b

Figure 11

Figure 12a

Figure 12b(1)

Figure 12b(2)

Figure 12c

Chapter 6
Analysis Interminable

*For this woman ... reading means stripping herself of every purpose,
every foregone conclusion, to be ready to catch a voice that makes itself
heard when you least expect it, a voice that comes from an unknown
source, from somewhere beyond the book, beyond the author, beyond the
conventions of writing: from the unsaid, from what the world has not yet
said of itself and does not yet have the words to say.*[1]

If *Céline and Julie Go Boating* has a utopian dimension, it is built upon
an ethics of reading. An invaginated structure, the film both turns within
itself and opens up to an outside. In this respect, I have argued that the film
might be understood as illuminating the relation between narrative and the
structure of phantasy. However, I have also argued that while the film
presents an opportunity for reading, and reading differently, it cannot determine this activity. With the lonely inwardness of every narrative object, it
cannot interrupt with finality the forms of repetition that drive it forward.
In other words, for *Céline and Julie,* and in fact all aesthetic work, the task
of deciding between ideological and utopian meanings cannot take place
outside of the activity of reading. This is not a question of identification,
sexual or otherwise. Rather it is an activity that occurs in the gap—spatial,
temporal, and historical—that divides reader from text, where meaning
differs and differs again.

By the same token, if phantasy is a form of protest, especially against the
socially given norms of identity, it is primarily an interior and private one.
Psychoanalysis, which often reduces history to a subjective interiority, has
not often given this protest a larger, cultural expression. Some of the contemporary political critiques of psychoanalysis have based themselves precisely
on this point: that its theoretical as well as therapeutic force will only
serve to reconcile the subject to "repression," social authority, and the
renunciation of desire.[2] Moreover, the attempts to develop classical psychoanalysis as a theory of culture—most notoriously represented by Carl Jung's
notions of myth and the collective unconscious, and Freud's no more satisfying notion of a "genetic" unconscious—have not proven fruitful.

Nevertheless, I have argued that phantasy is a cultural modality giving
expression to collective as well as individual desires with all their complex
ambivalences. As embodied in forms of mass cultural expression, it defines

and perpetuates the contradictory desires and aspirations of social life in ways that are neither exclusive, totalizing, nor readily apparent to spectators much less critics. When there is pleasure in narrative, it is defined by the peculiar ambivalence of phantasy life which gives form simultaneously to desire and its prohibition. The complex evolution of infantile beating phantasies examined in Chapter Four demonstrated both an implantation of power—the acculturation of the child to an ideological world divided by gender—and a canny evasion of that power to which the child will not be reconciled. Where desire inhabits representation, one finds the drive to remake an intolerable world, and this should be no less true for the public and collective narratives modeled on phantasy. In this respect, there are two reasons why the structure of phantasy presents an apposite model of narrative for ideological criticism: first because it provides a way of examining how desire historically inhabits narrative forms; second because the expression of desire is always driven by unmasterable contradiction, beautifully represented in Lyotard's statement that phantasy is at once form and transgression. I believe that psychoanalysis can contribute significantly to a historical and materialist analysis of mass culture, especially in terms of defining the modalities of desire underwriting its symbolic forms. However, the power of this analysis will not devolve from accounts of identification and spectatorship, especially where the spectator seems doomed dialectically to repeat the unfolding system of the text. Instead, I want to conclude by examining what psychoanalysis has to offer for a theory of critical reading, especially with respect to illuminating questions of sexual difference.

My first point, while obvious, is nonetheless fundamental. The special province of psychoanalysis is the study of the unconscious and the vicissitudes of desire. Despite any criticisms one may now make of Christian Metz's path-breaking studies on psychoanalysis and the semiology of film, his fundamental insight still convinces: that what psychoanalysis contributes to the study of film and ideology is the question of desire. While this idea informs all the essays collected in his book *The Imaginary Signifier,* it is most succinctly developed in "Story/Discourse (A Note on Two Kinds of Voyeurism)."[3] Metz states unambiguously that the economics of the film industry trades on a phantom and intangible commodity—the production of pleasure. The paradox of film-going, what keeps the theaters full and the industry developing apace, is that spectators exchange seven dollars for nothing more substantial than a psychological experience, or what Metz defines as "an *orientation of consciousness,* whose roots are unconscious, and without which we would be unable to understand the overall trajectory which founds the institution and accounts for its continuing existence" (IS 93). As a mass-produced experience of the imaginary, the cinema as a social and economic institution must modulate, according to Metz, between several regimes of desire. The ideal objective of this process is to maintain spectators in a state of regression, in the most precise psychoanalytic sense of the term. In Metz's analysis, from the standpoint of the industry the successful film is defined by a specific *visée de conscience* which is most appropriately compared to states of reverie or daydreaming; in short, phantasy.[4] By the same token, Metz insists that neither the form of the narrative film nor the context of reception can determine this experience; they merely stage, more or less successfully, the conditions where it may occur. In fact, in his view repetitive cinema-going has less to do with the desire to see particular films, than the desire to re-experience this condition of wakeful dreaming. Alternatively, Metz stresses that one can adopt a variety of positions of meaning and desire before any film, and that the film analyst in particular chooses to stand "outside the institution" (IS 138).

Raymond Bellour and Thierry Kuntzel have developed different approaches to textual analysis in this context while exploring the same question: how does the representation of desire inform the structure of filmic expression? In contrast to Metz's metapsychological approach, this is primarily a question of filmic signification, not spectatorial identification. Kuntzel examines directly the idea that narrative in the grip of desire resembles phantasy and that the desiring logic of narrative must be examined on the model of phantasy. However, both theorists work from the premise that narrative processes can be understood as replicating in their forms the structure of primal phantasy: Kuntzel understands filmic expression as modeled on the dream-work and the situation of the primal scene; Bellour sees narrative unfolding according to a symbolic Oedipal logic that recapitulates a phantasy of castration reconciling the desire of the male hero to the cultural law.[5]

These are not analogical arguments. Rather Metz, Bellour, and Kuntzel assert in different ways that psychoanalysis' premises concerning the unconscious forms of mental life have an intimate relation with cultural forms and institutions. Examining similarities between filmic expression and the primary processes, or comparing the situation of reception to the topography of mental life, does not necessarily presuppose a relation of mirroring or identity. Rather, what is in question is a logic of repetition in the Freudian sense of the term as unconscious replication. Cultural work in both production and reception is the result of the historical praxis of individuals and collectivities; it is the complex product, in both creation and interpretation, of unrealized desires. Therefore, the hypotheses that the structure of phantasy repeats itself in narrative, that the primary processes inform filmic expression or poetic language, or that the divisions of mental life inform the relation of spectator, projector, and screen, should not be surprising. For me, what is most open to question is the nature of this repetition.

Raymond Bellour explores this question in an essay entitled "Cine-Repetitions."[6] Bellour argues that repetition in the cinema involves a varied, complex logic that is incommensurable with relations of identity. Bellour divides the cinematic experience of repetition into three internal and three external forms. The first external form involves *répétition* in the French sense of the word as rehearsal or preparation for a final performance. The second form of external repetition is more fundamental to film. Unlike a theatrical experience—where each performance is unique, differing to a greater or lesser extent from the text of the play—"filmic representation is constituted by a printed text, the identity of which, ideally, is repeated absolutely unchanged" (CR 66). This situation is idealistic not only because screening conditions are themselves materially and historically variable, but also because a print deteriorates over time and with each projection. Nonetheless, despite, or perhaps because of, these editorial "corruptions," textual analysis in film no less than literature persists in the fantasy of basing itself on *the* text as if it had an originary and authenticating form.

I will address this problem more completely in a moment. However, Bellour's first form of internal repetition underlies this paradox where the desire for a unique experience of the text intensifies in proportion with the immateriality of the object. Here the illusion of movement, which accounts to a great extent for the perceptual density of cinematographic images, is based on the most material element of filmic repetition: the serialization of frames on the film-strip. Nothing divides the experience of the spectator from the reader more than the control exercised by the latter over the qualities of movement and time deriving from the regulated passage of the film-strip in projection.[7] By stopping the image and interrupting the ineluctable flow of time, the film analyst also breaks the circuit of desire whose goal is to keep auditoriums full. This is a convincing illustration of Metz's basic thesis that the power of desire in relation to the cinematographic image derives proportionately from a double absence pursued by the spectator: the quasi-hallucinatory photographic representation of an absent referent in space as well as the ineluctable slipping away of images in time.

The two other forms of internal repetition define what I call the horizontal and vertical organization of the film text with respect to narrative sense. In this respect they represent the fundaments of cinematographic language as a temporal art. "[The] camera," writes Bellour, "which cuts out its units in space also cuts them out in time, by means of a serialization comparable to the model of classical music, where the alternation of segments orchestrated on different levels assures the cohesion and the progression of the text."[8] This second form of internal repetition accounts for the horizontal and forward drive of the fiction film by organizing its narrative space through a logic of *alternation*, which Bellour defines as "a structure of opposition between two terms, which develops through the return of either one or both terms according to a process of more or less limited expansion: a/b/a', a/b/a'/b', and so on" (CR 67).

This form of repetition and difference characterizes the basic figures of cinematographic language, including point of view shots, shot/counter-shots, the regulated exchange of shot scales (close/distant) and movement (static/mobile), as well as the alternation of shots within and between diegetic locations. Just as important for my argument is Bellour's analysis of how this serial form of composition distributes narrative oppositions from one shot to the next. For example, in his analysis of a Biograph short by D. W. Griffith, *The Lonedale Operator* (1911), Bellour demonstrates how the film is organized from its most specific to most general level by a melodramatic ideal of heterosexual romance and a binary characterization of sexual difference.[9] Here alternation is used to define the idealized romantic couple (an engineer and a telegraph operator), only to threaten and subsequently reconfirm that idealized image. The initial series of shots defines the hero and heroine individually, then brings them together in the same frame as an image of potential union. Departing for work, they are gradually separated, first by alternation within the same diegetic locale (point of view cutting as the heroine waves off the departing train), and secondly between locations. As the locomotive absents the young hero, an arriving train introduces a sexual threat: a band of thieves. In the forms of alternation that ensue, the basic editing pattern is repeated and expanded with the sexually innocuous hero being replaced by the band of threatening thieves. In a classic example of the cross-cutting for which he is justly renown, Griffith begins to intercalate the two forms of alternation. On one hand, there is a series of alternated shots between the heroine and the thieves where she attempts to barricade herself in a set of adjoining rooms each time the thieves break into the space where she has currently retreated. This successive and violent penetration of frames is a thinly disguised image of attempted rape that recurs in a number of Griffith melodramas. On the other, an alternate syntagm develops through cross-cutting as the heroine telegraphs to a nearby station for help, and then as the hero charges to the rescue in his steam locomotive. The rescue occurs according to formula—in the nick of time. The thieves gain access to the same frame as the heroine and the audience fear the worst. Yet she holds them at bay with what appears to be a shining pistol. Just then the rescuers arrive and a close-up reveals the "pistol" to have been only a simple wrench. The criminals bow to the heroine and are absented from the frame, leaving the heroine and hero there alone together, presumably happy ever after. Or, at least until the next train arrives.

My resumé, which is far less detailed than Bellour's own analysis, is meant to demonstrate two points. First, the forms of alternation that drive the text forward from shot to shot also expand and replicate themselves on more general levels of narrative form and content. This represents the third variety of internal repetition in Bellour's synopsis, what he calls a "repetition-resolution effect." Through this effect, the most minute and the most global elements of narrative structure in film constantly interpenetrate and mirror one another as an effect of reciprocal development. More simply put, the forms of linear repetition that drive the narrative along a horizontal axis also duplicate themselves vertically across levels of narrative structure:

> What we must understand is that the force of alternation is entirely due to the fact that it always works more or less on the two levels at once, which means that it is constantly at the point of articulation between expression and content. . . . In fact, the extraordinary power of alternation lies in that it can work simultaneously and in complementary fashion both on the level of diegesis and on the level of specific codes, and that it can do so on multiple dimensions of the textual system going from the smallest to the largest elements. . . .
>
> The classical cinema, especially the American cinema, thus uses alternation very specifically as a kind of formal basic principle which is constantly and organically at work in the film, setting itself up, breaking off, re-establishing itself on various levels, displacing itself constantly from one level to another in order to ensure the movement which leads the film from its beginning to its end. The process of repetition-resolution, which I have shown to be in various ways the governing process in the organization of the classic American film, is thus determined, both on the level of the film as a diegetic whole and on the minimal level of the internal organization of the segment, by the phenomenon of alternation as the generalized form of narrative. (ASH 79–80)

My second point returns to the more fundamental arguments of this book. There is little doubt that *The Lonedale Operator* represents a narrative of attempted rape. By the same token, the film can be read as simply but effectively staging a masculine phantasy of castration. What allows the hero and heroine to come together, as it were, is the exorcising of a threat across the film's representation of femininity. The symbolizations that the film puts into play are so thinly disguised as to be parodic. The figure of woman is made to bear culturally the threat of castration, both as a threat against her body (violation and perhaps death, depriving the hero of possession of her) and as a threat she exercises in turn: the thieves stop dead in their tracks when they imagine the woman to "possess" the phallus (the gun). However, this possession is shown to be illusory; the woman must renounce even the fiction of power, swooning as the hero regains her in the frame through the force of his activity and his "superior" means of symbolization—after all, he drives the train.

The apparent silliness of the scenario renders it no less effective for the spectator in the auditorium. What is at stake here is another level of repetition, at once internal and external to the film, which reproduces intertextually a cultural scenario of sexual difference represented by unconscious phantasy, thus extending its historical power and permanence. The binary division of space and time by alternation reproduces a logic of representation that divides the man from the woman across a series of oppositions including activity/passivity, law/criminality, licit/illicit sexuality, finally sorting out positive and negative values until desire finds its "lawful" image redeemed in the final union of the chaste, heterosexual couple. In his magisterial analysis of Alfred Hitchcock's *North by Northwest* (1959), Bellour coins the term *le blocage symbolique* to describe the peculiar circularity shared historically and ideologically by the nineteenth-century novel and the twentieth-century fiction film as tautological manifestations of the binary machine. The Oedipal scenario that informs the most general levels of narrative content is also found, in Bellour's analysis, to replicate itself in the most minute and specific levels of the text, thus fueling the forms of desire that drive the progression of the narrative. In a spectacular effect of inversion, an unconscious phantasy of sexual difference of broad historical and cultural scope is also discovered as unfolding within the smallest details of an individual text. This is a striking example, as Bellour himself is entirely aware, of a historical process, emerging with the norm of the bourgeois family and an economic system based on industrial capitalism, that attempts to universalize an image of sexual difference where "the woman occupies a central place only to the extent that it's a place assigned to her by the logic of masculine desire" (ASH 93).[10]

This brings me, in a no less circular fashion, to Bellour's last category of external repetition and to the problem that opened this chapter. Bellour calls this last repetition "that of the cinema itself. It serves to designate, beyond any given film, what each film aims at through the apparatus that permits it: in the regulated order of spectacle, the return of an immemorial and everyday state which the subject experiences in his dreams, and for which the cinematic apparatus renews the desire. This repetition depending on a set of material and metapsychological conditions, will be all the more active when the film takes on not the representation—which would be impossible—but the fictionalization of that repetition through its 'work', sometimes so close to the work of dreams, with the psychic-figural operations and the diegesis indissolubly linked" (CR 71). At this point, Bellour refers to the arguments forwarded by Christian Metz in "The Fiction Film and its Spectator," and by Thierry Kuntzel in his two studies of the "film-work," that the objective of the fiction film is to organize a scenography of desire where the spectator may experience psychological regression; in short, as the opportunity to re-experience phantasy in the psychoanalytic sense of the term. The spectator "knows that he is 'at the cinema,'" writes Bellour, "Yet, in the shadow of that knowledge, the film does indeed repeat *his own* dream, his desire to dream. Similarly, by repeating itself the dream becomes metamorphosed to fulfill the phantasy . . . and from there to model itself on its most insistent form: desire as repetition, the desire of repetition" (CR 71–72).

Readers will have already been struck by the universalization of the spectator as male in this passage. Indeed, the very brilliance of Bellour's demonstration of the pervasiveness of a phantasy of sexual difference that collapses relations of sexual identity into an androcentric image of desire can be demoralizing for a counter-ideological criticism. This is especially true in Bellour's studies of the process of enunciation in Hitchcock's films. Here he notes that even in films like *Psycho* (1960) and *Marnie* (1964) where women characters occupy a central place,

> this place was determined by properly filmic means according to a very precise logic of enunciation: the same logic which in classical psychoanalysis is founded on a necessary differentiation between masculine and feminine sexuality, in order to finally fall back on the dominant model of masculine sexuality.
>
> This gets crystallized in a particularly striking way in Hitchcock's films, but I think it's a determining factor in the American cinema as a whole. Of course one would have to draw fine distinctions between specific directors, genres, periods or films. But a number of precise analyses . . . show clearly that the central place assigned to the woman is a place where she is figured, represented, inscribed in the fiction through the logical necessity of a general representation of the subject of desire in the film, who is always, first and last, a masculine subject. (ASH 94)

Thus in an essay like "L'Énoncer," the progression of the textual system of *Marnie* is described as based on a circuit of identifications where the figuration of woman serves as the collective image of a desire whose subject is produced as a narcissistic replication of male doubles whose origin is the camera itself.[11]

In judging Bellour's work, however, I am less interested in targeting his description of the narrative logic of Hollywood films (which I find to be compelling and convincing) than in asking the following question: does the circuit of masculine desire he describes as *le blocage symbolique,* where an image of desiring subjectivity is delegated by the camera to a chain of male protagonists, extend "beyond" the text to be repeated "in" the spectator? Or can the desire as/of repetition that Bellour refers to be understood differently? In Chapter Two, I criticized Bellour's notion of *le blocage symbolique,* as a totalizing model leaving little room for historical variability either between texts or spectators. This is also the basis of Janet Bergstrom's concern in an otherwise sympathetic interview. However, my question has less to do with interrogating Bellour's results than with what his idea of a textual *system* implies for a theory of critical reading. When Bellour integrates a theory of enunciation with his ideas concerning how fiction films derive their narrative logic from primal phantasy, the problems for ideological criticism are twofold: on one hand, the demonic force of repetition across narrative seems to repeat all too perfectly the logic of Oedipus and castration phantasy; on the other, the risk occurs of conceptualizing this process as replicating itself dialectically *in* the spectator as an extension of the circuit of (masculine) identifications established in this narrative logic. Indeed this extension is often presumed in the way that Anglo-American textual analysis has treated the problem of spectatorship and identification.

Whether or not psychoanalysis can support this notion of identification is a question I will hold to one side for the moment. Now it is important to clarify that this is not exactly Bellour's thesis. Both the splendors and miseries of Bellour's description of textual systems according to the logic of symbolic blockage devolve from his intricate examination of what Freud would call the force of Eros where repetition seeks to resolve itself into ever higher unities and more complex forms. In this respect, symbolic blockage comes to represent an imminently successful ideological process where the logic of castration phantasy replicates itself perfectly from the largest to smallest units of textual structure. Within Bellour's theory and methodology there seems little room to explore contradiction and disunity either within the films or their historical contexts.

Alternatively, Bellour is quite clear that his choices represent an ideal functioning of the system and that, since his historical scope is broad, there is a risk in covering over significant differences within and between films. Even if the logic of alternation is a fundamental aspect of film language as Bellour suggests, this does not mean that all films will be governed by the forms it takes in the classical Hollywood cinema. My analysis of *Céline et Julie vont en bateau* provides an illustrative counter-example. While the film develops initially using forms of alternation that are quite familiar in early melodrama, the forms of repetition it invokes nonetheless become an uncanny temporal and disunifying force where an other scene appears to derail the linear development of an Oedipalized narrative according to the repetition-resolution effect. Thus *Céline et Julie* could be characterized among the films that Bellour describes as remaining "totally foreign to that particular effect which superimposes repetition on resolution in order to allow for the development of the film, and which seems to me to be linked above all to the form of the hermeneutic narrative characteristic, on the whole, of the classical American cinema" (ASH 82). Moreover, in its particular inversion of a hermeneutics of suspense, it is also interesting how the film seeks to establish a circuit of identifications based on an image of *feminine* narcissism with quite different consequences for the desires attached to seeing and knowing, rendering the films as a utopia of an active desire, based on feminine autoeroticism, that is regained by subverting the phallic division that represses it.

However, this is a digression from the question at hand: should textual analysis base itself on a logic of identity where the forms of the text repeat themselves "in" the spectator, or a logic of difference where the reader confronts the text from "outside the institution." In this respect, Bellour's appeal to the work of Thierry Kuntzel in the last section of his essay on repetition is interesting. While the work of these two critics is complimentary in many ways, their positions as readers *vis-à-vis* the problem of the text is distinct. Kuntzel has explicitly based his notion of the film text on the model of phantasy and his idea of reading on the psychoanalytic concept of "working-through." Following the example of Roland Barthes's *S/Z*, Kuntzel refuses any idea of totality with respect to the text. In his few published essays, he avoids treating films as intelligible wholes; his readings are elliptical, taking the form of a strategic fragmentation that follows the semiotic paths opened by the text in a digressive way. Where Bellour conceives filmic signification as a hierarchical organization of interlocking parts, Kuntzel sees a process of dispersion or drift, and where Bellour proceeds by attempting to restore the intelligibility of a system, Kuntzel's readings take the form of a floating attention to the disunifying forces against which the text attempts to shore itself up.

However, I do not believe that the work of Bellour and Kuntzel represent opposed approaches; rather, for me they represent two sides to an equation concerning the relation of narrative structure to desire. This may be illustrated by referring again to Lyotard's *Discours, figure,* an important book for both critics: where Bellour is attentive to the figure-form, Kuntzel is more concerned with how the figure-matrix informs filmic signification. Kuntzel analyzes the oneric qualities of the fiction film through its rhetorical similarities to the primary processes (film-work as dream-work) and its situation of the spectator (regressively) in the place of the primal scene. Recall that Lyotard emphasizes how the structure of phantasy—in his own nomenclature, the figure-matrix—is thoroughly permeated by the primary processes: linguistic elements run counter to the rules of syntax; images are complex and highly worked over by condensation; its forms are multi-layered; it may seek to satisfy multiple and contradictory aims; and finally, the matrix combines, in often contradictory ways, multiple partial drives. In sum, for Lyotard the logic of phantasy is completely foreign to the logics of identity, totality, and unity. This is also how Kuntzel describes the closeness of film's heterogeneity in its matters of expression to the primary processes, drawing on Freud's metaphor of the "dream-work" to characterize what he calls the "film-work." If his observation rings true, then there is nothing essentially unifying in filmic signification with respect to the possible identifications of the spectator, nor is identification itself unifying as a subjective process. If films present an occasion to phantasy where the spectator experiences a state of psychological regression, for Kuntzel this state renders the temporality of reception as asynchronous with respect to the presentation-time of the film; in fact, Kuntzel refers explicitly to this state as an experience of *Nachträglich-keit,* or deferred action.[12] Therefore, in Kuntzel's textual analyses, there is no question of identifying either spectatorial positions or identification with textual figures. Rather his activity of reading is used to reflect on and to build speculatively on a theory of spectatorial experience based on the model of phantasy. Nor is there any sense of rendering the activity of reading as a recapitulation of an originary and authenticating experience. Instead, it becomes an activity of strategic fragmentation and reinscription, reconstructing the text in ever-renewable contexts of meaning.

This is another way of saying that for both Bellour and Kuntzel, the asymptotic relation between phantasy and narrative—not to mention the imaginary and the symbolic or desire and the law—has important, if paradoxical, consequences for textual analysis and the positions of reading it implies. Bellour beautifully describes this paradox as "le texte introuvable," a text that cannot be "found" because it is so difficult to cite. It is true that Bellour spends a good deal of time describing the contradictory status of filmic as opposed to literary analysis. Unlike literature, whose specificity seems undisturbed when translated into the (written) language of criticism, the specificity of filmic experience is entirely transformed by the work of textual analysis which drains time and movement from the image, reproducing it in stills, and constitutes the film in a (written) language that is fundamentally alien to it. Thus both the limitations and the fascinations of textual analysis in film derive from ineluctable factors of movement and time."On the one hand," Bellour writes, "it spreads in space like a picture; on the other it plunges into time, like a story which its serialisation into units approximates more or less to the musical work. In this it is particularly unquotable, since the written text cannot restore what only the projector can produce: a movement, the illusion of which guarantees the reality" (TI 82).

This paradox is neither an obstacle to, nor a liability for analysis. Instead it defines the terms where critical reading and knowledge of the text become possible. The citability of literature in the language of written interpretation guarantees neither that a critical reading will take place nor that, in Roland Barthes's perspective, a "text" will be derived from the originating work.[13] As Barthes demonstrated in a variety of his analyses, to reproduce the text of a work of literature—as a strategic simulacrum of the obdurate dynamics of its inner movements, its complex symbolic processes, and its relations to desire—the originating object will of necessity be destroyed and reconstituted in fragments. The contingent knowledge of the simulacrum thus produced can only be judged by its fragmentary and destructive character, not in relation to an originary object whose status will always be historically uncertain. It is in this sense that Bellour asserts that "the freeze frame, and the photogram that reproduces it, are simulacra; evidently, they never prevent the film from escaping, yet paradoxically they let it escape as text. Obviously, the language of analysis is in charge of the rest. Like any other analysis, it attempts to weave together, from the simulacra of frozen images, the multiplicity of textual operations" (TI 83).

Thus the peculiar knowledge of textual analysis is resolutely based on a relation of non-identity; it relies paradoxically on its strategic "distortions" of an original whose unverifiable status will never authenticate in turn an "exact" description. A similar paradox was addressed by Freud in a late essay titled "Constructions in Analysis" (1937d). Interestingly, in this article Freud returns to the problem of "historical truth" with respect to the status of primal phantasy. Since patients are divided both internally with respect to knowledge of themselves, and externally in space and time from the childhood events that precipitated their present crises, there is no way of verifying absolutely an interpretation of the patterns of repetition subtending their fragmentary representations and symptomatic behaviors. Psychoanalysis is always, then, a construction concerned less with a truthful picture than a contingent model whose claims for knowledge are necessarily fragile. In the same way that Metz and Bellour insist that the powers of desire in film and the fascinations of its analysis derive from the pursuit of an object that never ceases slipping away from perception and thought in space and time, so to does Freud insist that psychoanalysis cannot base itself on either a complete interpretation of the desires symbolized in the patient's representations, or a verification of the historical origins of primal phantasy. Here the paradox of the "unfindable" text—no less than the forms of time, movement, and repetition that underwrites its phantasmic status—rejoins again that of the place of primal phantasy in psychoanalysis. Both are absent objects and non-assignable origins, and therefore knowledge of them must derive from the contingent "constructions" of analysis. "That is why," Bellour writes, "[textual analyses] always seem a little fictional: playing on an absent object, never able, since their aim is to make it present, to adopt the instruments of fiction even though they have to borrow them. Film analysis never stops filling up a film that never stops running out: it is the Danaids' cask *par excellence*. This is what makes the text of the film an unattainable [*introuvable*] text . . ." (TI 83–84). Thus the text is not a pre-existing empirical entity that can be described, more or less exactly, or adequated through commentary. The analysis of a textual system does not repeat an experience of a film; rather it constructs the intelligibility of its object. Theoretical work only operates, then, as a disjuncture between the activity of reading and the object of study. This is one of Metz's and Bellour's most crucial contributions to the theory of textual analysis as a practice of reading, which bases itself on the de-constitution of the object and the creation of a fundamentally new entity rather than the interpretive conventions of criticism, commentary, or description.

These arguments clarify that any claims made for textual analysis as a theory-building activity are not based on a logic of identity, but rather of reading as difference. Still unaddressed are the implications of this idea for ideological criticism, especially with respect to sexual difference.

I have argued in all the preceding chapters of this book against a dualistic definition of sexual difference that would reduce the lived identities of men and women to the presumption of the two mutually opposed, self-identical categories of Man/Woman. While few have mourned the death of "man" in poststructualist thought, what happens if the category of "woman" is treated, like primal phantasy, as a non-assignable origin or a historical construction of analysis? On the surface, this question would seem to fly in the face of much feminist, psychoanalytic film criticism which seeks, in a mass culture that produces derogatory images of women and excludes them from positions of identification and desire, an empowering image of collectivity and unity. In her thought-provoking book, *"Am I That Name": Feminism and the Category of 'Women' in History,* Denise Riley argues that feminism has historically followed through and must still pursue the following gamble: that the category of " 'women' is historically, discursively constructed, and always relatively to other categories which themselves change; 'women' is a volatile collectivity in which female persons can be very differently positioned, so that the apparent continuity of the subject of 'women' isn't to be relied on; 'women' is both synchronically and diachronically erratic as a collectivity, while for the individual, 'being a woman' is also inconstant, and can't provide an ontological foundation. Yet it must be emphasised that these instabilities of the category are the *sine qua non* of feminism, which would otherwise be lost for an object, despoiled of a fight, and, in short, without much life."[14] For Riley, nothing is lost by insisting on the shifting historical discontinuities of the concept of womanhood or its fragile and asymmetrical relation with other historically mutable categories of personhood, soul, mind, body, nature, and society. Rather the indeterminacy of the concept stresses its status as a contested category where individuals engage in battles for rights of recognition and empowerment denied them in the reigning social, political, economic, and medical norms of identity.

In the same way, Juliet Mitchell and Jacqueline Rose have insisted on the indeterminacy of the figure of *the* Woman in both psychoanalytic theory and the phantasy life of individuals. Rose in particular has one of the most cogent and compelling critiques of arguments, most often derived from Michèle Montrelay and Luce Irigaray, that attempt to restore the self-identity of the woman with respect to the divisions of "phallic" subjectivity. At stake is a feminine specificity locating itself as an original and unmediated relation with either the maternal body or itself, an exact repetition or doubling that sees itself as a primal unity where the woman finds herself "before" division, as it were. The difficulty of this idea is that it restores to the woman a unity, coherence, self-identity, and fullness of being that no subject, as considered by psychoanalytic theory, could ever possess. As Rose insists, the importance of Lacan's notion of the Symbolic is that there is no "prediscursive" reality, no origin to which one can return; what is assumed to fall *before* language can only be understood as a retroactive understanding in *language*. Thus the problem of "femininity" as described by psychoanalysis (to which Freud's work is a fascinating testament) can belong to neither woman nor man. This is first because "the unconscious severs the subject from any unmediated relation to the body as such . . ., and secondly because the 'feminine' is constituted as a division in language, a division which produces the feminine as its negative term. If woman is defined as other it is because the definition produces her as other, and not because she has another essence. . . . [That] refusal of the phallic term brings with it an attempt to reconstitute a form of subjectivity free of division, and hence a refusal of the notion of symbolisation itself."[15]

What are the consequences of this idea for feminist criticism in particular and for the study of ideology in general? First and foremost that the work of criticism and the struggle for ideological change can only take place, indeed can only produce effects, within the terms of the Symbolic. Here is where most arguments concerning the politics of identification and distance come to grief, especially where they are led to assume the essential unity of gender positions. By the same token, in most psychoanalytically informed feminist film theory, the problem of identification and desire is delimited paradoxically by a formalist emphasis. Both Doane and Linda Williams, for example, assume that pleasure for women audiences is "textual" pleasure, though not explicitly in a Barthesian sense. As such their arguments are structured by three ideas: that there is no relation with the spectator that is not determined by the forms of the text; that the female spectator has an implicit ontological specificity and self-identity represented by kinds of identification proper to these forms; and that this self-identical subject is able to recognize forms of "authentic" female experience, no matter how occluded, in the artifacts of mass culture.

Cultural criticism does have an empowering role to play in the contestation of norms of identity and the creation of positions from which one may see, understand, desire, think, and act differently. This is why I have insisted, within the limited purview of psychoanalytic film theory, on critiquing simultaneously the methods of textual criticism—as protocols of reading that perpetuate positions and contexts for understanding and evaluating mass cultural artifacts—and an idea of identification as a unifying force with respect to either categories of spectators, or in the relation of spectator to text. In this respect, every act of criticism implies a repetition, and the particular forms of this repetition have profound consequences for the stakes of critical knowledge.

This idea is illustrated in two of the most pervasive critical strategies of Anglo-American textual analysis: that of symptomatic reading and of defining the "progressive" text. For example, Mary Ann Doane's version of symptomatic reading, as I described in Chapter Two, is informed by Louis Althusser's observations on epistemology and his emphasis on defining the aesthetic, the ideological, and the theoretical as different modes of cognition. The figure of distance plays an important role in Althusser, and in the rereading of his work by critics like Pierre Macherey, Terry Eagleton, and Fredric Jameson.[16] However, the implications of this figure for a theory of critical reading differ greatly from Doane's arguments. Briefly, the Althusserian position understands the specific social function of aesthetic work as an "internal distancing" of the ideologies it represents. There is always a disjunction between ideology—as the historically specific questions, problems, and conflicts defined within a culture—and the symbolic forms available to give imaginary representations and solutions to those problems. The result is that aesthetic work is always characterized by contradiction; its fictional responses to actual social conflicts is always marked symptomatically by equivocations, vacillations, and other "eloquent silences" that are available to a theoretically and historically informed reading. To the extent that the work of ideological and aesthetic signification is distinguishable, all aesthetic work makes legible the work of ideology by staging and attempting, usually unsuccessfully, to resolve its contradictions. The woman's film has no special place or function here with respect to other styles or genres. Nor would a modernist counter-cinema be necessarily exempt from a similar relation to ideology. The form of a text can never determine its relation to ideology. An ideology becomes readable in the eloquent silences of its aesthetic representations only by appropriating the text from a critical position able to describe and articulate historically these contradictions.

The problem with Doane's reading of the woman's film is that the argument concerning "film and the masquerade" tends to conflate the critical positions of symptomatic reading and the progressive text. This causes certain confusions in Doane's implicit theory of ideology, for the two positions presume different strategies of reading and different epistemological criteria. Arguments concerning the "progressive text" always invoke formal criteria that consider the text as a self-identical, autonomous object, where the epistemological function is considered a property of the texts themselves. As such the defense of certain styles or genres of the classical, Hollywood cinema as "progressive" relies implicitly on an empiricist position: in their contradictions, the films "foreground" or "defamiliarize" their relation to ideology in a self-evidential way. The "proper" spectator of these films has only to look to understand since ideological conflicts are won or lost *within* the battleground of the text. Doane's summary chapter illustrates this problem precisely.[17] To the extent that her own critical goal is "an attempt to expose 'those obvious truths' of femininity as they are inscribed within the woman's film and to defamiliarize them, to break down and subject to analysis their very obviousness" (DD 176), I believe her project is unqualifiably brilliant and successful. Moreover taking Doane exactly at her word, I also agree that what is most important is the activity of analyzing these tropes "in relation to processes of representation and meaning, delineating the positions from which texts become readable and meaningful to female spectators" (DD 176). The problem is that in her emphasis on subject-position as identification, Doane implies that these positions reside "in" the text as positions reproducible "in" the spectator.

Symptomatic reading, however, is a position taken with respect to the text from a position of critical difference. The symptomatic approach (to which Freud's hermeneutics has much to offer) is a genuine position of reading. In their relation to ideology, *all* texts (whether realist, progressive, or counter-cinema) are incomplete—perhaps failed, contradictory, or incoherent. Where the problem of meaning is concerned, the activity of the spectator engages the text by assuming a position of reading. For example, Pierre Macherey emphasizes the difference between reading as interpretation (where the critic simply fills in the gaps, claiming to produce a true, latent, or recondite meaning from the text's silences) and a materialist reading that produces a critical knowledge of the function of ideology within the text. A more complex and replete version of this position is represented by Stuart Hall's observation that any mass cultural "message" is received in a space of competing readings—the preferred, the negotiated, and the oppositional.[18] Thus the spectator can complete or challenge, even project an ideology into the film, according to conscious or unconscious reading contexts informed by his or her historical and social formation. It is also important to remember that readings are no less innocent than texts, nor are they any more complete or coherent self-sufficient positions. No less than the texts they appropriate and the meanings they generate, positions of reading are historical, complex and contradictory intertextual formations. Most of what we do as critics and educators is to establish positions and fight battles over what counts as knowledge and how meanings will be established and perpetuated. With respect to what I feel are the best aspects of Doane's work, it matters little what the "female spectator" as a position of identification essentially is. For Doane demonstrates convincingly how a historical image of the "female spectator" is created across these films, and more importantly, herself creates a critical position that makes this image readable. Doane does not give herself enough credit when she suggests that these relations are intrinsically "visible" within the woman's film. It is her critical activity that has rendered them so, and in fact, has created a position for the feminist spectator where one may not have existed before.

Beverly Brown and Parveen Adams have demonstrated how and why feminist theory would wish to define an authentic experience grounded in the female body and have demonstrated the political dangers of this position.[19] More appropriate for my argument here is that this version of the subject cannot be supported by either the psychoanalytic or Marxist theories appealed to, both founded by the desire to explain the experience of contradiction. The idea that individuals might act against their own interests, and take pleasure in doing so, is central to the thoughts and behaviors that united psychoanalysis and Marxism. Nor is it unthinkable, as Fredric Jameson points out, that spectatorial experience of, and pleasure in, the texts of mass culture could be characterized as simultaneously ideological and utopian.[20] Neither Marxism nor psychoanalysis are strangers to the association of one form of pleasure with self-destructiveness. While such an idea is surely and justifiably anathema to most feminist criticism of mass culture, is an unconscious nostalgia for an ontological grounding of subjective unity really an appropriate utopia for defining the collective aspirations of women in their social and historical multiplicity? The questions I would prefer to ask are: Can psychoanalysis help explain the multiple and contradictory experiences of identification and pleasure across sexual difference? And can psychoanalysis formulate a theory of reading that identifies the utopian as well as ideological dimensions of collective fantasy life represented in mass cultural representations?

In this respect, the analyses and arguments derived from textual analysis and metapsychological studies of cinema have opened a wealth of possibilities for understanding the *virtual* conditions of spectatorship and sexual difference. By stressing the term virtual I mean to emphasize the hypothetical nature of this knowledge, which is limited by the reigning formal concepts of text and of the cinematic apparatus. Only by outlining and comprehending these conditions—currently understood as properties of cinematic form, on the one hand, and as technology on the other—can a theory of identification be inaugurated. But just as films as cultural artifacts can be understood as "fantasy" but not "phantasy" in a strictly psychoanalytic sense, the terms of "identification" are similarly limited methodologically and conceptually. Contemporary film theory has far too easily forgotten that in their psychoanalytic specificity, studies of identification are limited to the psychic life of individuals. In many recent studies of sexual difference, assumptions are made about "male" or "female" spectators, conceived as entities identical to themselves and to formal conditions set by the text. Unquestionably, cinema-going actualizes desire, and relations of identity and sexual difference are forged "in" that desire "through" the experience of cinematic representation. But this experience is the property of historical subjects and must be analyzed as such. It can, in no decidable way, be understood as strictly identical to the forms of a text, patterns of enunciation, or the conditions set by the cinematic apparatus.

Alternatively, strategies and norms of *signification*, which are resolutely cultural artifacts and subject to greater historical permanence, are not prey to the protean quality of psychical life. Indeed part of the brilliance of Doane's analysis is her demonstration of the historical transformation in what she terms subject address and subject-position as figures of signification in this sense. Here the binary machine is understood as a historical given contributing to a dualistic construction of gender as well as the division and attribution of value-laden properties to representations of gender. In this manner, Doane's study of the woman's film demonstrates how all genres distribute, divide, and classify iconographic characteristics, patterns of plot development, and structures of point of view on the basis of a social and historical construction of sexual difference. But female spectators are not constructed here; only patterns of signification and position coded according to a binary model of gender. And Doane shows convincingly how ideology functions by seeking to proliferate this process of binary division, distribution, and classification in order to bolster its definition of sexual difference against ceaseless erosion and contradiction.

Thus films, like other cultural artifacts, do not produce subjects but symbolic positions of subjectivity, and these positions are virtual not actual. They demonstrate how ideology works to define and delimit the inventory of "identities" available to a culture. Indeed many historical individuals may accept and reconfirm their sense of gender and social position by identifying with these positions. But the possibilities of resistance, reconfiguration, re-reading, and in fact, a whole range of eccentric and non-contingent responses are equally possible. In the current state of psychoanalytic and cultural theory, the possibilities for the study of identification are extremely limited, while the ideological criticism of discursive formations provides a wealth of opportunities. In other words, the tools of discourse analysis enable an understanding of the norms of identity and desire that are the historical and ideological ideals of a culture. Similarly, these tools can help describe how specific subcultures and other collectivities identify themselves by challenging these norms in diverse and heterogeneous ways.

Therefore, in my view textual analysis as a form of critical reading should be informed by the following questions: Does it restore the logic of a system, or does it demonstrate the impossible attempt of a system to shore itself up against dispersion and loss? Does it restore the visibility of a hidden logic, or is it motivated by the ever renewable sense derived from recontextualization? Does it produce an interpretation motivated by the desire for reconciliation, or a reading based on irreconcilable contradiction? In contrast, if textual analysis verified its claims for knowledge as an exact description, that is, as a model that repeats exactly the functioning of the original it examines, this would be yet another form of uncanny repetition based on identification, where the unfolding of the text would realize itself completely in the mental activity of the spectator. This is how the methodology of textual analysis in the French school has often been adopted by Anglo-American film theory to analyze the forms of point of view and identification deemed proper to the fiction film. By the same token, Bellour's comment on women spectators in the interview with Janet Bergstrom is damaging only if one assumes that identification indeed implies a process where the forces of repetition unleashed by the fiction film inevitably complete themselves in the spectator. Alternatively, if Metz's comment that the film analyst stands "outside the institution" is taken seriously, one could reinterpret Bellour's statement to mean that women spectators are ideally placed as film theorists: psychologically they are exempted from participating in the Oedipal phantasies of fiction films if they can evade a masochistic response, and are thus able to reconstitute their pleasure in the forms of "sadism" sanctioned by the methodology of textual analysis. This has already been the conclusion arrived at by some critics, and I have argued that it is not entirely satisfactory. If the text is truly "unfindable," a non-assignable origin, and if textual analysis is to serve in facilitating redemptive as well as symptomatic readings, then all forms of identity must be relinquished. The interested simulacrum that textual analysis achieves through "constructions in analysis" must be understood not as repeating what the text means, but as presenting the opportunity to construct positions from which it can always be read and understood in new and unforeseen ways.

This also demonstrates how the emphasis on the problem of identification in studies of film and ideology has clouded understanding of the more radical aspects of Metz and Bellour's position on textual analysis and psychoanalytic theory. For in their view, textual analysis can tell us little about processes of identification since it aims to derive knowledge of the text's functioning by demolishing the mechanisms that sustain this experience. As a form of reading, the goals and methods of textual analysis will always be opposed and completely alien to the subjective experience of identification. This is often verified in the resistance to theory articulated by film students; namely the fear of relinquishing an unconscious pleasure, wonderfully expressed in the anxiety of one of Pierre Janet's patients who was afraid to read "for fear of getting the books dirty." Similarly, this attitude represents a misrecognition of the alternative pleasures of reading as a sanctioned epistemophilia organized by working-through the text and disrupting the uncanny repetition of the fiction film.

A first conclusion to be reached from this argument is that psychoanalytic film criticism must distinguish problems of identification and signification with much greater rigor. In *Totem and Taboo*, Freud characterizes neurotics as people whose phantasy life has withdrawn from the collective to take exclusively individual manifestations. This was his warning against taking too far psychoanalytic speculation on anthropological problems. A similar warning can be made for psychoanalytic film theory: one should not too forcibly generalize, in the analysis of collective representations, about the psychic economies and responses of actual spectators. As I have argued in the earlier chapters of this book, contemporary film theory has often totalized complex questions of sexual difference and identification within a singular unity which merges the "forms" of spectatorship with the "forms" of the text, or, just as badly, divides identification into two mutually exclusive forms, male and female. Here the question of "the spectator," which hypostatizes the collective in an image of false unity, is of little interest to a historical and materialist criticism.

In this manner, separating the problem of identity from that of identification is the main confusion of most studies of sexual difference. This is surprising since one of the most important discoveries of psychoanalysis is that the concept of identity is unknown to processes of identification, which is one of the principle points that Jacqueline Rose and Juliet Mitchell make in their Introductions to the volume on *Feminine Sexuality*. The self is never singular. Its internal divisions and contradictions, especially where sexual identification is concerned, can be quite complex as Freud's detailed analysis of infantile beating phantasies so uncannily demonstrates. This is why I have insisted that all processes of identification are transactional. They are complex structures where multiple temporalities and subjective relations coexist in contradictory ways that are radically other to binary relations. Thus one cannot classify identification simply as masculine or feminine, active or passive, sadistic or masochistic. In all sexed subjects, its processes comprise constantly permutable ratios between all these terms, which can never be strictly aligned with biological gender. Nor would any ontogenetic distinctions be possible; for example, masochism as the simple "property" of the female subject. Of course, from the standpoint of psychoanalytic film theory it is axiomatic that both the cinematic apparatus and the textual structure of films must appeal to the component instincts, above all the scopic and the auditory. Therefore, identification—its presence, its absence, its ennuis, thrills, in short all its peculiar vicissitudes—are the cinematic commodity par excellence. Psychoanalytic film theory has long recognized that the problems of pleasure and desire (which are not necessarily equivalent) would be its most specific area of inquiry, especially with respect to questions of ideology and sexual difference. However, identification is a psychical and strangely contingent process. It is a property of mentalities, of the psychology of individuals and collectivities, and cannot be considered as embodied in, or the product of, specific technologies or textual figures. In short, any speculation on the co-equivalence of formal textual features and actual processes of identification is undecidable.

There is another way of stating this idea. From a psychoanalytic perspective, *when* identification takes place its psychological forms can be defined—regression and disavowal as well as narcissistic reinforcement of the ego. But textual analysis can in no decidable way provide evidence of when, how, or if identification takes place in any spectator, nor in fact should it. In this one area "Brechtian" arguments—establishing epistemological criteria divided on the basis of textual forms—are red herrings that contribute very little to political criticism or ideological analysis. Similarly, while the actualities of identification remain slippery, the undecidability of this question becomes a powerful and empowering utopian figure of reading. Perhaps a text will repeat demonically the totalization of subjects within ideological figures, but every repetition presents simultaneously the possibility of difference.

Where psychoanalysis witnesses the ineluctable dispersion of identity in identification, textual analysis discovers the attempt to perpetuate, hold, and sustain the memory of historically based symbolic norms of identity through a binary model of sexual difference. In this process, the cinematic institution is only one among a regime of institutions and discourses. Similarly, the problems of identification and signification belong to separate domains sharing only a little territory in common. If the processes of identification and the force of the drives are irreducible to forms of unity and identity, then this is one way of acknowledging the variegate potentialities for resistance, refusal, and discontent, whether inchoate or not, that are always present historically in the sphere of reception. From the standpoint of the critic of mass culture, this discontentedness can never be verified in the structure of the text; yet it may blossom in the forms of its appropriation in a critical reading. Thus, psychoanalysis clarifies the inevitable failures and erosions of identity where ideological apparatuses want to contain these erosions within binary grids. Between erosion and defense, reading defines the utopian space of an interrupted repetition.

I wish to emphasize that my approach holds nothing in common with ideas concerning textual excess which still rely on a formalist model. If desire is the motor of contradiction in narrative, it is not necessarily historically legible. It must be rendered so through the activity of a reading sensitive to the logic of contradiction, its relation to desire, and its historical origins. Nor do I see my position as necessarily aligned with that of reader-response and other forms of "ethnographic" criticism. In this respect, I agree with Tania Modleski that criticism has a performative function that is at odds with the premises of reader-response studies. Modleski writes that

> reader response critics have countered textual critics by insisting that meaning resides not in any given text, but in readers as they interact with the text, though this meaning may be determined within a larger context—that of the interpretive community to which the readers belong. I have already discussed some of the limitations of this view for feminist criticism; but now I would like to go further and argue that another problem with such formulations lies in their assumption that an *already-existent* meaning resides *somewhere,* and that the critic's only job is to locate it (in the text, in the reader, in the interpretive community, or

in the relations among the three). On the contrary, a fully politicized feminist criticism has seldom been content to ascertain old meanings and (in the manner of ethnographers) take the measure of already-constituted subjectivities; it has aimed, rather, at bringing into being *new* meanings and *new* subjectivities, seeking to articulate not only what is but "what has never been." In this respect it may be said to have a performative dimension—i.e., to be *doing* something beyond restating already existent ideas and views, wherever these might happen to reside.[21]

Reading encounters the text as a relation of difference not identity. It not only renders as legible and meaningful aspects that were previously unforeseen, it also potentially creates the text anew while ideally transforming the larger discursive context where both text and reading are embedded. In this manner, reading is always an activity of intervention and creation—the possibility of counter-hegemonic collectivities to refunction and reconstitute the extant discourse of mass culture. This activity is agonistic, a battleground, and a situation of conflict whose outcome is always undecided. Oftentimes ideological norms take the high ground in this conflict because historically they have proliferated in a wide range of discursive contexts (political, educational, critical, journalistic) that reciprocally support one another. But a throw of the dice will never abolish chance. Every reading—especially the public ones we call teaching, lecturing, and publishing—demands a performative act and an ethical choice. One engages in commentary and so leaves the terms of language and knowledge in the historical state in which they were found, or one engages in critique in hopes of transforming the reigning norms of knowledge. The semiotic process is not just completed in the subject (repetition as identity), it is in itself transformed by critical practice. In this respect, every reader is a translator in the sense defined by Walter Benjamin in which the greatest crime is to leave language in the state where you historically found it.[22] Like the translator, the reader should encounter the text as a literally foreign object—divided from her or him both linguistically and temporally—whose sense is obdurate. By the same token, it is impossible to restore either an authenticating sense or a verifying historical origin. For in the work involved, the text is lost and recreated in a new form. This process should not be considered as distortion complimented by nostalgia for a lost, authentic language. Nor is the contrary idea of reading as restoring free play more desirable, since reading is never free. Rather, reading should be understood as an opportunity for transforming, if only in small ways, the reigning norms of knowledge and the forms of their transmission. The critic can intervene on the side of the system, demonstrate its uncanny efficiency for the ordering and exhaustion of desire, and finally complete a process that the text itself could not. Or the critic can push contradictions, search out their historical derivation; in short, recognize in the relation of desire to representation a temporal becoming as the site of unforeseen meaning.

Even though I have been arguing here for a renewed consideration of the value of psychoanalytic paradigms, I want to conclude this book with some thoughts about the limits of psychoanalytic accounts of subjectivity, including alternative accounts of the female spectator. Psychoanalysis must not be understood as a totalizing theory, and its limitations for a theory of ideology must be clearly recognized. Psychoanalysis can only consider the subject as a singular category whose divisions and complexities are bounded by the interiorized space of an actual or imagined body. But what about the multiple sets of discourse and institutional interpellations that delimit this "body" from the "outside" according to medical, legal, economic, "scientific," or even aesthetic designations? In the last instance, legal and juridical discourses superintend, as Foucault points out in *The History of Sexuality,* what rights of recognition and action are derived from these designations. This is demonstrated by two recent, interesting cases: one is the challenge of the chromosome test used by the International Olympic Committee "to insure femininity in the competitors"; the other involves the law suits initiated by the hermaphrodite Mark (née Brenda Margaret) Rees for the right to change his name, to establish a "single" genital sex, to have his medical expenses reimbursed by British Social Security, and to change his birth certificate to assure the right of marriage.[23] In each instance, the juridical process has held tenaciously to a binary definition of sexual difference that it expects to have confirmed by medicine in a tautological assurance of State power. However, these cases reveal that medical science has no means for reducing the spectrum of biological sex to two mutually exclusive "bodies," any more than sociology or psychology can similarly reduce the spectrum of practiced sexualities. The fascinating paradox here is the insistence that the body act as an unchallengeable, physical guarantee for an ideological construction of sexual difference that is attempting to preserve its own fictions concerning the body, "correct" sexual identity, and legal sexual practices. My point is that the problem of sexual identification must be understood within a historical and conjunctural analysis, itself open to multiple levels of contradiction. Most studies of film and ideology emphasize the intimacy of the text-spectator relationship, identifying the latter with the former, at the expense of understanding reading as difference. This might be the inheritance of psychoanalysis' underdeveloped sense of history and its emphasis on subjective interiority. For me, the activity of reading involves an attentiveness to the continual shifts in terrains of meaning, and the fault-lines dividing texts and readers as their historical and discursive environments evolve in disjunct and disparate ways.

In sum, to the extent that feminist film theory uses psychoanalysis to justify ontologically the specificity of femininity as devolving from the female body, it risks reproducing the very logic of domination that it has so far effectively challenged. While holding on to the powerful claims of Freud's discoveries, as well as those of psychoanalytic film theory, we must nonetheless acknowledge their limits. Subjectivity does not devolve from the body; it cannot be defined ontogenetically nor can it be simply divided into masculine and feminine identities assured from birth by chromosome count, hormonal balances, or types of genitalia. Subjectivity is defined by social and historical processes that are irreducible to singular categories, and its forms and potentialities are always in flux. Only on this basis can we recognize and defend the multiple possibilities of identity and desire, in film as well as other discourses and practices, that challenge patriarchal and capitalist ideologies. And only on this basis can we as critics produce new and unforeseen possibilities of knowledge, desire, and meaning in our readings of the texts of mass culture.

Notes

Preface

1. Laura Mulvey, "Visual Pleasure and Narrative Cinema," *Screen* 16.3 (Autumn 1975): 11; reprinted in Constance Penley, ed. *Feminism and Film Theory* (New York: Routledge, 1988): 57–68. My essay, "The Difficulty of Difference," was published in *Wide Angle* 5.1 (1982): 4–15.

2. See "The Spectatrix," Mary Ann Doane and Janet Bergstrom, eds., *Camera Obscura* 20/21 (1990).

3. (Urbana: University of Illinois Press, 1988).

4. See her "French Feminism in an International Frame," in *In Other Worlds* (New York: Routledge, 1988): 134–153.

5. Mulvey's argument is presented in her essay "Afterthoughts on 'Visual Pleasure and Narrative Cinema' Inspired by *Duel in the Sun*," *Feminism and Film Theory*, 69–79. For de Lauretis, see her *Alice Doesn't* (Bloomington: Indiana University Press, 1984), especially pages 103–157.

6. "Masochism and Male Subjectivity," *Camera Obscura* 17 (May 1988): 31–66. I discuss Silverman's essay in greater depth in Chapter Four.

7. "Subversive Melodrama and Oedipal Plots, or the Difference of Reading in *Céline et Julie vont en bateau*," *Art & Text* 34 (Spring 1989): 127–144.

8. A succinct statement of Bellour's position in the 1970s is the interview conducted by Janet Bergstrom, "Alternation, Segmentation, Hypnosis: Interview with Raymond Bellour" *Camera Obscura* 3/4 (Summer 1979): 71–103.

1. The Difficulty of Difference

1. Paris: Flammarion, 1977: 27–31, 42–43 and passim. Trans. Hugh Tomlinson and Barbara Habberjam (New York: Columbia University Press, 1987): 21–23 and 33–35. Hereafter cited as D.

2. See, for example, Jean-François Lyotard's comments on Hegel and Saussure throughout the first half of *Discours, figure* (Paris: Editions Klincksieck, 1974). Especially interesting is Lyotard's gloss on Marx's early critique of Hegel's *Philosophy of Right*, which focuses on how the logic of sexual difference comes to be organized in binary terms. See *Discours, figure*, 138–141.

3. (Urbana: University of Illinois Press, 1988). See especially Chapters Eight and Nine. Needless to say, these reservations apply to writing on film alone and are not *a fortiori* extendable to all of feminist and psychoanalytic theory. Important critical rereadings of Freud are represented in the work of Luce Irigaray and Shoshana Felman, for example,

both of whom are sensitive to Freud's complex and contradictory rhetoric, neither of whom imposes a logic of binary division on his thought.

4. *Screen* 16.3 (Autumn 1975): 6–18. Cited as VP.

5. Mulvey has reconsidered the "Visual Pleasure" argument, which dates from 1973, in several important essays: "Afterthoughts on 'Visual Pleasure and Narrative Cinema' Inspired by 'Duel in the Sun' (King Vidor, 1946)," *Framework* 15/16/17 (Summer 1981): 12–15 and "Changes," *Discourse* 7 (Fall 1985): 11–30. These essays have been collected in her book, *Visual and Other Pleasures* (Bloomington: Indiana University Press, 1988). Important and sympathetic critiques of Mulvey include Mary Ann Doane's "Misrecognition and Identity," *Ciné-Tracts* 11 (Fall 1980): 25–32; Kaja Silverman's "Masochism and Subjectivity," *Framework* 12 (1980): 2–9; Gaylyn Studlar's "Masochism and the Perverse Pleasures of Cinema," *Quarterly Review of Film Studies* 9.4 (Fall 1984): 267–282; Teresa de Lauretis's *Alice Doesn't* (Bloomington: Indiana University Press, 1984): 103–157; and Miriam Hansen's "Pleasure, Ambivalence, Identification: Valentino and Female Spectatorship," *Cinema Journal* 25.4 (Summer 1986): 6–32. Also see two special journal issues on sexual difference, *Oxford Literary Review* 8.1/2 (1986) and *Screen* 28.1 (Winter 1987).

6. J. Laplanche and J.-B. Pontalis, *The Language of Psychoanalysis*, trans. Donald Nicholson-Smith (New York: W. W. Norton and Co., 1973): 205.

7. This logic is only characteristic of Freud's texts before 1920. The theory of the drives was profoundly transformed by Freud's hypotheses concerning the death drive and primary masochism as represented in *Beyond the Pleasure Principle* (1920g) and "The Economic Problem of Masochism" (1924c). The implications of these later texts for my argument will be discussed in Chapter Four.

8. SE 14: 109–140. The original title of Freud's essay is "Triebe und Triebschicksale." Although *Trieb* is usually translated as "instinct," Freud also uses the term *Instinkt* and seems to distinguish between them in other writings. In *The Language of Psychoanalysis*, Laplanche and Pontalis suggest that a distinction should be made between the drives [*Triebe*] on one hand, and the instincts [*Instinkts*] on the other, on the basis of ideas that begin to be developed more clearly in "Triebe und Triebschicksale" (214–217). In this case, the term instinct should be preserved for the classical, biological sense of genetically inherited patterns of behavior and response. The term drive [*Trieb*], however, belongs only to psychoanalysis as one of its essential concepts. The fate of the drives is a consequence of the particular history of each individual in their relation to society. While originating in something like a sexual force, the drives are only comprehensible through their organization into components and their attachment to particular unconscious ideas or representations. I will maintain this distinction even though the translations of the Standard Edition are inconsistent on this point.

9. See Jacqueline Rose's interesting argument in "Paranoia and the Film System," *Screen* 17.4 (Winter 1976/77): 85–104. Also see Lacan's essays "The mirror stage as formative of the function of the I" and "Aggressivity in psychoanalysis" in E: 1–29.

10. "Pleasure, Ambivalence, Identification," 11. I am deeply indebted to Hansen's reading of Freud and of suggesting ways of understanding his arguments outside of the Lacanian paradigm that is particular to contemporary film theory.

11. Cf. *Three Essays on the Theory of Sexuality*, SE 7: 150. Two important scholars, Gaylyn Studlar and Kaja Silverman, have addressed this problem from divergent points of view, and I must admit that my sympathies reside with Silverman's position. In a critique of Studlar's reading of Gilles Deleuze's *Masochism: An Interpretation of Coldness and Cruelty* (trans. Jean McNeil [New York: George Braziller, 1971]) in the essay "Masochism and the Perverse Pleasures of Cinema," Silverman notes that "Studlar conflates Deleuze's

oral mother with the pre-Oedipal mother of object relations psychoanalysis, and extrapolates from that conflation a highly dubious argument about the origin of masochism. According to Studlar, that perversion has its basis in the (male) child's relationship with the actual mother prior to the advent of the father, a relationship predicated upon his helpless subordination to her, and the insatiability of his desire for her. Masochistic suffering consequently derives from the pain of separation from the mother, and the impossible desire to fuse with her again, rather than from the categorical imperative of the Oedipus complex and the symbolic law. This is a determinedly political reading of masochism, which comes close to grounding that perversion in biology" ("Masochism and Male Subjectivity," *Camera Obscura* 17 [May 1988]: 66). By the same token, in opposing masochism to sadism as a model of filmic pleasure, Studlar fundamentally misconstrues my critique of Mulvey in the original version of this chapter (first published in *Wide Angle* 15.1 [1982]: 4–15), reinvoking an agonistic logic of binary terms that I insist must be rejected. I will return to this problem in greater detail in Chapter Four.

12. Of particular interest, among many relevant essays, are Freud's accounts of the case history of the "Wolf Man" (1918b [1914]), and the analysis of the phantasy of "'A Child is being Beaten'" (1919e). Both will receive commentary later in this book.

13. A number of interesting essays have been published on the eroticization of the male body in film and television, especially from the point of view of homosexual desire. Among the most thought-provoking are: Steve Neale's "Masculinity as Spectacle," *Screen* 24.6 (November–December 1983): 2–116 and "Sexual Difference in Cinema," *Oxford Literary Review* 8.1/2 (1986): 123–132; Richard Dyer's "Don't Look Now—the Male Pin-Up," *Screen* 23.3/4 (September/October 1982): 61–73; and Andrew Ross's "Masculinity and *Miami Vice*," *Oxford Literary Review* 8.1/2 (1986): 143–154.

14. Beverly Brown and Parveen Adams have cogently defined and criticized this problem in feminist politics in their essay, "The Feminine Body and Feminist Politics," *m/f* 3 (1979): 35–50. Also see my *Crisis of Political Modernism*, 249–262.

15. See in particular *Totem and Taboo* (1912–1913), SE 13: 7–161. I will return to this problem in Chapters Three and Five.

16. SE 21: 106. Compare, for example, this footnote from *Three Essays on the Theory of Sexuality*: "It is essential to understand clearly that the concepts of 'masculine' and 'feminine' whose meaning seems so unambiguous to ordinary people, are among the most confused that occur in science. It is possible to distinguish at least three uses. 'Masculine' and 'feminine' are used sometimes in the sense of activity and passivity, sometimes in a biological and sometimes, again, in a sociological sense. The first of these three meanings is the essential one and the most serviceable in psychoanalysis. When, for instance, libido was described in the text above as being 'masculine,' the word was being used in this sense, for an instinct is always active even when it has a passive aim in view. The second, or biological, meaning of 'masculine' and 'feminine' is the one whose applicability can be determined most easily. Here 'masculine' and 'feminine' are characterized by the presence of spermatozoa or ova respectively and by the functions proceeding from them. . . . The third, or sociological meaning, receives its connotation from the observation of actually existing masculine and feminine individuals. Such observation shows that pure masculinity or femininity is not to be found either in a psychological or biological sense. Every individual on the contrary displays a mixture of the character-traits belonging to his own and to the opposite sex; and he shows a combination of activity and passivity whether or not these character-traits tally with his biological ones." (SE 7: 219–220).

17. Compare Mulvey's argument in this respect with Peter Wollen's "Godard and Counter-Cinema: *Vent d'est*," which is perhaps the most direct and influential manifesto for a

"Brechtian" conception of political modernism in the cinema. Wollen's essay was originally published in *Afterimage* 4 (1972) and has recently been anthologized, along with "Visual Pleasure and Narrative Cinema," in Philip Rosen, ed., *Narrative, Apparatus, Ideology* (New York: Columbia University Press, 1986): 120–129.

18. Whether a term like "fetishistic scopophilia" has a precise sense in the context of Freudian theory or whether it must rest as an interesting neologism on Mulvey's part is also uncertain. In Freud's own important essay on "Fetishism" [(1927e), SE 21: 152–157] there is no evidence to characterize this perversion as a "passive" form of looking. On the contrary, it is characterized by a profound degree of psychical activity. Moreover, the point that is most important for Freud, and indeed most important for any theory of ideology, concerns the problem of *Ichspaltung*, or the splitting of the ego where the subject simultaneously holds contradictory and mutually exclusive beliefs. Contrary to the view promoted in contemporary film theory, the splitting of the ego is not a "result" of the castration complex, nor is this phenomenon peculiar only to fetishism. Fetishism is only the clearest example of this phenomenon. In short, the splitting of the ego is for Freud a more general and wide spread condition, representing one of the ego's strongest means of defense against traumatic events of all kinds. See his late essay, "Splitting of the Ego in the Process of Defense" (1940e [1938]), SE 23: 275–278.

19. For an interesting discussion of this concept in relation to film, see Thierry Kuntzel, "*Le Défilement*: A View in Close Up," trans. Bertrand Augst, *Camera Obscura*, 2 (Fall 1977): 51–65.

2. The Return of the Exile

1. I am thinking in particular of the work of Stephen Heath. While still obviously committed to psychoanalytic paradigms, and one of the earliest and most interesting importers of Lacan to film theory, Heath has nonetheless produced some of the most sensitive and interesting critiques of psychoanalysis. See his "Difference," *Screen* 19.3 (Autumn 1978): 51–112 and *The Sexual Fix* (London: Macmillan, 1982). More recently, this ambivalence has been cogently expressed by Mary Ann Doane in her *The Desire to Desire: The Woman's Film of the 1940's* (Bloomington: Indiana University Press, 1987); cited hereafter as DD. See especially pages 13–22.

2. See "Le Blocage symbolique" and "Énoncer" in *L'Analyse du film* (Paris: Editions Albatros, 1979). The latter has been translated by Bertrand Augst and Hilary Radner as "Hitchcock, the Enunciator," *Camera Obscura* 2 (Fall 1977): 67–91. The former will appear in Mary Quaintance's translation in *The Analysis of Film* (Bloomington: Indiana University Press, forthcoming). I will return to this problem in Chapter Six.

3. Janet Bergstrom, "Alternation, Segmentation, Hypnosis: Interview with Raymond Bellour," *Camera Obscura* 3/4 (Summer 1979): 97.

4. Respectively: Jacqueline Rose, "Paranoia and the Film System," *Screen* 17.4 (Winter 1976/77): 85–104; Miriam Hansen, "Pleasure, Ambivalence, Identification," *Cinema Journal* 25.4 (Summer 1986): 6–32; Mary Ann Doane, *The Desire to Desire: The Woman's Film of the 1940s*.

5. The best statement of Williams's position is " 'Something Else Besides a Mother': *Stella Dallas* and the Maternal Melodrama," *Cinema Journal* 24.1 (Fall 1984): 2–27; for Modleski, "'Never to be thirty-six years old': *Rebecca* as Female Oedipal Drama," *Wide Angle* 5.1 (1982): 34–41. I feel strongly that the principal influence on this point of view, which understands narrative structure as staging and then attempting to contain the terms of its own negation and critique, is the work of Stephen Heath. See in particular his essay,

"Narrative Space," *Screen* 17.3 (Autumn 1976): 68–112, and my account of Heath's work in *The Crisis of Political Modernism* (Urbana: University of Illinois Press, 1988): 180–220.

6. As cited by Doane in "Film and the Masquerade: Theorising the Female Spectator," *Screen* 23.3/4 (September/October 1982): 74; cited hereafter as FM. The "lecture" in question—for these texts were never meant for oral presentation—is from *The New Introductory Lectures on Psychoanalysis* (1933a [1932]), SE 22: 112–135.

7. See for example, "Misrecognition and Identity," *Ciné-Tracts* 11 (Fall (1979): 25–32 and "Film and the Masquerade," as well as *The Desire to Desire*.

8. Trans. Ben Brewster, *Screen* 16.2 (Summer 1975): 14–76. This important essay is also part of Metz's book *The Imaginary Signifier* (Bloomington: Indiana University Press, 1982): 1–87; cited as IS.

9. The first interior citation is from "Some Psychical Consequences . . ." (1925j), SE 19: 252; the second is from *The New Introductory Lectures on Psychoanalysis* (1933a), SE 22: 125.

10. The interior citation is from "Women's Exile," *Ideology and Consciousness* 1 (May 1977): 65.

11. There is a danger here of confusing the problem of primary narcissism as described by Lacan with secondary identifications associated with the castration complex. In short, the association of the types of identification linked with the castration and Oedipus complexes to the *stade du miroir* is deeply problematic. The particular branching off of masculine and feminine identifications that is the product of these complexes is only possible by placing at risk a narcissistic and autoerotic foundation *already* in place. This foundation has nothing to do, in either Freud or Lacan, with a phallic identification. In her reading of Irigaray, Doane is postulating an ontogenetic division of the sexes—that must be present from the first—on the basis of the castration complex.

12. Doane characterizes this situation in the following terms: "The relation between the spectator and the image, grounded in an absence, is characterized by the lure and fascination of presence. The narcissism of the imaginary relation consists in its dyadic nature and hence its resistance to the intrusion of the triangular (or Oedipal) structure of the symbolic. Lacan has consistently associated aggressivity with narcissism, primary identification and the imaginary: 'Aggressivity is the correlative tendency of a mode of identification that we call narcissistic, and which determines the formal structure of man's ego and of the register of entities characteristic of his world.' The aggressivity stems from the alienation via an image specific to the mirror phase which constitutes itself as 'a primary identification that structures the subject as a rival with himself' . . . . The imaginary component of the cinematic signifier would seem to entail that the supposedly placid or pacifying effect of movie spectatorship is actually haunted by a veiled aggressivity. As Jacqueline Rose argues, aggressivity and paranoia are latent to the cinematic system, becoming manifest only when the stability of that system is threatened" (DD 128). The interior citations are from Lacan's *Écrits*: 16 and 22. The Rose essay referred to is "Paranoia and the Film System." Following Rose, it will be important for Doane that the structure of paranoia always comprises a threat to the film system.

13. Doane is following Samuel Weber's reading of Freud in "The Sideshow, or: Remarks on a Canny Moment," *Modern Language Notes* 88.6 (December 1973): 1102–33.

14. Trans. Leon S. Roudiez (New York: Columbia University Press, 1982).

15. This complex process, where the camera must reassert its control of the narrative as an agent of the masculine protagonists, is described by Doane in the following terms: "In

tracing the absence of the woman, the camera inscribes its own presence in the film as phallic substitute—the pen which writes the feminine body. The two scenes demonstrate the technical fluency of the camera in narrating the woman's story, extended to the point of ejecting her from the image. In its foreclosure of a signifier—here, the woman's body—from the symbolic universe, the camera enacts its paranoia as a psychosis. It is as though, in a pseudogenre marked as the possession of the woman, the camera had to desperately reassert itself by means of its technical prowess—a prowess here embodied in the attribute of movement. The projection scenes discussed earlier effect a cleavage, a split between the image of the woman's desire (linked to stills—photographs or sketches without movement) and what is projected on the screen (in *Caught*, the machinery of industry, capitalist enterprise; in *Rebecca*, the image of Maxim's memory of her before the black satin dress). In each case, it is the man who has control of the projector and hence the moving image. Thus, the films construct an opposition between different processes of imaging along the lines of sexual difference: female desire is linked to the fixation and stability of a spectacle refusing the temporal dimension, while male desire is more fully implicated with the defining characteristic of the cinematic image—movement. The two scenes in which the camera inscribes the absence of the woman thus accomplish a double negation of the feminine—through her absence and the camera's movement, its continual displacement of the fixed image of her desire. Invoking the specific attributes of the cinematic signifier (movement and absence of the object) around the figure of the woman, the films succeed in constructing a story about the woman which no longer requires even her physical presence" (DD 170–171).

16. "Is There a Feminine Aesthetic?," *New German Critique* 10 (Winter 1977): 127; cited in Doane, "Misrecognition and Identity," 30.

17. Joan Riviere, "Womanliness as a Masquerade" in *Psychoanalysis and Female Subjectivity*, ed. Hendrik M. Ruitenbeek (New Haven: College and University Press, 1966): 213; cited in FM 81.

18. *Social Text* 1.1 (Winter 1979): 130–148; reprinted in his *Signatures of the Visible* (New York: Routledge, 1990).

19. As I was completing this chapter, Doane's essay "Masquerade Reconsidered: Further Thoughts on the Female Spectator" appeared in *Discourse* 11.1 (Fall–Winter 1988–89): 42–54. In this interesting and provocative article, Doane responds to criticisms from Patrice Petro and Tania Modleski concerning the epistemological consequences of her arguments in "Film and the Masquerade." Here she emphasizes, more strongly than in her other work, the importance of a retroactive critical and feminist reading for delineating new positions of reading. "There is a difference," Doane writes, "between the critical act and the act of reception. . . . It is all a question of timing. Feminist critical theory must be attentive to both the temporality of reading and the historicity of reading. What has to be acknowledged is that there are, in fact, constraints on reading, constraints on spectatorship. Social constraints, sexual constraints, historical constraints" (51). Further on, she stresses that the *how* of critical reading—which I take to mean its methodological and logical premises—are as important as the reading itself. I believe that this represents an important shift with respect to her earlier positions which I look forward to seeing articulated in other essays.

20. "Masochism and Male Subjectivity," *Camera Obscura* 17 (May 1988): 31–67. I discuss Silverman's argument at greater length in Chapter Four.

21. From the last stanza of Heinrich Heine's *Die Nordsee*, second cycle, section 7, "Fragen":

The waves murmur their eternal murmur,
The wind blows, the clouds fly,

The stars twinkle, indifferent and cold,
And a fool waits for an answer.

In *Heinrich Heine: Selected Verse*, ed. and trans. Peter Branscombe (New York: Viking Penguin, 1968): 83.

3. Reading Freud . . . Differently

1. Trans. Jacqueline Rose in Juliet Mitchell and Jacqueline Rose, eds., *Feminine Sexuality: Jacques Lacan and the école freudienne* (New York: W. W. Norton and Co., 1985): 151; cited hereafter as FS.

2. *Cinema Journal* 24.1 (Fall 1984): 2–27; cited as SEB. Although I will comment critically on this essay, I believe that Williams's position on sexual difference and sexual identification has shifted subsequently in important and interesting ways. See for example her recent book *Hard Core: Power, Pleasure, and the "Frenzy of the Visible"* (Berkeley: University of California Press, 1989), especially Chapter Seven.

3. (Berkeley: University of California Press, 1978); cited as ROM.

4. A somewhat different, more critical view of Kristeva is presented in Kaja Silverman's *The Acoustic Mirror* (Bloomington: Indiana University Press, 1988): 72–140 et passim.

5. The interior citation is from Ruby Rich in discussion with Michelle Citron and others, "Woman and Film: A Discussion of Feminist Aesthetics," *New German Critique* 13 (1978): 87.

6. I am referring here to the "identity theory of knowledge" that is a central component of much of contemporary film theory. See my *The Crisis of Political Modernism* (Urbana: University of Illinois Press, 1988), especially Chapters Seven and Eight.

7. I believe that Juliet Mitchell implies a similar distinction by dividing Freud's work on sexuality into two phases: the first organized around the question of infantile sexuality (1890s to 1919), the second around the problem of sexual difference (1920 to 1940). See her introduction to *Feminine Sexuality: Jacques Lacan and the école freudienne*, especially page 9. Later, I will argue that the case study of the Wolf Man (1918b [1914]) and the essay "'A Child is being Beaten'" (1919e) comprise the fundamental linch-pins for these two phases.

8. As I mentioned in a note to Chapter One, the *Standard Edition* has often been criticized for translating both *Instinkt* and *Trieb* as "instinct," thereby confusing two terms that Freud took care to differentiate. In my own account, I have tried to distinguish systematically between these terms by referring to *Trieb* as drive and by citing in brackets the original German where necessary. For an illuminating discussion of these terms, see the entry "Instinct (or Drive)" in Jean Laplanche and J.-B. Pontalis's *The Language of Psychoanalysis*, trans. Donald Nicholson-Smith (New York: W. W. Norton and Co., 1973): 214–217.

9. Another problem with the translation of Freud in both English and French, which is not often commented on in psychoanalytic literature and which causes much confusion in film theory, involves the term *Schaulust* and its derivative *Schaulustiger*. These are important and often used words in Freud's writings on the drives, whose simplest and most exact translation would be "visual pleasure" and "onlooker" or "spectator." Strachey's weakness for technical vocabularies leads him to translate *Schaulust* as both "voyeurism" and "scopophilia." A serious problem occurs because the scopic drive [*Schautrieb*] is a fundamental component of infantile sexuality in both boys and girls, yet the connotations of Strachey's translation choices often confuse it with its development as a perversion. In

the original German, and throughout his writings, Freud clearly distinguishes between what is normal for the scopic drive and what constitutes its development in a perverted form. Moreover, Freud uses the French word "*voyeur*" in limited contexts, indicating that he himself reserved the term for specific situations.

What this means for film theory is that if one wishes to examine cinematic articulations of the scopic drive and the problem of visual pleasure, one cannot begin with the idea that women are somehow excluded from the field of *Schaulust* and the position of a *Schaulustiger*. In the infantile sexuality of both boys and girls, the scopic drive operates as a fundamentally active form linked to the autoeroticism of childhood. This active autoeroticism, so closely tied to the child's narcissistic interests, leads to the castration complex. However, even if, with the onslaught of the problem of sexual difference, one hypothesizes that the positions of looking in boys and girls will take different forms, there is no immediate justification for associating the perversion of voyeurism with either position. In sum, although there is little doubt that various articulations of the scopic drive must be understood as structured around the problem of sexual difference, they cannot be described as simply divided across the oppositions of male/female, subject/object, or active/passive. I will discuss this problem in greater depth in the next chapter.

10. See, for example, Freud's baroque yet fascinating description of the interrelations of autoeroticism, narcissism, and scopophilia in "Instincts and their Vicissitudes" (SE 14: 129–133).

11. From "Instincts and their Vicissitudes," 128 as cited in Mary Lydon's translation of Jean-François Lyotard's "Fiscourse Digure: The Utopia Behind the Scenes of the Phantasy," *Theatre Journal* 35.3 (October 1983): 341; cited hereafter as FD. This article comprises pages 327–354 of Lyotard's *Discours, figure* (Paris: Éditions Klincksieck, 1974).

12. This argument found its first elaboration in *Totem and Taboo* (1912–1913) on pages 115–116, written a year earlier. Here Freud clearly places narcissism in the developmental argument of the *Three Essays*, situating it on the cusp, as it were, between the stages of autoeroticism and object-choice. Similarly, one can see the importance of Lacan's theory of "le stade du miroir." For as the first division between the sexual and ego-instincts, narcissism describes the situation where the fragmented and partialized drives coalesce around the finding of an object; namely, the subject's own ego.

13. See "Freud: Ideology and Evidence" in ROM: 141–158.

14. See, for example, the entry for "Instinctual Impulse" in *The Language of Psychoanalysis*, 222–223.

15. There is another way of representing this problem. Freud himself remarked that his case histories read like novels. The narrative positions he adopted, above all in the works devoted to sexual difference, are therefore extremely informative. When Freud wishes to illustrate the awakening and confrontation with problems of sexual difference, he always tries to project himself into the mind of the child. Where the thought processes of boys are concerned, Freud feels at liberty to depict them as reported speech. He sits comfortably within the minds of boys and, projected into that interior space, to relinquish his position as enunciator to them. (Chodorow reiterates Karen Horney's observation that Freud's understanding of feminine development was "completely isomorphic with the traditional psychoanalytic picture of the four-year-old boy's view of girls . . . [ROM 144].) However, Freud cannot conceive a similar position for girls. Their "unrepresentability" is consistently remarked upon. Their "thoughts" are not as accessible or imaginable and must be reflected on from the outside as a disinterested observer. Thus within the positions of enunciation described in Freud's own texts, he "identifies" with boys—creates positions of enunciation for them, imagines and recreates their thoughts subjectively—while girls cause problems that require objectification in the discourse of science.

Not only representations of sexual difference but also the Freudian conception of the subject is at stake here. Only two options are available in this rhetorical schema. Freud speaks from inside the mind of the boy and he observes hypothetically, from the outside, the dilemma of the girl. In either case Freud's notion of the subject is cut off from social and historical understanding. Freud's "characters" act as if there were no mise-en-scène and no other players on the stage. I believe this is the main point of Chodorow's critique. Consequently, her emphasis is on the active object-relations organized historically within the space of the family which thus perpetuates certain patterns of gender difference and the sexual division of labor under patriarchy. In Freud, the parents are often invoked as ghosts and phantasms, sometimes as Freud's observational delegate (as in the case of Little Hans [1909b]) but never as historical actors who relate, direct, stage, and otherwise contribute to the never-ending story of sexual difference. Thus Freud barricades himself within a particular notion of the individual, a historical inheritance but unrecognized as such and universalized in Freud's thought. Within that interiorized space of mind and body there are fascinating problems, questions, complexities, and many stories to be told. But outside of it—in the form of ideology, culture, history—little can be imagined. In sum, where there is history in Freud's thought, it unfolds literally within the individual. Here one can see clearly the relation between some of Freud's most tenaciously held ideas: the "origin" of component-instincts "within" privileged erotogenic zones on the body; the linear unfolding of the phases of sexual development as a process coded within, on, and over the body; and most scandalously, the theory of phylogeny and racial memory. Freud's assumptions concerning the integrity and self-sufficiency of the individual as a concept—even as he divided and fragmented the subject within that concept—blinded him not only to problems of femininity, but also to the possibilities for understanding, through psychoanalysis, the historical dynamics of social collectivities. For Freud, the patriarchal family and the heterosexual, gender roles it defines are normative paths from which neurotic individuals have deviated. Where Chodorow or Laing, for example, comprehend the family as a historical and ideological machine—a complex set of relations that formulates and reproduces gender difference as well as sexual division and hierarchy— Freud sees the prehistorical unfolding of phylogeny—with a specific attribution of roles, actions, and position—according to a predetermined and timeless timetable.

16. In her introduction to the anthology on *Feminine Sexuality* Juliet Mitchell accurately points out that the first phase of Freud's work on sexuality is marked by a contradiction devolving from his belief in parallel and symmetrical paths in the Oedipus complex for boys and girls. She emphasizes that behind this idea "lies a notion of a natural and normative heterosexual attraction; a notion which was to be re-assumed by many psycho-analysts later" (FS 10). By the same token, everything that Freud writes on the theory of the drives from the *Three Essays* to "Instincts and Their Vicissitudes" and beyond runs counter to his idea of an equivalency between the sexes. At the root of this tension lies the notion of bisexuality. Mitchell more or less agrees with my position, but believes that Freud's ideas change after 1920; then bisexuality becomes a product of sexual undecidability, or the fragile and incomplete nature of Oedipal identifications.

17. Josef Breuer, interestingly enough, seems not to have been bound to mapping active and passive processes to a gendered terminology. The comparison is all the more striking when one recognizes Freud's enormous debt to Breuer's "Theoretical Section" in the *Studies on Hysteria* for the theories of cathexis—the binding of energy—and all the neurological speculation from the "Project for a Scientific Psychology" (1950a [1887–1902]) to *Beyond the Pleasure Principle*. Breuer's point, simply put, is that perceptual/mental life is intrinsically active, seeking only to maintain an equilibrium between inflowing (perceptions) and outflowing (motor activity) excitations. From this Freud derived his "principle of constancy" which eventually involved into the "pleasure principle." There are thus two

forms of activity in mental economy characterized by psychoanalysis. One maintains the constant enervation necessary for functioning; the other, more characteristic of the drives, is active in its aims and is constantly seeking cathexis. This is a fundamental point in the *Three Essays*: "We have defined the concept of the libido as a quantitatively [excitation and relaxation of tension] variable force which could serve as a measure of processes and transformations occurring in the field of sexual excitation. We distinguish this libido in respect of its special origin from the energy which must be supposed to underlie mental processes in general, and we thus also attribute a *qualitative* character to it [dynamic formation of components]" (*Three Essays*, 217). That Freud could not divorce the sense of "masculinity" from "activity" is the residue of an inability to give up completely a notion of causality and temporality that psychoanalytic experience continually refuted.

18. See her *Speculum de l'autre femme* (Paris: Éditions de Minuit, 1974) as well as "Woman's Exile: Interview with Luce Irigaray," trans. Couze Venn, *Ideology and Consciousness* 1 (May 1977): 62–76.

   Nancy Chodorow sees the problem in another way: "The classic Freudian account of the oedipus complex is imbued with an inexorable logic following from two basic assumptions about sex and gender: first, Freud defines gender and sexual differentiation as presence or absence of masculinity and the male genital rather than as two different presences; second, Freud maintains a functional/teleological view of the "destiny" reserved for anatomical differences between the sexes. Patriarchal assumptions about passivity and activity, and the necessity for men to aggress sexually, are cloaked in the idiom of 'nature'" (ROM 157–158).

19. Interior citation is from Janine Chasseguet-Smirgel's "Feminine Guilt and the Oedipus Complex," in J. Chasseguet-Smirgel, ed., *Female Sexuality* (Ann Arbor: University of Michigan Press, 1970): 118.

20. The female genitals, of course, are subject to their own powerful and material network of significations that figure prominently in both masculine and feminine phantasies. In historicizing classical Freudianism, castration as "absence" of a penis can be understood not as "symbolized" by the female genitals, but as a symbolic construction attributed to them. Obviously, for Freud the vagina provoked something of a mystery that is full of symptomatic manifestations in his writings. At the same time, Freud's work provides many examples of the symbolization of the female genitals as organized in the phantasy life of women in ways that are not necessarily reducible to the problem of absence of a penis. Examples are found in "A Case of Paranoia Running Counter to the Psycho-Analytic Theory of the Disease" (1915f) and "Some Psychical Consequences of the Anatomical Distinction between the Sexes," as well as other essays. The point is that if in Freud's work the woman's body is made to bear the mark of castration, this mark is not necessarily organized around terms of negativity, lack, or "unrepresentability." Rather, female genitality is organized precisely if complexly and contradictorily according to a discursive "positivity" in Foucault's sense. All the terms associating castration and female genitality in Freud pose no threat whatsoever to representation; they are in fact *produced* in discourse, part of whose objective is to limit the possibilities of female subjectivity. Freud may not have understood this well, but psychoanalysis provided one of the first theories able to articulate and comprehend the problem. By the same token, this helps clarify Lacan's reworking of the problem of castration as a lack-in-being in relation to the symbolic order as experienced by all individuals.

21. In his 1938 essay on *Les Complexes familiaux* (Paris: Navarin, 1984), Lacan accords no special privilege to the patriarchal family. Rather, despite the numerous roles and attributions in family groups, Lacan asserts that its "essential traits" derive from laws and interdictions of two fundamental types: "authority, if not concentrated as the patriarchal

type, then at least as represented by a council, a matriarch, or her male delegates; kinship modes of heritage and succession, often transmitted distinctly through a paternal or maternal line" (15, my translation). However, while Lacan's rereading of Freud's theory of sexuality seems to displace the role of phylogeny, the teleological thrust of this theory returns through Lacan's adoption of Hegel's dialectic (as taught by Alexandre Kojève) as the logical principle underwriting his theory of identification. Each phase is thus dialectically overcome and incorporated into the higher unity of the phase that follows. Paradoxically, in this early work Lacan refines and systematizes Freud's teleological tendencies, where Freud's text itself is much more open to contradiction. Chodorow, for example, notes that while mothering serves in the reproduction of the family and of ideological gender-positions, it simultaneously generates "tensions and strains" that erode that process (ROM 211). Chodorow, who is closer to Freud's own arguments, I think, sees the drives as a force that continually erodes the identification processes that seek to define and contain them. Lacan's allegiance to Kojève, on the other hand, leads him to subordinate this force to a dialectical *aufhebung*.

22. Although Lacan's seminar on female sexuality is deeply problematic in many ways, I believe that Mitchell and Rose justifiably stress his acute analysis of two fundamental points. First they emphasize that the seminar is an important antihumanist critique of the subject that radically undercuts any understanding of masculinity or femininity as self-identical and mutually exclusive positions; and second, that the phantasy of "the Woman" is an imaginary construction of patriarchal culture in which the impossible desire for a coherent subjectivity is symptomatically played out. I will discuss these points at greater length in the next chapter.

23. *Personal Services* was inspired by the memoirs of Cynthia Payne, whose early years are protrayed in *Wish You Were Here* (David Leland, 1987), a very different film about the revolt against phallocentric power.

24. The most condensed example of this tautological thinking is found in one of Freud's last writings, *An Outline of Psychoanalysis* (1940a): "We are faced here by the great enigma of the biological fact of the duality of the sexes: it is an ultimate fact for our knowledge, it defies every attempt to trace it back to something else. Psychoanalysis has contributed nothing to clearing up this problem, which clearly falls wholly within the province of biology. In mental life we only find reflections of this great antithesis; and their interpretation is made more difficult by the fact, long suspected, that no individual is limited to the modes of reaction of a single sex but always finds some room for those of the opposite one, just as his body bears, alongside of the fully developed organs of one sex, atrophied and often useless rudiments of those of the other. For distinguishing between male and female in mental life we make use of what is obviously an inadequate empirical and conventional equation: we call everything that is strong and active male, and everything that is weak and passive female. The fact of psychological bisexuality, too, embarrasses all our enquiries into the subject and makes them harder to describe" (SE 23: 188).

4. Metamorphoses

1. Trans. Horace Gregory (New York: Viking Press, 1958): 95.

2. See his *Le Mythe de Tirésias* (Leiden: E.J. Brill, 1976). The variant analyzed by Brisson reads as follows: "According to an elegiac poem by Sostratus, Tiresias was originally of the feminine sex. She was born and raised by Chariclo. At the age of seven years she was walking in the mountains. Apollo desired her. And for the price of her favors taught her music. When she had learned it she no longer gave herself to Apollo. Thus the god turned

her into a man, so that she would be tested by Eros. And the young girl, changed into a man, rendered judgment for Zeus and Hera as recounted above. And thus having become again a woman, she fell in love with Kallon, an Argian, from whom she bore a child who, because of the wrath of Hera, was afflicted with strabism. This is why he was named Strabo. Consequently, having mocked a statue of Hera, she was changed into an ugly man, such that she came to be called Pytho (Monkey). Zeus took pity and she was changed again into a mature woman, and thus traveled to Troezen. There she was desired by Glyphios, a peasant, who attacked her while she was bathing. But surpassing the young man in strength, she strangled him. Poseidon, who held Glyphios as a favorite, committed her to the Moirae so they could pass judgment. The Fates changed her into Tiresias and rescinded her gift of prophecy. She relearned the art of divination guided by Chiron, and attended a banquet celebrating the marriage of Peleus and Thetis. There took place a beauty contest between Aphrodite and the Graces—Pasithea, Kalea, and Euphrosyne. Asked to judge, Tiresias bestowed the prize on Kalea who married Hephaestus. This is why the wounded Aphrodite changed him again into a woman, an old spinner. But Kalea gave her beautiful hair and brought her to Crete. There Arachnos fell in love with her, and being united with her boasted of having made love with Aphrodite. The goddess, angered by this thing, changed Arachnos into a weasel and Tiresias into a mouse. This is why one says the mouse eats little, because she was originally an old woman. And the mouse is a divinatory animal because of Tiresias. That the mouse is a prophetic animal is shown by two facts: their sharp cries which give sign of an approaching storm; and their flight from houses that are threatening to collapse" (Brisson, 78–81), my translation.

3. "Enunciation and Sexual Difference, Part 1," *Camera Obscura* 3/4 (1979): 58. Also see her essays "Sexuality at a Loss: the Films of F. W. Murnau," *Poetics Today* 6.1/2 (1985): 185–203 and "Androids and Androgyny," *Camera Obscura* 15 (Fall 1986): 37–66.

4. *Feminine Sexuality: Jacques Lacan and the école freudienne* (New York: W.W. Norton and Co., 1985): 26; cited as FS.

5. Interior citation is from Jacques Lacan's "The Meaning of the Phallus," as translated by Jacqueline Rose in FS 74–85.

6. In particular, I will address Lyotard's chapter "Fiscours, digure, l'utopie du fantasme" in *Discours, figure* (Paris: Éditions Klincksieck, 1974): 327–354; translated by Mary Lydon as "Fiscourse Digure: The Utopia Behind the Scenes of the Phantasy," *Theatre Journal* 35.3 (October 1983): 333–357, cited hereafter as FD. Kaja Silverman's essay is published in *Camera Obscura* 17 (May 1988): 31–68; cited as MMS. It is interesting to read Lyotard and Silverman together, for while the former ignores the dimension of sexual difference that the latter gives such brilliant expression, Lyotard gives more thorough expression to the utopian dimension of phantasy that Silverman outlines.

7. "Le Fantasme dans 'On bat un enfant'," *Cahiers pour analyse* 7 (March–April 1967): 74; my translation.

8. Table Two is adopted from Jean François Lyotard's "Fiscourse Digure," 338.

9. A reconsideration of Freud's stages according to my speculations would be tabulated as follows:

Male. I (uncs):   "My father is beating the other child . . ."

II (cs) :   "I am being beaten   by my father . . ."

(uncs):   "I am loved (genitally) by my father . . ."

Female. I (cs) : "My father is beating the other child . . ."

II (uncs): "I am $\begin{bmatrix} \text{being beaten} \\ \text{loved (genitally)} \end{bmatrix}$ by my father. . ."

In the case of the boy, a primary repression would set in between stages I and II, thus accounting for a regression that intensifies his anal eroticism while forging a topographical split between the two versions of stage two. In the transition to stage III, a secondary repression would transform the conscious level of phantasy by substituting the mother for the father. Then, as Freud himself suggests, the girl's primary repression would set in between the third and second stages where *her* incestuous desire for the father is most strongly expressed. For the girl, the transition between I and II would be marked by disavowal rather than repression.

10. Lyotard's description would also be adequate for my speculations concerning an unconscious first stage in the boy's phantasy. A degree of caution is warranted here, however, since Lyotard excessively places verbalization on the side of consciousness and plastic expression on the side of the unconscious, thus posing a binary opposition which his own argument does much to deconstruct. Despite the power and eloquence of Lyotard's other arguments, this opposition is the product of an avant-gardism that believes, in an unqualified way, in the critical capacity of works of art. It should be clear later on that, in my view, the utopian function of aesthetic work can only be redeemed through a critical reading; one cannot simply presume *a priori* that this function is a defining property of the aesthetic. A more critical view of Lyotard is presented in my essay "Reading the Figural," *Camera Obscura* 22 (1990).

11. *Masochism: An Interpretation of Coldness and Cruelty*, trans. Jean McNeil (New York: Georges Braziller, 1971): 28–29; cited in MMS 57.

12. *Masochism in Sex and Society*, trans. Margaret H. Beigel and Gertrud M. Kurth (New York: Grove Press, 1962): 41. Silverman's analysis occupies pages 51–56 of "Masochism and Male Subjectivity."

13. I am thinking in particular of the argument presented by Fredric Jameson in his essay "Reification and Utopia in Mass Culture," *Social Text* 1.1 (Winter 1979): 130–148 and reprinted in Jameson, *Signatures of the Visible* (New York and London: Routledge, 1990), as well as Tania Modleski's redemptive reading of romance fiction in *Loving With a Vengeance* (New York: Methuen, 1984).

14. It is likely that Sergei Pankeiev is the male patient discussed in "'A Child is being Beaten'." By the same token, Freud's analysis of the stratifications of the phantasy lends itself readily to a description in Lyotard's terms. The figure-image derives from the manifest content of the phantasy ("a child is being beaten on its naked bottom") which finds itself invoked in a variety of narrative guises, including popular literature from the *bibliothèque rose*. The figure-form, the basic narrative architecture of the phantasy, is capsulized in the third stage. The figure-matrix is reconstructed in the second stage of unmitigated incestuous desire for the father which has been subject to primary repression brought about by the castration complex.

15. FD 357; the interior citation is from J.B. Pontalis's "L'Utopie freudienne," *L'Arc* 34 (1968): 14.

5. The Difference of Reading

1. Jean Laplanche and J.-B. Pontalis, *Fantasme originaire, Fantasmes des origines, Origines du fantasme* (Paris: Hachette, 1985): 75; my translation.

2. *Fantasme originaire*, 61, my translation; hereafter cited as FO. This essay has recently been reprinted in English translation as "Fantasy and the Origins of Sexuality" in *Formations of Fantasy*, eds, Victor Burgin et al. (New York: Methuen, 1986): 5–34. While this is an adequate translation, I feel that there are enough distortions to warrant using my own translations exclusively.

Also, a short remark on nomenclature might clarify my argument at the outset. Standard Anglo-American psychoanalytic usage, introduced by Susan Issacs and others, distinguishes between "phantasy" as the staging of unconscious desire and "fantasy" as the (self-)conscious narration of desire of the subject to itself in daydreams. Laplanche and Pontalis argue against this strategy, claiming that Freud saw no real difference in structure between unconscious and conscious *Phantasie*. They drive home this point in their French title (*Fantasme originaire, Fantasmes des origines, Origines du fantasme*) which examines the "origins of fantasy life" in relation to the originary and unconscious "primal phantasy" [*fantasme originare*] and the conscious daydreams called the "family romance" [*fantasmes des origines, Familenroman*]. Nevertheless, the function of the unconscious in aesthetic forms like film or the novel, which are social and collective in ways that an analysand's imaginary life is not, pose problems that require terminological care. If the narrative structure of *Céline et Julie vont en bateau* seems strikingly analogous to Laplanche and Pontalis's model of phantasy, this does not mean that the film is informed by the unconscious in the same way as the daydream, for example. In this respect, I find it expedient to distinguish between "phantasy" in its specific psychoanalytic sense and "fantasy" as a narrative structure produced for social collectives.

Thierry Kuntzel, more than any other film theorist, has worked through the implications of comparing film narrative to phantasy in several important essays, including: "The Film-Work," *Enclitic* 2.1 (Spring 1978): 38–62; "The Film-Work, 2," *Camera Obscura 5* (Spring 1980): 7–68; "Sight, Insight, Power," *Camera Obscura* 6 (Fall 1980): 91–110; "Le Défilement: A View in Close-Up," *Camera Obscura* 2 (Fall 1977): 51–65; and "A Note Upon the Filmic Apparatus," *Quarterly Review of Film Studies* 1.3 (August 1976): 266–271. Also see my essay, "The Figure and the Text," *Diacritics* 15.1 (Spring 1985): 34–50.

3. "From the History of an Infantile Neurosis," (1918b [1914]), SE 17: 3–122.

4. In the history of psychoanalysis, this form of memory-repetition was originally encountered in *female* "narrators," especially in the *Studies on Hysteria* (1895d). Josef Breuer's account of the case of Fräulein Anna O—with her peculiar form of self-alienation and her unconscious repetition, day by day, of events transpiring exactly a year before— presents particularly interesting parallels with the narrative system of *Céline et Julie vont en bateau*.

5. On the adaptation of psychoanalytic "plots" by the American cinema, see Marc Vernet's "Freud: effets spéciaux-Mise en scène: U.S.A.," *Communications* 23 (1975): 223–234 as well as Mary Ann Doane's *The Desire to Desire: The Woman's Film of the 1940s* (Bloomington: Indiana University Press, 1987).

6. Figures 1, 4 and 12 are abbreviated samples of the sequences in question; some sequential shots are omitted.

7. My argument might be clarified with a brief digression on the parallel narratives of *Céline et Julie*. The plot of the first film was sketched out by Juliet Berto (Céline) and Dominique Labourier (Julie) with Jacques Rivette's participation. The plot of the "other film" is a melodrama scripted by Eduardo de Gregario from a pastiche of material from Henry James. In the "mythology" of *Céline et Julie*, the following scenario is repeated daily in the mysterious house on rue du Nadir aux Pommes. It is the birthday of a little girl, Madlyn, who lives with her father, Olivier (a wealthy widower played by Barbet Schroeder, the producer of the film!), her aunt Camille (Bulle Ogier), a governess named Sophie

(Marie-France Pisier), and a nurse played alternately by Céline and Julie. On her death-bed, Madlyn's mother made Olivier vow not to remarry as long as Madlyn lived. It is evident that all three women in the house are competing aggressively for the attention of Olivier and we, with Céline and Julie, discover that the scenario always ends with Madlyn's murder. What we only eventually learn is that she is killed thrice over—suffocated by Camille (whose bloody handprint is doubly impressed on Madlyn's pillow and on Céline/Julie's shoulder when they "return" from the other film) and poisoned by Sophie, and it is suggested, Olivier, through a daily guessing game the prize of which are candies that have been injected with a drug. Initially, it is through the agency of the candies—which Céline or Julie always have in their mouths when "returning" from the house—that the scenes from the other film are summoned.

8. In their essay, Laplanche and Pontalis map this structural situation, where the relation between primal phantasy and reverie is reproduced within the form of phantasy itself, in the following way:

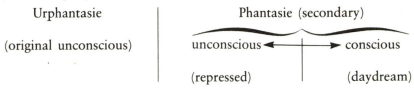

Urphantasie | Phantasie (secondary)

(original unconscious) | unconscious ⟵——⟶ conscious

(repressed) | (daydream)

By the same token, I would argue that the narrative "fantasy" of *Céline et Julie* is also mapped here with the plot in the House of Fiction as structurally equivalent to the "unconscious" strata of phantasy and the plot of investigation as equivalent to the conscious strata.

9. "Interview with Jacques Rivette in *La Nouvelle Critique* No. 63 (244), April 1973" in Jonathan Rosenbaum, ed., *Jacques Rivette: Texts and Interviews* (London: British Film Institute, 1977): 53.

10. "The narrative voice or the impersonal 'He' " in *The Siren's Song*, trans. Sacha Rabinov-itch (Bloomington: Indiana University Press, 1982): 216. I thank Hillis Miller for pointing me towards Blanchot's work in this context.

11. Jonathan Rosenbaum, et al., "Phantom Interviewers over Rivette," *Film Comment* 10.5 (September–October 1974): 22.

12. I will refer to Joan Riviere's translation published in *Collected Papers*, vol. II (London: The Hogarth Press, 1971): 366–376; cited as RRW. James Strachey's reworking of this translation, found in SE 12: 145–156, is somewhat less satisfying than Riviere's original work.

13. "Time Overflowing. Interview with Jacques Rivette from *Cahiers du cinéma*, No. 204, 1968" in Rosenbaum, *Jacques Rivette*, 37.

6. Analysis Interminable

1. Italo Calvino, *If on a winter's night a traveller* (London: Secker and Warburg, 1982): 188–189.

2. I am thinking in particular of Michel Foucault's critique of psychoanalysis as confession as a strategy of power in *The History of Sexuality*, trans. Robert Hurley (New York: Vintage Books, 1980), as well as Gilles Deleuze and Félix Guattari's critique of the centrality of Oedipus and the castration complex in their *Anti-Oedipus*, trans. Robert

Hurley, et al. (Minneapolis: University of Minnesota Press, 1983). Both critiques have much to recommend them and should be seriously engaged. However, in their polemical thrust they misrecognize the function of phantasy, and psychoanalysis' account of it, as a site of resistance equal in power to their alternatives.

3. Trans. Celia Britton and Annwyl Williams (Bloomington: Indiana University Press, 1982): 89–98; cited hereafter as IS.

4. See the chapter titled "The Fiction Film and its Spectator: A Metapsychological Study," especially the last two sections on "Film and Phantasy" and "The Filmic *Visée*" (IS 129–142).

5. The best statement of Kuntzel's position is found in his essays "The Film-Work," *Enclitic* 2.1 (Spring 1978): 38–62, and "The Film-Work, 2," trans. Nancy Huston, *Camera Obscura* 5 (Spring 1980): 7–68. The most thorough exposition of Bellour's argument is his analysis of *North by Northwest*, "The Symbolic Blockage," trans. Mary Quaintance in *The Analysis of Film* (Bloomington: Indiana University Press, forthcoming). Metz, Bellour, and Kuntzel coedited the influential dossier on cinema and psychoanalysis published in *Communications* 23 (1975), where most of these essays originally appeared.

6. *Screen* 20.2 (Summer 1979): 65–72; cited as CR.

7. Thierry Kuntzel provides an interesting account of this problem, especially where sexual difference is concerned, in "*Le Défilement*: A View in Close-Up," trans. Bertrand August, *Camera Obscura* 2 (Fall 1977): 51–65. However, the most fundamental statement of this paradox remains Raymond Bellour's "Le Texte introuvable," *Ça Cinéma* 7/8 (May 1975): 77–84. I will return to this fascinating essay, cited in my translation as TI. An English translation has been published as "The Unattainable Text" in *Screen* 16.3 (Autumn 1975): 19–27.

8. Janet Bergstrom, "Alternation, Segmentation, Hypnosis: Interview with Raymond Bellour," *Camera Obscura* 3/4 (Summer 1979): 77; cited as ASH.

9. Bellour's analysis is summarized in his interview with Janet Bergstrom. The complete analysis has been published as "Alterner/raconter" in Raymond Bellour and Patrick Brion, eds., *Le Cinéma américain: analyses de films*, vol. I (Paris: Flammarion, 1980): 69–88.

10. A more exact, if more technical, way of describing Bellour's thesis is to state that as he moves from the most general to the most specific levels of filmic narration in his analysis of *North by Northwest*, he discovers the structural logic of castration phantasy reproducing itself asymptotically on the plane of content and expression. "This principle, regulating the narrative's fate," writes Bellour, "owes its strength largely to the way in which the narrative never ceases by segments, by fragments, to be resolved on to itself, as it were, by partial effects of symmetry, of circularity and compression. These constitute so many successive micro-resolutions where the major resolution of the narrative seems to be echoed and reflected following an effect of continuous-discontinuous reverberations, through an interlocking mechanism of the whole back with the part. Outlining this operation of repetition and its difference resolved in the psycho-analytical perspective into which it is inscribed, this is what I have designated by the phrase *blocage symbolique*" (CR 70). This logic reproduces itself from level to level in the narration, not only in the dualistic structure of themes, actions, and conflicts, but also in the organization of segments that drives the narrative forward according to the repetition-resolution effect, and in the organization of space within segments according to varieties of alternation.

Bellour also explores this process in nineteenth century fiction in his recent book, *Mademoiselle Guillotine: Cagliostro, Dumas, Oedipe et la Révolution Française* (Paris: La Différence, 1989).

11. Trans. Bertrand Augst and Hilary Radner as "Hitchcock, the Enunciator," in *Camera Obscura* 2 (Fall 1977): 67–91.

12. I discuss these ideas in much greater depth in my essay, "The Figure and the Text," *Diacritics* 15.1 (Spring 1985): 34–50.

13. See his essay, "From Work to Text," trans. Stephen Heath in *Image-Music-Text* (Glasgow: Fontana, 1977): 155–164. Bellour specifically discusses Barthes's argument in the essay on the *texte introuvable*.

14. (Minneapolis: University of Minnesota Press, 1988): 2.

15. *Feminine Sexuality: Jacques Lacan and the école freudienne* (New York: W.W. Norton and Co., 1985): 55–56.

16. For a relatively concise and critical overview of the Althusserian positions on art and ideology, see Tony Bennett's *Formalism and Marxism* (New York: Methuen, 1979). For an account of contemporary film theory's reading of Althusser, see my *Crisis of Political Modernism* (Urbana: University of Illinois Press, 1988): 67–110.

17. *The Desire to Desire: The Woman's Film of the 1940s* (Bloomington: Indiana University Press, 1987): 176–183; cited as DD.

18. See his "Encoding/decoding" in *Culture, Media, Language*, eds. Stuart Hall et al. (London: Hutchinson, 1980): 128–138. Macherey's position is outlined in *A Theory of Literary Production*, trans. Geoffrey Wall (London: Routledge and Kegan Paul, 1978).

19. "The Feminine Body and Feminist Politics," *m/f* 3 (1979): 35–50. Also see *The Crisis of Political Modernism*, 221–270. One way of explaining Brown and Adams's position is to say that feminist experience is not reducible to femaleness. Certainly, the easiest way to identify women as a collective social and political group is through an identification with the body. My argument with this position has less to do with an easily refuted biological essentialism, than the attempt to reduce what is surely a multiple and complex experience of oppression to an ontological singularity that easily conforms to the binary norms of capitalism and patriarchy. Here feminism risks the classical error of a Marxism that projected an idea of "the proletariat" as a similarly self-identical subject capable of a self-consciousness that would ultimately recognize and rectify the causes of its oppression. But this self-consciousness can never be assured *a priori* in the singularity of a bodily or social experience. Like class consciousness, feminist consciousness is not guaranteed by the fact that one is born a woman or a worker. Rather one must arduously work out the theoretical and practical tools for understanding the determinations common to an experience that is complexly and historically differentiated across gender, race, class, and national identities.

    For a recent, thought-provoking account of these problems, see Judith Butler's *Gender Trouble: Feminism and the Subversion of Identity* (London and New York: Routledge, 1990).

20. See his important essays "Reification and Utopia in Mass Culture," *Social Text* 1.1 (Winter 1979): 130–148, reprinted in *Signatures of the Visible* (New York and London: Routledge, 1990), and "Pleasure: A Political Issue" in *Formations of Pleasure* (London: Routledge and Kegan Paul, 1983): 1–14.

21. "Some Functions of Feminist Criticism, or The Scandal of the Mute Body," *October* 49 (Summer 1989): 13–14. The interior citation is from Bonnie Zimmerman's "What Has Never Been: An Overview of Lesbian Feminist Criticism," in Elaine Showalter, ed., *The New Feminist Criticism: Women, Literature, Theory* (New York: Pantheon, 1985): 200–224.

22.   I am referring, of course, to his fascinating essay, "The Task of the Translator," trans. Harry Zohn in *Illuminations* (New York: Schocken, 1977): 69–82.

23.   An overview account of the challenge of the chromosome test can be found in Alison Carlson's "Chromosome Count," *Ms.* (October 1988): 40–44. On the Mark Rees case see Victor Andolfi's "Mark Rees, femme malgré lui," *Libération* (21 October 1986): 19.

Index